Composing Diverse Identities

Narrative inquiries into the interwoven lives of children and teachers

D. Jean Clandinin, Janice Huber, Marilyn Huber, M. Shaun Murphy, Anne Murray Orr, Marni Pearce, and Pam Steeves

Routledge
Taylor & Francis Group

LONDON AND NEW YORK

First published 2006
by Routledge
2 Park Square, Milton Park, Abingdon, Oxon OX14 4RN

Simultaneously published in the USA and Canada
by Routledge
270 Madison Ave, New York, NY 10016

Routledge is an imprint of the Taylor & Francis Group, an informa business

© 2006 D. Jean Clandinin, Janice Huber, Marilyn Huber,
M. Shaun Murphy, Anne Murray Orr, Marni Pearce, and Pam Steeves

Typeset in Galliard by
HWA Text and Data Management, Tunbridge Wells
Printed and bound in Great Britain by
The Cromwell Press, Trowbridge, Wiltshire

British Library Cataloguing in Publication Data
A catalogue record for this book is available from the British Library

Library of Congress Cataloging-in-Publication Data
A catalog record for this book has been requested

ISBN10: 0–415–36218–0 (hbk)
ISBN10: 0–415–39747–2 (pbk)
ISBN10: 0–203–01246–1 (ebook)

ISBN13: 978–0–415–36218–4 (hbk)
ISBN13: 978–0–415–39747–6 (pbk)
ISBN13: 978–0–203–01246–8 (ebook)

Contents

Acknowledgements

Many children, teachers, families, and administrators accepted our invitations to engage in narrative inquiries with us. As our relationships developed, so too, did our inquiries as children, teachers, families, and administrators invited us into their schools, classrooms, and, at times, into their homes. Their invitations for us to live alongside them as they composed their lives in and outside of schools shaped our understandings. We are deeply grateful to the children, teachers, families, and administrators at Ravine Elementary School and at City Heights School. Without them these narrative inquiries would not have been possible.

Our research is situated within the theoretical background created by John Dewey, Joseph Schwab, Jean Clandinin, and Michael Connelly. Their writing gave us ways to inquire into our experiences alongside the children, teachers, families, and administrators.

Two Social Sciences and Humanities Research Council of Canada research grants awarded to Jean Clandinin and Michael Connelly supported our research. This financial support allowed us to live in the schools over time, to complete doctoral work, and to attend conferences where we have shared aspects of this research. The University of Alberta's financial support in a research grant to Jean Clandinin enabled the "Writing School Lives" conference in Whistler, BC, in the summer of 2004. Being able to gather together as a whole group, to write together, and to collaboratively conceptualize this book changed each of our lives, as teachers, as teacher educators, and as narrative inquirers.

Lauren Starko has been alongside us since the beginning of this work. She transcribed our research conversations and our teleconference calls. As this book took shape, through multiple revisions, Lauren's expertise and patience brought it together. Cherie Geering also supported our work through the setting up of teleconference calls, the organization of flights and conference materials.

Many of our friends at the Center for Research for Teacher Education and Development at the University of Alberta helped to sustain our passions for this research through their responses to our stories and by sharing their stories with us.

Our families and friends have supported us throughout this research. To all of them, from all of us, our deepest thanks.

D. J. C.

J. H.

M. H.

M. S. M.

A. M. O.

M. P.

P. S.

Introduction

Questions around what it means for teachers and children to compose lives in schools have been embedded within our work as teachers and researchers for many years. These questions are shaped by questions about the nature of experience itself, the nature of schools, the nature of teachers' and children's knowledge, and the relationship of language and experience. These questions form a backdrop to our work, shaping inquiries such as the one we describe in this book.

Through years of studying philosophers' and psychologists' views on experience and through years of studying the lives of children and teachers in schools, we came to a narrative understanding of experience, an understanding that owes much to John Dewey's work. We took our narrative understandings of experience with us into the schools central to this inquiry. These understandings helped us make sense of the lives of the children, administrators, teachers, and families who lived in these schools.

Our view of experience helped us to pay attention not to experience conceptualized as vagrant shards, but rather to narrative threads of experience unfolding and enfolding within the embodied persons who lived in these schools. Our understanding is a deeply narrative one conceptualized within a Deweyan view of experience with temporal dimensions, personal-social dimensions, and dimensions of place. As each person's experience unfolded over time, we were attentive to temporal unfoldings. We were, at the same time, attentive to the personal, that is, to the interaction of the personal and social, embodied in the person. And we were attentive to the interactions of the embodied person with the social, that is, to the social, cultural, institutional narratives and to the minute-by-minute particularities of ongoing events. We also attended to the places where lives were composed, lived, and relived. Increasingly we became attentive to the ways that language shaped the social, cultural, and institutional narratives and how those narratives, in turn, shaped the individual person. The stories we live and tell are profoundly influenced by the lived and told narratives in which we are embedded. In all of these ways, this book is about trying to understand more about the nature of experience, particularly experience as it is lived out and considered from multiple vantage points in North American school contexts at the start of the twenty-first century.

This book is also about trying to understand diverse individual's experiences as they are lived out in dynamic relation to people, places, and things in and outside of schools. In order to understand these interwoven and relational experiences our intention was to work as a research group in one school so we could position ourselves alongside multiple participants who were themselves positioned in multiple ways within a school. At first, two of us worked in one school, positioning ourselves alongside one teacher, several children, and a few mothers. When we realized the complexity of what we were trying to do, more researchers joined us and we moved into another school, positioning ourselves alongside school administrators, several teachers, children, and families. We stayed for 18 months, building on prior relationships and continuing our relationships even after we no longer went to the school each day. In this way we felt we could begin to understand the complexities of experience as people lived in relation with each other and within the social, cultural, and institutional narratives of these schools.

Our purpose in this research was to understand more about experience, teachers' and children's knowledge, and how we might study experience and knowledge using a narrative inquiry research methodology. However, as we did this work, we became caught up in the moral questions about how children's, teachers', administrators', and families' experiences, and, therefore their lives, were being shaped. The schools where we worked were urban schools which were becoming increasingly multicultural, with children's and families' lives embedded within diverse religious, linguistic, cultural, and social narratives. Many of their lives were in marked moments of transition, transitions that shaped interruptions. We noticed that while some interruptions shaped more educative life possibilities, using Dewey's terms, other interruptions shaped miseducative life experiences, narrowing the possibilities from which individuals composed their lives. We were in the schools as new mandated policies for assessment began to filter down the metaphoric conduit and began to interrupt, in profound ways, the lives being lived there. Perhaps because these policies with their new prescribed practices were being so sharply defined, perhaps because we were in intense and intimate relationships with children, families, teachers, and administrators, our awareness was heightened and we began to see the ways these shifts in institutional plotlines were shifting lives. We realized we wanted to attend to how these policies were shaping lives and to what we could learn by attending to the broader landscape as well as to the individual narrative life compositions.

In this book, readers will meet many characters: children, teachers, families, administrators, and a group of researchers. It is narrative accounts of all of these lives in motion that fill the pages of this book.

Plotlines convolute and spiral, lives intertwine, coincidences collide, seemingly random happenings are laced with knots, figure eights, and double loops, designs more intricate than the fringe of a silk rebozo. No, I couldn't make this up. Nobody could make up our lives.

(Cisneros 2002: 429)

Chapter 1

A narrative understanding of lives in schools

We watch Lia come into the classroom, late again. She flings her backpack onto a hook, takes off her coat, and sighs as she heads, first for the teacher's unoccupied desk where she drops the late slip on the corner and then for her desk. It's 9.15 a.m. and the singing of the national anthem has finished. The announcements are ending. We watch as Lia puts her head down on her desk, an audible sigh registering her feelings. She lifts her eyes; her face seems to show she knows she's late but not too late. At least she still has time to exchange her book for the home reading program before her teacher gathers the children in the cozy corner.

Later in the morning, as children are spread out around the room, we go over to where Lia is working. She still feels edgy and, kneeling beside her, we ask what made her late for school. Sighing, she gives us one more telling of her story. It is an unfolding story, one we've come to know over the past months. This morning, a particularly frosty morning in this northern Canadian city, Lia describes how the family car would not start. Her father, frustrated, finally gets it started and insists that Lia gets her brothers to their classrooms before going to her own. She's already late when they leave home. As Lia recounts what happened she says that the national anthem was already playing when she and her brothers entered through the big front door. A school rule is that when the anthem is playing everyone has to freeze, hands at their sides, standing tall. She thought for a moment that she might sneak down the hallway anyway but decided against it. She knew she was supposed to be a model for her young brothers and she knew she was supposed to check in at the office for a late slip for each of them. She also knew the school rule about the national anthem was an important cultural rule in her new country, Canada. Lia and her family arrived from Somalia about a year and a half ago and she was still trying to fit into this new school in this new country. After checking in at the office, getting the late slips, Lia took first one brother and then the other to their classrooms. As she gave the late slips to each teacher she explained to them what happened. Finally, she arrived in her classroom.

From earlier told stories we knew that her father would have insisted it was a girl's job to take care of her brothers. She explained earlier about some cultural and religious practices that situated her as a girl in relation to boys, women in relation to men.

(Interim research text based on field notes, Fall 1999)

When Janice and Jean met Lia they were in the midst of an ongoing narrative inquiry (Clandinin and Connelly 2000) trying to understand the bumping up of children's lives with teachers' lives, children's lives with stories of school, and teachers' lives with stories of school (Clandinin and Connelly 1996). Carefully positioning themselves alongside one teacher in one multicultural urban classroom in western Canada, they were able to attend to ways in which this bumping reverberated in and through lives (Huber *et al.* 2003). It was tensions such as the ones Lia experienced that helped Janice and Jean to stop and attend to the intersections and the bumping up of lives in schools. They were interested in exploring and coming to understand what happened in these moments of tension. As they began to pay attention to what happened in these moments, they realized these moments could shape children's and teachers' lives and could also shape the classroom curriculum.

Attending narratively to teachers' and administrators' lives in school

Huber and Clandinin's living alongside Lia, her teacher Emily, and the 27 other children in a Year 3/4 classroom[1] at City Heights School grew out of an ongoing program of research that connects back with the writings of John Dewey (1938) and Joseph Schwab (1969, 1971, 1973, 1983). Dewey's concept of experience, that is, his criteria of interaction and continuity, and of situation, shaped a background for Connelly and Clandinin's (1988) understandings of teacher knowledge as embodied, relational, temporally composed, and lived out in particular times and places. As Clandinin and Connelly developed these understandings of teacher knowledge by working alongside teachers in schools, they came to realize that teacher knowledge was a narrative construction composed in each teacher's life and made visible in their practices. They wrote of teacher knowledge as "personal practical knowledge" (Clandinin and Connelly 1995: 7) which they described as: "that body of convictions and meanings, conscious or unconscious, that have arisen from experience (intimate, social, and traditional) and that are expressed in a person's practices" (1995: 7). Attending to personal practical knowledge helped them to develop a language for understanding how teacher knowledge was held and expressed. For example, the language of images, practical principles, personal philosophies, metaphors, narrative unities, rhythms, and cycles became a way to speak of the knowledge teachers held.

In the opening story of Lia we showed some small sense of her teacher's personal practical knowledge as it found expression in the rhythms of a school day. We learned that morning was a time when children brought back school books they had taken home to read. This kind of rhythm created a space for children to make a transition from life outside of school to their lives in school. We also learned there was a cozy corner where children gathered to tell stories and to learn together. Gathering the children there as an early morning rhythm let us see the important place of this rhythm in the teacher's knowledge. Lia knew this rhythm in her teacher's practice as she entered the room, hung up her backpack, went to her desk, and became part of whatever was happening. She expected no disciplinary action for her late arrival. The teacher's knowledge which shaped these rhythms came from a personal philosophy which welcomed children whenever they arrived and invited them to join in with the activities of their classmates when they were ready.

While personal practical knowledge was seen as a dialectic between the personal and social within an individual's life, as teachers lived their lives both in and out of schools another dialectic between the personal and the social was lived out. The social of school, most often called school contexts, was conceptualized by Clandinin and Connelly (1995) through the metaphor of a professional knowledge landscape:

> A landscape metaphor is particularly well suited to our purpose. It allows us to talk about space, place, and time. Furthermore, it has a sense of expansiveness and the possibility of being filled with diverse people, things, and events in different relationships. Understanding professional knowledge as comprising a landscape calls for a notion of professional knowledge as composed of a wide variety of people, places, and things. Because we see the professional knowledge landscape as composed of relationships among people, places, and things, we see it both as an intellectual and a moral landscape.
>
> (1995: 4–5)

The professional knowledge landscape was understood as a landscape narratively constructed with historical, moral, emotional, and aesthetic dimensions. The landscape metaphor brought attention to the relational, temporal, and shifting nature of school contexts. Through Clandinin and Connelly's (1995) work alongside teachers and administrators they identified different epistemological and moral places on the professional knowledge landscape. They described these two different places as "in-classroom" and "out-of-classroom" places (p. 14). In-classroom places were described as safe places, places where teachers lived out their stories of who they were and who they were becoming as they interacted with children. Out-of-classroom places were described as prescriptive, professional places shared with other teachers, and as places where teachers were expected to hold certain, expert knowledge.

The differences between in- and out-of-classroom places became apparent in Lia's story as she entered the school on this frosty late fall morning. As she and her brothers entered the building, they went into an out-of-classroom place, the front foyer of the school, where an out-of-classroom rhythm of rigidly set times of arrival and of respecting the national anthem were being lived out. Different stories shaped the out-of-classroom place and, even though Lia momentarily wondered about sneaking past the office and down the hallway, she seemed to know there was no flexibility around these rhythms. Seeming to know the inflexibility of these rhythms, Lia quieted her feeling of wanting to get to her classroom and, instead, modelled for her two younger brothers how to live out a story that fit with the plotlines of late attendance in the out-of-classroom place.

As Clandinin and Connelly (1995) and others (Davies 1996; Rose 1997) with whom they inquired into the professional knowledge landscape learned, as teachers moved between in- and out-of-classroom places they experienced dilemmas, felt tensions as their personal practical knowledge bumped against the storied knowledge context of the landscape. Maintaining their focus on teachers' experiences on the professional knowledge landscape, Clandinin and Connelly (1996: 24) wrote of "teacher stories – stories of teachers – school stories – stories of school" as a way to describe teachers' dilemmas as they moved between in- and out-of-classroom places.

Teachers' stories, their personal practical knowledge, are the stories teachers live and tell of who they are and what they know. Some teachers' stories are "secret stories," stories told only to others in safe places both on and off the school landscape. Some teachers' stories are "cover stories" (Clandinin and Connelly 1995: 25), stories told to maintain a sense of continuity with the dominant stories of school shaping a professional knowledge landscape.

Not only is personal practical knowledge a narrative life composition but so too is the professional knowledge landscape a narrative composition of school stories and stories of school. When teachers enter the professional knowledge landscape they enter into a place of story. School stories are described as the ongoing stories composed by teachers, children, families, administrators, and others as they live their lives in school. Stories of school are the stories composed by others and told to others about what the school is about. For example, in the story of Lia above, one of the stories of school was that the school was a welcoming place for children, parents, and the community. The foyer inside the big front door where Lia and her brothers entered had a coffee pot, a bench, and reading materials. A school story told by children was that they did not feel welcomed in the school foyer. The doors to each of the smaller side entrances used by children as they entered and left the building were locked by the time Lia and her brothers arrived on this school morning. Instead, the big front door was the door they were made to enter when they were late and the office was a place to visit when a late slip was needed. These stories structured the professional knowledge landscape of City Heights School and offer a way to understand the tensions experienced in the bumping up of lives.

In their work alongside teachers and administrators, two narrative ways Clandinin and Connelly (1995) understood how these tensions appeared on the landscape were described as "competing stories" and "conflicting stories" (p. 125). Competing stories are understood as teachers' stories that live in dynamic but positive tension with the plotlines of the dominant stories of school. These stories live alongside one another in ways that allow for change and possibility in both teachers' stories and stories of school. An example of competing stories appears in our earlier story of Lia in that the story of school of being "on time" was shaped by different plotlines in Lia's in- and out-of-classroom place. In the in-classroom place she was welcomed whenever she arrived. In the out-of-classroom place, she knew her late arrival, despite a good reason, would be questioned and that a silent reprimand was given through the issuing of the late slips. Conflicting stories are understood as teachers' stories that collide with the dominant stories of school. Conflicting stories are often short-lived as teachers are unable to sustain them in the face of the dominant stories of school. Indeed, as Clandinin and Connelly (1995: 157) wrote: "Professionals could live and tell ... [conflicting] stories only at their peril. Often they told cover stories." In our story of Lia we have a sense that in her decision to not sneak down the hallway she, too, had some knowing of the peril of trying to live out a story in conflict with the dominant stories of school which said that children who were late needed to get a late slip from the office. What was not clearly visible in our story of Lia was that the late slip she dropped on the corner of Emily's desk, like other late slips dropped there by children before and after Lia, was lost in the midst of the papers, teaching supplies, and resources scattered across the desk.

As Connelly and Clandinin (1999) continued to spend time alongside teachers, inquiring with them about their experiences in schools, what teachers often spoke of seemed to be not only their knowledge, their personal practical knowledge, and their contexts, the professional knowledge landscape, but also how their contexts and knowledge were intimately woven into their stories of who they were and who they were becoming. In this way, Connelly and Clandinin (1999) realized that teachers seemed to be talking about their identities. Teachers asked questions such as "Who am I in my story of teaching?", "Who am I in my place in the school?", "Who am I in children's stories?" This attention to identity led them to develop a narrative concept of "stories to live by" (p. 4) to conceptually bring together personal practical knowledge, professional knowledge landscapes, and teacher identity. Stories to live by is a term that allows us to "understand how knowledge, context, and identity are linked and can be understood narratively" (p. 4).

For Connelly and Clandinin (1999: 4), stories to live by refers to identity which is "given meaning by the narrative understandings of knowledge and context." For teachers and administrators, stories to live by are "shaped by such matters as secret teacher stories, sacred stories of schooling, and teachers' cover stories" (p. 4).

Teacher identity is understood as a unique embodiment of each teacher's stories to live by, stories shaped by knowledge composed on landscapes past and present in which a teacher lives and works. Stories to live by are multiple, fluid, and shifting, continuously composed and recomposed in the moment-to-moment living alongside children, families, administrators, and others, both on and off the school landscape. We do not wish to imply that teachers' stories to live by are floating or ungrounded or easily changed. Stories to live by are threaded by plotlines shaped by teachers' personal practical knowledge and the landscapes on which they live. Teachers' stories to live by offer possibilities for change through retelling and reliving stories. This retelling and reliving is a restorying that changes their stories to live by.

As we began to think more deeply about narrative understandings of identity, we were led to other authors who were also trying to understand the connections between experience and narrative conceptions of identity. Kerby (1991: 34) offered a psychologically based narrative concept of identity:

> We see that the mere saying of "I" tells us very little about identity and continuity, though it does seem to presuppose them, or at least beg the question of them. The important question to ask someone who says "I" is very often "Who?" rather than "What?" – sometimes we ask it of ourselves.

Kerby drew attention to the ways self-identity is dependent upon "the *coherence* and *continuity* of one's personal narrative" (1991: 6; emphasis in original). Carr (1986) also pointed towards continuity and coherence in the unfolding of a life. He reminded us, as did Dewey (1938), that experience is both temporal and situated.

> Our lives admit of sometimes more, sometimes less coherence; they hang together reasonably well, but they occasionally tend to fall apart. Coherence seems to be a need imposed on us whether we seek it or not. Things need to make sense. We feel the lack of sense when it goes missing. The unity of self, not as an underlying identity but as a life that hangs together, is not a pre-given condition but an achievement. Some of us succeed, it seems, better than others. None of us succeed totally. We keep at it. What we are doing is telling and retelling, to ourselves and to others, the story of what we are about and what we are.
>
> (Carr 1986: 97)

In the living and telling of their stories, Connelly and Clandinin (1999) saw teachers trying to develop a narratively coherent account of themselves in the sense Carr wrote. As Carr (1986: 96) noted, this is "a constant task, sometimes a struggle, and when it succeeds it is an achievement." Carr explained the narrative coherence of a life-story as a struggle with two aspects: "one to live out or up to a plan or narrative, large or small, particular or general; the other to construct or choose that narrative." As we tried to understand teachers' and our own stories to live by, we saw teachers and ourselves struggling with both aspects.

One way of thinking about stories to live by is that they are the stories teachers live and tell. In both the living and in the telling there is a struggle for narrative coherence. Sometimes in reflection teachers begin to retell their stories, that is, to actively understand that they are writing their lives, as Heilbrun (1988) suggested. The retelling of their stories is only part of what Connelly and Clandinin (1990) called a restorying process. There is also a reliving part of restorying. In reliving their stories, teachers may begin to imagine themselves in new ways and to change their practices, the ways they live in the world. As they gain a deeper awareness of their stories to live by, they begin to shift those stories as they continue to go about their days.

Stories to live by sometimes have contradictory plotlines. Similar to competing and conflicting stories that live between teachers' stories to live by and their landscapes, competing and conflicting plotlines can live within a teacher's stories to live by. When these contradictory plotlines compete with one another, they can, for the most part, be sustained. When these contradictory plotlines conflict with one another tension becomes apparent, shaping awakenings that can lead to retellings and relivings of teachers' stories to live by.

This earlier work (Clandinin and Connelly 1995; Connelly and Clandinin 1988, 1999) began with understanding teachers' knowledge as personal practical knowledge, then grew to include the metaphor of the professional knowledge landscape as a way to understand how teachers' personal practical knowledge shaped, and was shaped by, their particular school contexts, and lastly stories to live by became a conceptual way to narratively understand the connections among teachers' knowledge, contexts, and identity. In the midst of work alongside teachers and administrators, new questions of children's stories to live by became foregrounded. Huber and Clandinin began to wonder about children's stories to live by, stories shaped by children's knowledge and context. They wondered, for example, about the stories Lia lived by. How were her stories to live by shaped by personal, social, and cultural narratives?

Beginning to attend narratively to children's lives in school

As they (Huber *et al.* 2003) shifted their focus to children's identity-making, they identified moments in which children's constructions of identities were visible. They noted that children worked to figure out their identities by asking questions of each other, by asking questions of teachers, by engaging in a playful way with teachers and each other, and by metaphorically laying their stories alongside particular poems or books. As they attended to children's stories to live by, they realized teachers' stories to live by often served as a context that shaped or interacted with the children's stories. They sharpened their focus and began to attend to the meeting of teachers' and children's stories to live by in in-classroom places in order to see what could be learned from studying the bumping up of children's and teachers' life identities and stories of school. For example, what could they learn if they attended closely to Lia's experience as her life stories bumped against the stories of school at City Heights and her teacher's stories to live by as they lived alongside one another in the in-classroom place of their Year 3/4 classroom? In time, as they lived alongside Emily and the Year 3/4 children at City Heights, they saw these bumping places, these places of tension, as occurring in both the in- and out-of-classroom places. In part, and at that time, they understood this bumping as a negotiation of stories to live by as teachers and students engaged in curriculum making.

Attending to curriculum making as negotiating a curriculum of lives

We're gathered in the cozy corner on this cold January afternoon. It is close to the end of the day and we've come together to share literature. Children work each day with literature, joining with one another in spaces throughout the room and in the hallway, sharing books and talking about their connections with the stories. Today it's Lia's turn to share and she pulls out *Whoever You Are* (Fox 1997) to read a few pages from it to her classmates. We smile as we watch for this is a book Lia has shared before, several times. Lia often talked about liking this book because it included "more than white people."

We think back to an early September morning when the children were gathered in the cozy corner. Emily, the teacher, gathered the children as part of a classroom rhythm during which she shared a piece of literature as an entry point and invitation for the children to write, draw, paint, and talk about their similarities and differences. It was early in the year and Emily wanted the children to find ways to think about who they were in relation to other children in their classroom. She chose a colourful picture book, *Whoever You Are*, by Mem Fox as a way to begin the year by making a space for the children to talk about who they were. On that September morning we had no idea that this book would become so important to the curriculum Lia was making in this multicultural classroom.

(Interim research text based on field notes, January 2000)

As Janice and Jean lived alongside the children and Emily in their classroom they gradually began to awaken to the curriculum making that was occurring. They positioned themselves in a tradition of curriculum studies grounded in John Dewey's (1938) ideas of experience and Joseph Schwab's (1973) ideas of curriculum commonplaces. In their 1988 description of the curriculum commonplaces, teacher, subject matter, milieu, and learner, Connelly and Clandinin wrote: "The commonplaces are a set of factors or determinants that occur in statements about the aims, content, and methods of the curriculum. Taken as a whole they serve to bound the set of statements identified as being curricular" (p. 84). Establishing this way of looking at curriculum, that is, in terms of the four commonplaces, Clandinin and Connelly (1992) acknowledged their starting point in their work on personal practical knowledge was the teacher. As they shifted their attention to the professional knowledge landscape, they were attending to both teacher and milieu. We followed their lead when they wrote that they worked from:

A Deweyan view of the curriculum from a teacher's vantage point (Clandinin, 1986; Connelly and Clandinin, 1988). Dewey's (1938) notion of "situation" and "experience" enabled us to imagine the teacher not so much as a maker of curriculum but as a part of it and to imagine a place for contexts, culture (Dewey's notion of interaction), and temporality (both past and future contained in Dewey's notion "continuity").

(Clandinin and Connelly 1992: 365)

Clandinin and Connelly suggested curriculum "might be viewed as an account of teachers' and children's lives together in schools and classrooms... [In this view of curriculum making] the teacher is seen as an integral part of the curricular process ... in which teacher, learners, subject matter, and milieu are in dynamic interaction" (1992: 392). They drew our attention to the centrality of lives in the negotiation of curriculum making. We share their "vision of curriculum as a course of life" (1992: 393) and as we played with this idea of curriculum as a course of life, we began to imagine how curriculum could be seen as a curriculum of life, perhaps a curriculum of lives. Thinking in this way, of course, makes the composition of life identities, stories to live by, central in the process of curriculum making. It was in this way that we began to deepen our understandings of the interactions among the teacher, the milieu, and children. And as we attended to children's lives, we attended to multiple plotlines within each life, plotlines of child as learner, as learner of subject matter, as learner of his/her life, of his/her stories to live by.

Returning to the story of Lia and the book *Whoever You Are* (Fox 1997), we saw the negotiation of a curriculum of Lia's life. In the field notes on which we based our interim research text, we saw the rhythm of a classroom milieu in which shared reading, a time when children shifted from quiet, on their own reading to sitting side-by-side or in small groups to read, was part of the daily rhythm. The choice of what was read in shared reading often spilled over from quiet reading as some children brought those books into the small group space of shared reading. After Emily introduced the book *Whoever You Are*, Lia had an opportunity to read and discuss the book multiple times over the course of the year. Shared reading eventually flowed into a time when the whole class gathered to celebrate the literature they read, to talk about ideas, to read pages loved because of language, ideas, or images, to sing, and to act out favourite parts of text. Even in January, Lia was continuing to share parts of *Whoever You Are* when the class celebrated literature. The spaces Emily made through literature, gatherings, and conversations enabled the beginning of a negotiation of Lia's curriculum making. As Lia talked about the book there was a sense of a meeting of her life stories with the lives of the characters. It included, as she said, "more than white people." In her continued returnings, Lia seemed to be awakening to how the classroom presence and honouring of a book that contained characters like her was threaded into possible new tellings of who she was. As she carried this book with her and frequently shared it, she engaged in possible experimentations with who she imagined she was and who she imagined she might become. She was able to see children who physically resembled her, to see that children had similarities and were worthy of love, and was able to see what was possible in this new country. Over time these experimentations became new tellings of her stories to live by. In this way her identity and the in-classroom curriculum making were negotiated as her life stories interacted with the stories her teacher was living by.

As they began their research study at City Heights School, Jean and Janice were attending mostly to what happened in the in-classroom place. However, as they lived alongside Emily, Lia, and the children in this Year 3/4 classroom, they began to attend more closely to the shaping influence of the out-of-classroom place. In this way, they began to see that teachers' stories to live by were nested within stories of school and school stories and that attending to this nestedness was important in trying to understand the meeting of the diverse lives of teachers, children, families, and administrators as their lives met in schools. With these puzzles in the foreground, puzzles of how children's stories to live by are shifted as they bump into teachers' and administrators' stories to live by and stories of school, we framed new puzzles around these bumping places, these places of tension, and how these places of tension sometimes interrupted children's, teachers', administrators', and families' stories to live by.

Michael Connelly and Jean Clandinin framed a research proposal to the Social Sciences and Humanities Research Council of Canada around these questions. The study proposal underwent ethics review at the University of Alberta and was approved. At the time of approval, a number of doctoral students expressed an interest in framing their research within the context of this study. Shaun Murphy, Marni Pearce, Anne Murray Orr, Marilyn Huber, and Vera Caine began to imagine who they might be in the context of the study and working alongside Jean Clandinin. Pam Steeves had recently completed her doctoral work and expressed an interest in continuing to engage in research while she worked as the Horowitz Scholar in Teacher Education. Janice Huber, part of the work at City Heights, left the University of Alberta to begin work as an assistant professor at St Francis Xavier University. She expressed an interest in continuing to engage the puzzles she had begun to explore alongside Jean, Emily, and the children at City Heights. In this way, some of the researchers knew others over time in various ways while others came to know one another through the collaborative and relational work that unfolded. This book is one of the outcomes of this shared passion for understanding the complex interwoven nature of lives in school.

In the chapters that follow we take up these puzzles, puzzles of the interwoven lives of children and teachers, as we inquire into the lives of children, teachers, families, and administrators in a second urban multicultural school, Ravine Elementary School.

Coming to Ravine Elementary School

As we began to engage these puzzles around tensions and interruptions in children's, teachers', and families' stories of school, we realized we would need to find a school open to inquiring into these difficult and complex puzzles. We knew we needed to find a school with certain characteristics but also a school where we knew staff and had the possibility of negotiating the kinds of relationships where, even in the moments of difficult tensions, people would stay engaged with the inquiry. There were a number of schools that came to mind.

First, we wanted to find a school where children's and families' lives were ones of diversity. We knew that the story of school told to us by district personnel of the kind of school we were interested in would be around plotlines of "low socio-economic levels," "inner city," "multicultural," "a high percentage of second language learners," and "low achievement." We knew the school we wanted to work in would be named in this way but we did not want to come to know the lives of children, families, and teachers in terms of these plotlines. We wanted, rather, to attend to their lives and the complex ways they were composing them.

Secondly, we needed to find a school where we could develop the kind of research relationships necessary to allow us to stay with the inquiries and that would allow us, as researchers, to live alongside our participants. We knew the principal, Jeanette, at Ravine Elementary School.[2] Many of us knew her over time as she moved from one school to another. We knew her in different relationships: as friend, as graduate study classmate, as co-instructor, and as research participant in other studies. Ravine Elementary School was a school where we knew children and families lived lives of diversity. When, as a group, we wondered about Ravine Elementary School as the school where this work might unfold, Jean contacted Jeanette and they met informally to talk about the possibilities for such a large group of researchers to undertake such a complex and tension-filled inquiry at the school. Jeanette expressed interest and said she would support our application to the school district for permission to work in her school. District permission was given to begin the inquiry in September 2002. In the next chapter we share a more complete description of the ways this narrative inquiry unfolded in the school.

Revisiting our research puzzles

Returning to our earlier research at City Heights, we realized we wanted to understand more about what happened to teachers', children's, families', and administrators' lives as they met in in-classroom and out-of-classroom places on school landscapes. As their lives met, and sometimes bumped and jarred against each other, we wondered how these meetings sometimes reverberated through and shaped each person's identity, their stories to live by. As teachers, teacher educators, and researchers, we particularly wanted to understand how children's stories to live by were shaped and reshaped, storied and restoried, through their interactions with teachers' and administrators' stories to live by. Furthermore, we wanted to understand how school stories and stories of school shaped children's stories to live by. And we wanted to attend to how teachers' and administrators' stories to live by were shaped by bumping against children's stories to live by. For the first time in our work, we paid attention to families' stories and stories of families as we attended to the lives in motion that comprised the storied lives on storied school landscapes.

Our research puzzles were shaped and reshaped by our growing understandings that the curriculum being made in schools is a curriculum of lives, that is, in schools, teachers', children's, administrators' and families' lives are being storied and restoried. What happens in schools is an identity-shaping process; lives are written and rewritten, storied and restoried. The identities, the stories to live by of children, teachers, administrators, and families are all being expressed, and, in those expressions, become open to being restoried, to being silenced, to being erased, to being shifted in educative and mis-educative ways. Attending to the complex, unfolding, shifting interplay among children's stories to live by, teachers' stories to live by, subject matter, and milieu became another way for us to understand our research puzzle as a puzzle in how curriculum making can be understood.

In the chapters that follow we take up these interconnected research puzzles as we come to know some children's, teachers', administrators' and families' lives at the same time as we reflectively and reflexively come to know more about our own lives.

Chapter 2

Working alongside children, teachers, parents, and administrators in relational narrative inquiry

Melissa, a Year 3 student new to City Heights School, asked, "Who are you and why do you come to our classroom?" We responded, "We're trying to understand more about schools and classrooms by thinking about the different people who come to them." "What kind of differences?" Melissa wondered. In retrospect, as we spoke of cultural and lifestyle differences, our responses seemed vague. Melissa continued and asked, "Are you going to learn from adults, like other teachers, in the school?" "Yes," Janice said, "but mostly we want to learn from children and families in the class." Melissa seemed surprised and wondered, "The children?" We spoke of learning a lot from paying attention to what children were saying and writing. Melissa said, "Oh, so the children will be like teachers too?"

(Field notes, November 22, 1999)

Melissa's questions and our vague responses lived with us as we engaged in this study at Ravine Elementary School. Melissa's wonder about who children become in narrative inquiries compels us to ask ourselves who we are in this work and who we are in relation to the participants. It also made us think about the relational responsibilities we undertook as we lived alongside children, teachers, families, and administrators and what we were asking for as we became characters in their stories. Melissa's seemingly simple question opened up many questions of the complexities of engaging in a narrative inquiry alongside children, teachers, families, and administrators. In this chapter, as we describe the narrative inquiry we undertook at Ravine Elementary School, we try to deepen understandings about relational narrative inquiry.

As we read our field notes and told remembered stories of experiences at Ravine Elementary School we saw that Melissa's conversation with Janice and Jean three years earlier was echoed in the questions and wonderings of children and families at Ravine Elementary School. In what follows, we put forward imagined wonderings from the vantage points of a child, a teacher, a mother, and the staff as they met this group of researchers in the school year.

On Julie's first day of school in Year 1 she wondered to Anne about what Anne was writing as she sat quietly outside the gathering of children who were being read to. We wondered if Julie, like Melissa, was trying to figure out who we were, who she could be with us, and how our presence might shape the lives of children and the teacher in that classroom story.

On Vera's first day, as she spoke to the children in the Year 3/4 learning strategies classroom about taking photographs of who they were and who they were becoming, we wondered how Kristi, as teacher, might have felt about Vera's shaping influence in the classroom. We wondered if Kristi felt that Vera's presence might interrupt her imaginings she held of how the year might unfold with the Year 3/4 children.

As Marni met with Aaron's mom at her home, we wonder how she storied Marni as a person both in the school alongside her son and in her home as someone alongside both her and her family.

On the first school organization day we wondered how the staff might have felt about how the group of researchers who sat amongst them would shape the story of school and their lives over the year. Did they wonder about how vulnerable they might become? Did they feel excitement and a sense of possibility at what they might learn from engaging in narrative inquiry?

We carried these wonderings and questions, begun in our work at City Heights, within us and they shaped a place to begin our exploration of the methodology of narrative inquiry as it was lived out at Ravine Elementary School.

Narrative inquiry

When Connelly and Clandinin (1985) first began to engage in research alongside teachers and children in classrooms in the early 1980s, narrative inquiry, with its relational qualities, was still a somewhat questioned practice. However, as later noted by Connelly and Clandinin (1990: 2), while narrative inquiry was, at that time, becoming a more common research methodology in educational studies, in fields of study both in and outside of education (Carr 1986; Crites 1971; Mitchell 1981; Polkinghorne 1988), it already had "a long intellectual history." One way to understand openings shaped in the field of education for the continuing development of narrative inquiry as a research methodology can be understood by tracing shifts in dominant conceptualizations of knowledge and research. For example, as the dominant conceptualization of knowledge as objective began to shift toward understandings of knowledge as personal, as embodied in people, and as shaped and reshaped through their experiences in situations (Belenky *et al.* 1986; Bruner 1986; Connelly and Clandinin 1985; Dewey 1938; Johnson 1987, 1989; Polanyi 1958), questions of knowledge as understood in these experiential, contextual, temporal, and narrative ways were not only seen as increasingly legitimate in the field of education (Carter 1993; Clandinin 1986; Connelly and Clandinin 1988; Eisner 1988; Elbaz 1983; Witherell and Noddings 1991) but began to shape research in more collaborative, school-based directions (Clandinin and Connelly 1988; Clandinin *et al.* 1993; Hollingsworth 1994; Miller 1990). Yet, while these new views of knowledge and these more collaborative kinds of research brought researchers back into schools, they also opened up new questions about the positionings of researchers and participants and about complex ethical dilemmas that shaped not only the research process but what researchers came to know and write about (Borland 1991; Clandinin and Connelly 1988; Fine 1987; Harding 1988; Lincoln and Guba 1989; Lyons 1990; Noddings 1986; Personal Narratives Group 1989). These new questions continued to shape narrative inquiry as a research methodology.

Harder to describe, harder to find adequate words for, was how a narrative inquiry unfolds. What is the process narrative inquirers engage in as they inquire alongside participants? Unlike research methodologies beginning with, and then proceeding to answer, carefully crafted questions, narrative inquiry was messy and emergent, often creating, as Eisner (1991: 172) wrote, a collage rather than the "construction of a building." Narrative inquiry was also messy in the sense described by Schön (1983) as researchers and teachers lived alongside one another in classroom and school places. Schön's metaphor of a swamp drew attention to the uncertainty as well as the particularity which researchers experienced as they inquired alongside teachers in classrooms. Like entering a swamp – a changing, often tenuous, yet deeply interesting, alive, and complex landscape – researchers who choose to come down from the "highlands" of their university positions to live in the muddiness alongside teachers in classrooms understand classroom lives of teachers and children from a unique perspective, a perspective only possible by being positioned alongside those in classrooms.

In these ways, narrative inquiry called for a kind of living alongside that pushed against earlier research notions of distance and objectivity (Phillips 1987; Thorndike 1927). It was a decidedly relational form of inquiry. In Connelly and Clandinin's (1990) exploration of experience and narrative inquiry, they wrote of their unfolding relational living with co-researchers in the following way:

> We found that merely listening, recording, and fostering participant story telling was both impossible (we are, all of us, continually telling stories of our experience, whether or not we speak and write them) and

unsatisfying. We learned that, we, too, needed to tell our stories. Scribes we were not; story tellers and story livers we were. And in our story telling, the stories of our participants merged with our own to create new stories, ones that we have labelled *collaborative stories*. The thing finally written on paper (or, perhaps on film, tape, or canvas), the research paper or book, is a collaborative document; a mutually constructed story created out of the lives of both researcher and participant.

(1990: 12; emphasis in original)

This description of narrative inquiry as shared relational work and as an evolving co-construction was what guided us as we planned for and began to work with the children, teachers, families, and administrators at Ravine Elementary School. However, we were also guided by the university requirements for ethics clearance for working with human subjects. These university requirements were not designed for relational forms of inquiry. Complying with these university requirements we composed an ethics review complete with a letter of informed consent for working with children and families as well as for working with teachers and administrators. The letters of informed consent described how we would be participating in life in in-classroom and out-of-classroom places as well as, in some cases, out-of-school places. We described how we would be engaging in tape-recorded research conversations, writing field notes, collecting school documents and children's work, and having the children take photographs. We worked to negotiate relationships, always mindful of the human subject ethical guidelines. Negotiating these relationships and questions asked within them, such as the ones asked by Julie and Melissa, kept us awake to how the children, teachers, families, and administrators saw us as co-researchers, how they saw themselves as co-researchers, and how we saw ourselves as co-researchers engaged alongside participants in relational narrative inquiry.

In earlier writing Huber and Clandinin (2002) explored an ethic of relational narrative inquiry as they inquired into the bumping up of dominant human subject ethical guidelines in their relational narrative inquiry with children as co-researchers at City Heights School. They wrote:

As we entered into co-researcher relationships with children we began to be very thoughtful about what plotlines were shaping us as teacher researchers, as researcher teachers, as researchers. Attending to the maintenance of relationships with children, now and in the future, became, for us, a first consideration. For us, as Clandinin and Connelly (2000) wrote, we need to reframe ethical concerns into concerns of relational responsibility. We realized that our attentiveness to relationship could conflict with dominant stories of what "good" teachers and "good" researchers do. Plotlines for good researchers do not often attend to the aftermath for children's lives as their first concern. As relational narrative inquirers engaged with children as co-researchers, we realized that it was here that we needed to attend.

(2002: 801)

As we entered into relational narrative inquiry with people at Ravine Elementary School, we did so attentive to Huber and Clandinin's (2002) call for an ethic of relational narrative inquiry. We knew that negotiating this ethic did not come with a recipe of specific steps to follow but, instead, called us to stay "wakeful, and thoughtful, about all of our inquiry decisions" (Clandinin and Connelly 2000: 184). Entering into Ravine Elementary School and into inquiry relationships between and among teachers, children, families, administrators, and one another meant that we did so caring about the aftermath of each teacher's life, each child's life, each family member's life, each administrator's life, each of our lives. Negotiating an ethic of relational narrative inquiry took us, as Behar (1996) wrote, toward understandings as well as complexities we might not have otherwise experienced. For example, in both the living and telling of our narrative inquiry we continued to face questions of the differences between positioning ourselves as judging or more deeply understanding a teacher's, child's, family member's, administrator's, or researcher's lived or told stories.

As the upcoming chapters show, in trying to stay wakeful to all that was unfolding around and within us, there were many moments when we were able to inquire into our or participants' felt tensions. There were, as well, moments we could not or did not stay wakeful to in our living. We imagine these complexities of negotiating an ethic of relational narrative inquiry in multi-layered inquiries such as the one we undertook at Ravine Elementary School will continue to shape the methodology of narrative inquiry. As we wrote this book, talking often and thinking hard about the complexities of negotiating relational narrative inquiry among teachers, children, families, administrators, and researchers, we were reminded of Bateson's (2004) sense that our willingness to learn is, at least in part, shaped through a process of

entertain[ing] multiple points of view and even to hold[ing] two [or more] apparently conflicting points of view... . This is increasingly necessary for living in a world of high diversity and rapid change, which presses us all toward either confusion or insight.

(2004: 252)

A three-dimensional narrative inquiry space

Through our research we came to understand experience as narratively constructed and narratively lived out. Because we see experience narratively, we study experience narratively. In other words, we see narrative as both phenomenon and method (Connelly and Clandinin 1990). Thinking narratively, for us, is thinking within a metaphorical "three-dimensional narrative inquiry space" (Clandinin and Connelly 2000: 49). Dewey's (1938) work shapes our thinking about narrative inquiry. We engaged in this inquiry mindful of his concept of experience and Clandinin and Connelly's (2000) conceptualization of narrative inquiry. They described their terms as:

> personal and social (interaction); past, present, and future (continuity); combined with the notion of place (situation). This set of terms creates a metaphorical three-dimensional narrative inquiry space, with temporality along one dimension, the personal and social along a second dimension, and place along the third. Using this set of terms, any particular inquiry is defined by this three-dimensional space: studies have temporal dimensions and address temporal matters; they focus on the personal and the social in a balance appropriate to the inquiry; and they occur in specific places or sequences of places.
>
> (2000: 50)

The personal-social dimension points us inward and outward; inward "toward the internal conditions, such as feelings, hopes, aesthetic reactions, and moral dispositions" (Clandinin and Connelly 2000: 50) and outward "toward the existential conditions" (p. 50). Moving backward and forward points us "to temporality – past, present, and future" (p. 50). Place "attends to the specific concrete physical and topological boundaries of inquiry landscapes" (p. 51).

Connelly and Clandinin had not made this metaphor of a three-dimensional narrative inquiry space explicit in their early studies. It was as they and others (Bach 1993; Craig 1992; Davies 1996; Huber 1992; Kennedy 1992; Murphy 2000; Pearce 1995; Rose 1997; Sewall 1994; Steeves 1993) worked and lived alongside teachers and children that they realized such a metaphoric space would help them represent not only the wholeness of their lives and the lives of the participants with whom they engaged but would help them engage in the unfolding experiences that have temporal, personal, social, and place aspects. Even in their early work as narrative inquirers they wanted to represent people not as taken apart by analytic categories but as people who were composing lives – lives composed over time and full of richness and complexity. For example, when Clandinin (1986) was working on her doctoral dissertation, at one point she realized she had, by analyzing the images emerging from her two participants' lives, lost sight of the wholeness of their lives. In an attempt to give an account of each of them she struggled with what she called a characterization, "a holistic account" (p. 120). She wrote that the interpretive accounts she developed did not "allow me to give a picture of Stephanie that reflects the harmony and flow I saw in her practices and in her personal practical knowledge which minds those practices" (p. 120). Later, as Clandinin and Connelly (2000) continued to struggle with how to understand storied life experiences, stories to live by, as whole-life compositions, they developed the metaphor of a three-dimensional narrative inquiry space.

By engaging in a relational narrative inquiry in Lia's Year 3/4 classroom, Jean and Janice's relationships with Lia became woven into who they were and who they were becoming as teacher educators and as researchers. Many of the field notes of life in the Year 3/4 classroom at City Heights School documented stories of Lia, of her life there and outside of school, and of the thoughts and wonderings that attending to Lia's stories shaped for Janice and Jean. As we pulled this field note forward and placed it within the three-dimensional narrative inquiry space, we wanted to show something about how Lia's experiences raised questions about the bumping up of her life with the stories of school shaping City Heights. Identity threads of Lia and of her teacher, Emily, are visible. So, too, are plotlines of dominant stories of school at City Heights. As we did this, we were called to think more deeply about the interconnected set of plotlines visible in the field note. By inquiring into the field note by moving backward, forward, inward, outward, and attending to place, we were able, first, to be responsive to Lia by imagining the felt tensions she experienced as she pulled open the heavy wooden door at the school's front entrance, as she and her brothers stood at attention in the hallway as the anthem played, as she and her brothers waited in the office for their late slips, as she took each brother to his classroom and offered an explanation to each teacher, as she finally arrived in her own classroom, her actions showing that she felt tension about how the morning started.

As we entered into the midst of stories at Ravine Elementary School, we entered not only into the midst of school stories and stories of school but into the midst of the lives of teachers such as Kristi, of children such as Julie, of family members such as Aaron's mom, and of administrators such as Jeanette. We entered into the midst of the stories they were living, telling, reliving, and retelling of their lives in in- and out-of-classroom places and in in- and out-of-school places. We also entered into the stories we, as researchers, were composing and recomposing. As narrative inquirers, being in the midst of these nested stories brought us into the midst of uncertainty. As described by Clandinin and Connelly (2000: 145-6):

> Part of the narrative inquirer's doubts come from understanding that they need to write about people, places, and things as *becoming* rather than *being*. Their task is not so much to say that people, places, and things are this way or that way but that they have a narrative history and are moving forward. The narrative research text is fundamentally a temporal text – about what has been, what is now, and what is becoming.
>
> (emphasis in original)

Negotiating relationships with participants

With narrative inquiry, connections amongst storied lives, past, present, or imagined future often precede participation. As storied in Chapter 1, while some of the researchers and teacher and administrative participants knew one another prior to beginning narrative inquiries at Ravine Elementary School, other researchers and teacher and administrative participants did not know one another. None of the researchers knew the child and family participants prior to the inquiry. As we began to talk with Jeanette and the staff about inquiry possibilities, threads of interest between particular teachers and particular researchers became visible. In some situations, these threads were shaped in imagination as researchers began to talk with teachers about living alongside them in in-classroom places and, for example, of wanting to explore the place of conversation, photography, or sharing literature in shaping spaces for identity and curriculum making with children.

In the fall of 2002, as researchers lived in classrooms and in the school, connections, sometimes shaped by children's interactions with the researcher in the in-classroom place or sometimes shaped as researchers had opportunities to come to know family members of children in classrooms, drew child and family participants into inquiry with particular researchers. As narrative inquirers, these stories of connection shaped a background for negotiating relationships with participants. Not only did these connections shape possible places for beginning to negotiate relationships but, over time, as stories were lived and shared between participants and researchers, these unfolding stories continued to shape ways in which relationships were composed and recomposed.

Attending to the negotiation of relationships with participants as the inquiry unfolded was important, both in the living and in the telling of the inquiry as we composed research texts. The three-dimensional narrative inquiry space provided a field we as narrative inquirers played in, enabling a space for imagination in relationship. As narrative inquirers we were mindful of our continuing need to be responsive in this place in the way Buber (1937) described in a relationship of "I and thou." Realizing the complexity, mystery, and fragility of researcher/participant relationships lived in this way, we attempted to attend to our participants' lives with all of our own.

Buber's (1937) description of an I–Thou relationship between teachers and students drew attention to teachers' living of respectful relationships with students by the ways they attended to the uniqueness of each student and the situations she or he experienced in the classroom. His sense of an I–Thou relationship shaped a way for us to think through how we, as narrative inquirers, lived alongside teachers, children, families, administrators, and one another at Ravine Elementary School. Not unlike Buber's descriptions of the place of respect in an I–Thou relationship, respectful relationships in narrative inquiries are not pre-scripted, based on a pre-determined plan. Instead, respect as one aspect of relational narrative inquiry, is a thread pulled forward, a thread continuously negotiated throughout the inquiry. Buber's notions of respect in relationships shaped the field texts we composed and the ways we worked with these field texts to compose research texts. In Chapter 1 our inquiry into Lia's experiences on the crisp fall morning she and her brothers arrived late to City Heights School offered a way to think through Buber's (1937) I–Thou relationship as an aspect of relational narrative inquiry. Negotiating an I–Thou relationship with participants called us to engage with our hearts as we felt our and participants' stories, our ears as we heard our and participants' stories, our eyes as we became witness to the living of our and participants' stories.

In attending to threads of narrative connection as the narrative inquiry unfolded, we were not seeking narrative connections as a way to live or to tell of a smooth, happily ever after inquiry. Instead, our seeking of narrative connections helped us, as researchers, to more deeply understand the experiences of participants and ourselves as well as the particularities of the multiple and interconnecting contexts shaping our inquiry. Negotiating relationships with participants while attending to threads of connection opened spaces where the lives of the participants and our lives as researchers shaped the questions, wonderings, and emerging inquiry threads that moved our narrative inquiry forward.

Multiple storied lives played a part in determining the way lives and stories unfolded. Clandinin and Connelly's notion of the "negotiation of narrative" (1988: 281) helped us to stay wakeful about the multiple storylines shaping participants' lives, our lives, and the school context. As Clandinin and Connelly tried to understand the breakdown of a research relationship in an earlier study between a teacher, Ellen, and a graduate student/researcher, Charles, they turned to their earlier work with "narrative unities" (Clandinin 1985; Connelly and Clandinin 1985) as a way to understand what had happened. Describing narrative unity "as a continuum within a person's experiences which renders life experiences meaningful through the unity they achieve for the person" (1988: 280), they traced the narrative unities of Ellen and Charles. This tracing led them toward new insights about the relationship between Ellen and Charles, particularly the discontinuity shaped in the meeting of their lives. Ellen, knowing a story of Clandinin's earlier work and relationship with Stephanie, imagined a similar experience with Charles. Charles, however, "remained an outsider to the classroom" (p. 280), focusing his energies not on negotiation of their relationship but, instead, on gathering the "data" he needed for his study. As Clandinin and Connelly (1988) noted:

> one research partner anticipated a new narrative unity, began it, and felt betrayed by it while the other continued with an ongoing narrative unity revising it only to the point of encompassing a new set of school data according to his image of himself as researcher.
>
> (1988: 281)

Understanding the tensions between Charles and Ellen from the vantage point of narrative unities, they wrote:

> collaborative research constitutes a relationship. In everyday life, the idea of friendship implies a sharing, an interpenetration of two or more persons' spheres of experience. Mere contact is acquaintanceship, not friendship. The same may be said for collaborative research which requires a close relationship akin to friendship. Relationships are joined, as McIntyre implies, by the narrative unities of our lives.
>
> (1988: 281)

Attending to the multiplicity of stories to live by shaping participants' and our lives significantly deepened our understandings of the experiences of participants, of the continuities and discontinuities they experienced as they composed their lives in the school, and of the temporal ways in which their and our stories to live by were negotiated narratively as relationships developed, generating a "new shared narrative" (Clandinin and Connelly 1988: 281) between participants and researchers.

Greene (1995: 1) named this multiplicity in her life, in her stories to live by, in the following way:

> The quest involves me as woman, as teacher, as mother, as citizen, as New Yorker, as art-lover, as activist, as philosopher, as white middle-class American. Neither my self nor my narrative can have, therefore, a single strand. I stand at the crossing point of too many social and cultural forces; and, in any case, I am forever on my way. My identity has to be perceived as multiple.

What Greene drew attention to was that not only is her identity multiple through the various storylines shaping and reshaping the composition of her life, but these storylines, these multiple identity threads, do not exist in isolation from one another or from the broader social and cultural milieu in which she lives.

Engaging in narrative inquiry alongside participants called us to stay wakeful to the multiplicity of our identities, to the multiple identity threads each participant was negotiating, as well as to the broader social, cultural, and institutional plotlines at work in our and participants' contexts. We were called to attend to the multiple narrative unities of participants' and our lives as a way to not hide, deny, or silence the multiplicity of participants' and our life compositions or the shared narrative unities being co-authored between us.

By looking over time at our narrative inquiries we often came to see interconnecting threads. As Clandinin and Connelly (2000: 67–8) wrote:

It was being in the field, day after day, year after year, that brought forth a compelling sense of the long-term landscape narratives at work. This too is one of the things that narrative inquirers do in the field: they settle in, live and work alongside participants, and come to experience not only what can be seen and talked about directly but also the things not said and not done that shape the narrative structure of their observations and their talking.

Being in the field, being alongside participants as a way to come to know and understand interconnecting threads within, between, or across lives, was another aspect of our narrative inquiry. This particular aspect of negotiating relationships with participants helped us to be attentive as we lived in the field, composed field texts, and worked with our field texts to compose interim research texts and research texts.

Negotiating relationships at Ravine Elementary School

In May 2002 Jean asked Jeanette, the principal of Ravine Elementary School, how we might best connect with teachers in the school who would be open to having a narrative inquirer living alongside them in their classroom. Jean knew Jeanette from other relationships and previous projects at Ravine Elementary School and other schools. Pam had been at the school for several years after Jeanette first arrived at Ravine Elementary School. Pam and Jeanette continued to be in conversations at the school after Pam's narrative inquiry officially ended. Marni and Jean were involved with Jeanette in an alternative teacher education project at the school. With Jeanette's arrival the staff became accustomed to having research and teacher education projects at the school.

Jeanette suggested the team of researchers meet over lunch with small groups of teachers to describe their inquiry interests. Jean, Marni, Shaun, and Anne began to engage in a series of conversations about research possibilities with teachers. In that way, Lian, a Year 5/6 teacher, became a participant with Shaun. Laura, a Year 1/2 teacher became a participant with Anne. Shaun, Anne, and Jean participated in some late spring 2002 activities at the school to gain some sense of the school context. Shaun and Anne spent a short amount of time in Lian's and Laura's classrooms to begin to create classroom relationships with them. Because of the multi-age groupings in the school, they met some of the children who would be with Lian and Laura in the fall of 2002. Gale, a Year 1/2 teacher who was returning to the school and was known to some of the research group from earlier projects and courses, spoke with Marni and Jeanette about joining the inquiry. In this way, Gale and Marni began working alongside the children and families in Gale's Year 1/2 classroom in the fall of 2002.

In September 2002, Vera became interested in the possibilities of visual narrative inquiry (Bach 1998; Caine 2002) as a way of understanding experience and Jean approached Kristi and Jeanette about the participation of Kristi and the children in the Year 2/3 learning strategies classroom. In that way Kristi and her students became part of the project. By the winter of 2003 another teacher had approached Jean about the possibility of his becoming involved in the project. Jean approached Jeanette and asked if some teachers would be interested in telling their stories of learning to teach children of diversity. In that way Marilyn became involved in research conversations with Suzanne, Jim, and Sally. Jean and Jeanette engaged in research conversations stretching across the school year. Jeanette also engaged in research conversations focused on particular classrooms and teachers with Marni, Shaun, and Anne over the school year.

Over the year, the group of researchers participated not only in in-classroom places but also in out-of-classroom places in activities and events such as professional development days, staff meetings, school department meetings, school assemblies, parent teacher meetings, school open houses, special school-wide events, including the fall barbeque, the Christmas concert, and the penny carnival. We moved comfortably in hallways, staffrooms, playgrounds, and the office area. We also participated in out-of-school places including children's homes, children's events, community activities, and teachers' homes and gathering places.

As we began to live alongside teachers in their classrooms, we became involved in the life of the classroom. We helped with planning, organizing materials and resources, teaching small groups of children, responding to children's work, and so on. As we came to know the children in each classroom we began to develop special relationships with some children. We eventually invited these children to participate in more intensive ways in the inquiry. In Lian's class, Shaun eventually came to work intensively with Erica, Cheyenne, Catrina, Dylan, Leo, and Travis. In Gale's class, Marni came to work intensively with Aaron and Sadie. In Laura's class, Anne came to work intensively with Julie, Fareda, James, and Bob. Vera worked with all of the students, 14 boys in the Year 2/3 learning strategies classroom.

The researchers also negotiated relationships with some families of the children with whom they worked. They met the families at open houses and meet the teacher nights. They talked with families and gained their permission for their children to participate. Children, families, teachers, and administrators signed consent forms.

In informal ways our research group continually negotiated relationships with all members of the school staff, including the school secretaries, lunchroom supervisors, and custodians. As the year in the field at Ravine Elementary School came to a close many relationships continued to unfold. Anne had an intermittent series of classroom and student visits throughout the 2003–4 school year. Marni, Marilyn, and Shaun maintained some contact with children, families, and staff. In part, this happened as research texts were shared back with participants. Jean and Pam participated in an after school autobiographical book club with interested staff members over the 2003–4 school year. Marni, Pam, and Jeanette continued to work on a pre-service teacher education project.

Living in the field

As described earlier, our narrative inquiry at Ravine Elementary School emerged from both an evolving theoretical background as well as from the wonderings and inquiry puzzles we each carried in us as the inquiry began. The theoretical background shaping our narrative inquiry, described in Chapter 1, attends to the work of Clandinin and Connelly, alongside graduate students, teachers, children, and administrators, beginning in the early 1980s at Bay Street School, an urban school in Toronto. It was in this context that Jean, alongside a classroom teacher, Stephanie, and the children with whom she worked, engaged in long-term school-based relational inquiry (Clandinin 1986) trying to understand something more about teachers' "personal practical knowledge" (Connelly and Clandinin 1988: 25) and the ways in which curriculum might be understood as "an account of teachers' and students' lives over time" (Clandinin and Connelly 1992: 392). This early work built on Schwab's (1970) four curriculum commonplaces – teacher, learner, subject matter, and milieu – and, in particular, foregrounded teachers and learners. The next study in this program of research built upon narrative conceptualizations of personal practical knowledge as a way to further understand the milieu in which teachers lived and worked. Clandinin and Connelly (1995) developed the metaphor of a "professional knowledge landscape" as a way to study the nested and interconnected milieus experienced by teachers as they engaged in curriculum undertakings with children. These experiential, narrative conceptualizations and language lived in us as we lived in the field, composed or co-composed field texts, and as we composed research texts.

Another background also shaped our narrative inquiry at Ravine Elementary School. Our telling of this background pulls forward traditions shaped, reshaped, lived, told, and retold at the Center for Research for Teacher Education and Development, traditions of gathering with graduate students, faculty, and visiting professors, at both a weekly "research issues table" and in ongoing "works-in-progress groups." Often referred to as "the kitchen table" (Steeves 2004) by past and present participants at the Center, these two gathering spaces invited us into a process "of knowing through relationship, or relational knowing, [which] involves both the recall of prior knowledge and the reflection on what knowledge is perceived or present in social and political settings" (Hollingsworth 1994: 77–8). At the research issues table at the Center, participants co-shaped a conversation space in which stories of experiences of becoming researchers, both those spoken and written down, were shared and responded to. In works-in-progress groups we shared writing-in-progress. In both of these spaces of inquiry, while each participant brought self-authored stories or pieces of writing to share with others, because of the responses given back to our stories, our knowing became deeply relational. Constructing knowledge in this way required an "integration of voices," a process in which each person's knowing was interwoven with the "knowledge they felt intuitively was personally important with knowledge they ... learn[ed] from others" (Belenky *et al.* 1986: 134). Learning to live, tell, relive, and retell stories of relational knowing as narrative inquirers, that is, stories in which our ideas were not owned but shared, shaped, recomposed, and reknown through relationship and conversation, held an important place in the inquiry.

Two ways we carried this relational knowing in us and among us as we entered into and lived at Ravine Elementary School are described as we story our improvised meetings at "the pit," a circular space built into the centre of the school. As well, our more formal research meetings at the Center table, research meetings in which we participated both in-person and through teleconferencing, were also spaces shaped by wanting to stay at the messy, complex work of knowing in relation.

Another possibly more silent story weaving across the chapters of our book reveals our livings, tellings, relivings, and retellings of ourselves and of our knowing as deeply shaped in relation, in our living, moment by moment, alongside teachers, children, families, and administrators at Ravine Elementary School. This kind of relational knowing acknowledges the vital place of participants as they engaged with us in relational narrative inquiry.

Methodological challenges in the midst

Engaging in this work at Ravine Elementary School brought forward methodological challenges of relational narrative inquiry alongside teachers, children, families, and administrators. In what follows we attend to some of the methodological challenges we faced as a group of researchers.

The first challenge was intricately involved with knowing that narrative inquiry is relational inquiry (Clandinin and Connelly 2000; Connelly and Clandinin in press; Huber and Clandinin 2002; Mickelson 2000). By this, we attend to how narrative inquirers enter into landscapes and attempt to negotiate ways of living alongside research participants. At Ravine Elementary School our intention was to negotiate relationships that allowed us to live alongside teachers, administrators, children, and families and to hear their stories in their own terms, following their own plotlines. Each researcher positioned him or herself in ways that allowed him or her to hear the stories of a teacher and administrator; or a teacher and several children; or a teacher, several children, and some family members. Not only did this negotiation involve the shaping of multiple relationships that evolved over time but, as well, it engaged us in the complex work of continually attending to multiple lives as they unfolded over time.

A second challenge involved the need to thoughtfully negotiate ways to enter into the midst of an ongoing story of school at Ravine Elementary School and to learn to stand alongside multiple people as they lived their lives. As we worked alongside children, families, teachers, administrators, and each other as researchers we needed to remind ourselves that individuals are also in the midst of their lives. Participants' lives did not begin when we, as researchers, arrived. Nor did they end when we left. As we entered into inquiry spaces at Ravine Elementary School we needed to attend thoughtfully to how we shaped, and imagined we might shape, the lives of children, teachers, families, and administrators that were being composed alongside of our lives. We also needed to attend thoughtfully to how we moved away from their lives at the end of the study. For each of us it was difficult to leave the relationships we negotiated at Ravine Elementary School. As described earlier, in many ways, these relationships continued.

A third challenge was learning to live with a skin-tingling kind of awareness to all that was happening. Maxine Greene (1995) wrote of wide awakeness; it was this kind of wide awakeness that we felt needed to live within and among us. As a group of researchers we all knew a story of school and we all had a deeply felt embodied sense of school. We knew it was possible that we would sleep through, that is, be inattentive to, the tensions that might seep through the ongoing stories to live by as they were lived out at the school. One way of trying to stay wide awake was to employ diverse methods to compose field texts with participants in order to allow us to hear and see and feel the tensions as children's, families', teachers', administrators', and our storied lives bumped against one another and against institutional, social, and cultural stories. In addition to working with a range of field texts we also worked closely with one another in order to stay awake and to keep finding alternative ways of understanding the storied lives we were encountering. As a research group we came together often to share stories, transcripts, field notes, photographs, and other forms of field texts, and to respond to each other's stories. In that way we stayed awake to possible moments and places of tension. We say more about this in upcoming sections of this chapter.

A fourth methodological challenge: in the midst of composing field texts

Because we saw ourselves as living in the midst of multiple stories being lived and told by multiple people, one of our challenges was to find ways of composing field texts that would allow us to slow down the moments to which we wanted to attend. We thought about our field texts as situated within the three-dimensional narrative inquiry space and we realized that this process helped us to understand the lived and told experiences of our participants in relationship with us. We also wanted to think about field texts that would allow us to slow down the living so we could look back and try to recompose the moment of living from a future time and space.

Transcripts of research conversations, field notes, and researcher journals were all field texts we composed at Ravine Elementary School. We also collected field texts composed by participants such as the Ravine Elementary School handbook, newsletters, report cards, student work samples, student writing, and memory box artefacts. A third kind of field text we composed was more intentionally a co-composition between researchers and participants.

In earlier research with which we have been involved (Clandinin 1986; Clandinin and Connelly 1995; Clandinin, Davies, Hogan, and Kennard 1993; Connelly and Clandinin 1999; J. Huber 1992; J. Huber and Whelan 2000; M. Huber 2000; Murphy 2000; Murray Orr 2001; Pearce 1995; Steeves 2000) we engaged in research conversations with diverse participants, including pre-service teachers, experienced teachers, children, and administrators. As described by Clandinin and Connelly (1994: 422), research conversations

> are marked by equality among participants and by flexibility to allow group participants to establish the form and topics important to their inquiry. Conversation entails listening. The listener's response may constitute a probe into experience and takes the representation of experience far beyond what is possible in an interview... . Once again, we see the centrality of relationship among researchers and participants.

Both individual and group research conversations were forms of co-composed field texts among participants and us in this narrative inquiry. However, as described by Huber *et al.* (2004: 194–5), in our narrative inquiry we wanted to find ways of attending to both lived and told moments of experiences:

> In previous work we conceptualized narrative interlappings as what happens when we tell our stories in conversation or write them in narrative accounts that move across or within individuals' experiences. As one story resonates with another in the telling, new plotlines in lives become visible or old plotlines are seen in new ways. However ... we came to see that narrative interlappings are also a way to understand the living of stories. We cannot understand a moment where a teacher researcher's and child's story to live by bump up against each other without trying to understand how this moment of bumping reverberates back through the stories of each person. In the living, our stories to live by are side by side ... and, as the moment of experiencing unfolds, each story shapes the other in ways that we cannot predict or fully understand in the moment.

In our narrative inquiry at Ravine Elementary School we worked alongside children and teachers to create co-composed field texts which captured "the [lived] moments where … [researchers' and participants'] stories to live by touch and are understood as resonating back across each person's stories in particular moments in time and place" (Huber *et al.* 2004: 195).

For example, we created at least three of these more intentional co-composed field texts. Anne created an innovative approach of working alongside Year 1/2 children reading children's literature with them. Working from her relational knowing of children in the classroom she carefully selected children's literature that would draw out their stories. Attending to the children's lives Anne watched their friendships, their writing, and their talk and, based on what she imagined might be a narrative thread in their unfolding lives, Anne chose books to share with them. These books and the conversations among the children and Anne became a kind of field text that brought Anne as researcher and particular children together over almost two years. The multiple readings of the images, plotlines, and characters of these particular books were a shared plotline between Anne and each child. The actual book called up experiences from both researcher and participating child and became a kind of co-composed field text. While some of the ways Anne and the children co-composed these field texts are visible in this book, more are visible in her dissertation (Murray Orr 2005).

Shaun, working with Lian and the Year 5/6 children, co-composed found poetry drawn from the children's report cards (Murphy 2004). These co-composed field texts are described more fully in Chapter 8 where we explore the negotiation of a curriculum of lives. Shaun, sensing Lian's and the children's tensions around report cards, began to imagine ways of exploring these tensions. Over the past few years, found poetry had been a topic in conversations about composing research texts at many research issues conversations at the Center for Research for Teacher Education and Development. Researchers such as Raymond (2002) and Steeves (2000) both used found poetry in their research texts as a way to represent their field texts.

Working from transcripts of research conversations with participants, Raymond and Steeves wrote found poems as a kind of interim research text, a text "situated in the spaces between field texts and final, published research texts" (Clandinin and Connelly 2000: 133). In their narrative inquiries, Raymond and Steeves, drawn toward learning more about found poetry as interim research texts, explored the found poetry work of Ely *et al.* (1997) as well as Butler-Kisber (1998).

In 1999, Lynn Butler-Kisber presented a seminar at the Center about her experiences of developing found poetry as she pieced together a participant's story embedded in a variety of field texts. Working with a "narrative chain" she composed of the participant's embedded story, Butler-Kisber showed, read, and talked about her process of composing a "found poetic form"

(1998: 10) by working with the participant's words in the narrative chain as well as rewatching videotapes of their research conversations. In a later published paper based on her work, Butler-Kisber (2002: 233) described her process of composing found poetry in the following way:

> Creating found poetry is not a linear procedure… . As I selected words and phrases from the chained narrative, I experimented with the words to create rhythms, pauses, emphasis, breath-points, syntax, and diction. I played with order and breaks in an attempt to portray the essence of her story while inherently "showing more." As in any type of writing, it was necessary to reshape it over time.

In 2003 Butler-Kisber again visited the Center for Research for Teacher Education and Development for several months and Center members, including members of this research group, explored both her ideas and Dillard's (1995) ideas on found poetry. Shaun drew on these ideas as he and Lian created a way for the children to co-compose field texts of found poetry from their report cards as they inquired into their experiences. The found poetry was the result of this inquiry and became a kind of co-composed field text (Murphy 2004).

A third approach to co-composing field texts was explored by Vera, Kristi, and the 14 boys in the Year 2/3 learning strategies classroom. When Vera arrived the classroom was engaged in the study of a provincially mandated Social Studies unit on community. As Vera entered into life in the classroom she began to engage the children in camera work, a literacy process of linking images with writing. Ewald (2001: 12) described this camera work process as "provid[ing] a much-needed opportunity for the students to bring their home lives into school." In Ewald's work, as children documented their daily lives, their families, communities, or particular issues, interests, or dreams, in both photographs and writing, they were simultaneously learning about photography techniques such as using a camera, developing film, negatives, prints, reading photographs, framing, symbols, time, point of view, and so on.

In an early field trip, Vera and the children played with framing ideas and images of community. When they returned to the school these ideas and their imagined framings became part of the planned curriculum focus on community. With the financial support of the research project Vera provided each child with a camera and black and white film. Their task was to take photographs of what each boy saw as his community. After the photographs were developed Vera heard each child's stories of the photographs, including details about his purposes for taking them and how they connected to his understandings of community. Together, Vera and each child made a book which told their stories around the photographs of community. In this process both the photographs and the books were co-composed field texts.

We see this co-composition in the way Vera focused the children's attention on exploring their stories of community. They took the photographs and Vera and each child composed a visual and textual book of each child's story of community. The visual and textual books became a kind of co-composed field text (Caine 2002).

Moving from field texts to research texts

As described by Clandinin and Connelly (2000), narrative inquirers move from being in the field and composing field texts to working with field texts to compose interim research texts and research texts. As we began to compose interim research texts we realized our attention was drawn to identifying moments of tension, moments and places where children's and family's stories to live by bumped against stories of school, where teachers' stories to live by bumped against children's, researchers', and others' stories to live by, and so on. We also began to see how our own stories as researchers, as teachers, and as teacher educators were being interrupted and shifted. We often identified these "bumps" as marked by tensions. We began to identify moments and places of tension in people's experiences and then began to identify stories of school that shaped those bumps, stories such as character education, attendance, teachers' stories, and school stories. We also identified the complexities of stories of children and children's stories and saw how we could understand these complexities by seeing the nestedness of teachers' stories with children's stories. We saw how fictionalizing shaped stories, lived and told, and we attended to that shaping influence. These became chapter themes for us. As we began to pull these tensions together, we first attended to many children's and teachers' experiences. Attending to a multiplicity of lives and experiences helped us understand the experiences in deeper and more complex ways. In our research text, we drew only on a few of the many experiences as we tried to show these tensions.

At first we talked mostly about how these bumping places interrupted children's, teachers', families', administrators', and researchers' stories to live by as a mis-educative experience (Dewey 1938). Gradually, we realized that sometimes these bumping places shifted children's stories to live by in more educative ways. For example, in Chapter 9, as we inquired into the bumping up of Dylan's stories to live by with the story of school of attendance, we became more awake to ways in which this bumping shaped additional bumping places between his teacher's (Lian's) stories to live by and his principal's (Jeanette's) stories to live by with the story of school of attendance. It was in this reverberating of the bumping up that we saw how the narrative unities within and among Dylan's, Lian's, and Jeanette's stories to live by began to push at the dominant story of school of attendance. As well, as we talked together we realized it was often difficult to know whether a bump reverberated in educative or mis-educative ways. In the midst of so many unfolding lives we could only watch closely over the time we were engaged with the children, teachers, families, and administrators to see how stories to live by were shifted, changed, or interrupted.

Negotiating relationships among the researchers

As previously suggested, our research on the storied school landscape of Ravine Elementary School was nested within a relational framework of narrative research threads winding backwards and forwards through time, across places. As described earlier, some of the researchers had a prior and sustained presence at Ravine Elementary School. As stories of these earlier times and relationships were shared among the research group, the long-ago threads expressed in Ravine Elementary School in the rainbow images, kites, teddy bears, and hallway tiles painted by each student and teacher over the past years, reminded us that as we began to participate in the life of the school, who we each were and were becoming as researchers would also become woven into the storied fabric of the school. Teachers, children, family members, and administrators came to know us, and we them, as our lives met both in the context of the school and outside of the school as well as, in some situations, in home places.

As a group of researchers, as we negotiated relationships with teachers, children, family members, and administrators, we were simultaneously engaged in negotiating relationships with one another. Soon after we began the research at Ravine Elementary School we were drawn to a circular pit area opening onto each pod of classrooms in the school. This space became a place to gather, coffee in hand, throughout the day, to talk about our inquiries. Having this informal, improvised out-of-classroom place in the school shaped an important aspect of living in relation with one another as researchers. In looking back from the vantage point we had as we wrote this book we realized that, while this space shaped a gathering place where we could talk, wonder, explore, question, and puzzle over moments lived in the school and stories heard, told, and shared, it also shaped who we were becoming as researchers with one another.

As we looked back, we did so with a deeper recognition of the ways in which this space gave us courage to try to live and to see things from, as hooks (1984) described, both the centre and the margin while being immersed in the midst of what was happening all around. Being researchers in the school positioned us, in so many ways, in a place of privilege. Unlike our experiences in our teaching lives and unlike each of the participants in our inquiries, while we were, as much as we could, trying to live alongside teachers, children, family members, and administrators, participating in activities and the routines of school and classroom life, we were doing so not with the intensity nor with the responsibilities shaping participants' days there. Yet this kind of living, this living in the midst, was also not easy. Within us we each carried knowing of teaching, some of us carried knowing of parenting, some of us carried knowing of living in administrative roles. This knowing was always present, always in us, always storylines we could, and did at times, slip into. Gatherings and conversations at the pit helped us keep at the hard work of puzzling over what we were experiencing. Day after day, as we gathered in the pit and as our relationships grew and changed, our courage to try to stay awake to our inquiry puzzles deepened as we listened to one another's uncertainties. It was in this way that our inquiry found ways to breathe and move. In this way, as Heilbrun (1999: 102) described, the improvised meetings around the pit became a kind of liminal space, a threshold space "never designed for permanent occupation ... [as] those of us who occupy thresholds, hover in doorways, and knock upon doors, know that we are in between destinies." This space, then, and the processes of narrative inquiry, shaped, lived, and reshaped there, was vital as we engaged in composing field texts while also glimpsing possibilities of future research texts.

As we worked together, we connected to the wonderings and puzzles others were involved in. Doing so shifted our thinking about the moments we were living and trying to write about of our experiences in the classrooms, in the school, and in conversation spaces both in and outside of the school. Listening to others in the midst of living and telling meant that some threads were picked up and others dropped. As one of us told a story of what we saw happening, it sometimes drew a resonant thread to others' emerging stories with their participants. For example, as we describe in Chapter 6, over time we each came to know Amit, not only through our interactions with her but more so through Jeanette's stories of Amit. However, it was not until we began to more tightly hold onto the resonant threads across our told stories of Amit and Jeanette that the complexities and insights we explore in Chapter 6 became increasingly visible.

In addition to meeting in the pit, we also met frequently at the Center for Research for Teacher Education and Development. Sometimes all of us were able to be present in the Center and at other times some of us were connected via teleconference. In these conversations we shared stories of what we were doing, stories of children, teachers, administrators, families, and ourselves. In all of this, we shared moments of celebration and places of tension.

As we entered onto the landscape of Ravine Elementary School, we did so living and telling stories of ourselves as researchers trying to compose stories of co-authoring our knowing in relation with children, teachers, families, administrators, and one another. The kitchen table traditions shaped in our research lives at the Center lived in us, shaping our thinking and knowing throughout the inquiry. The experiences, stories, thoughts, vulnerabilities, and dilemmas shared by so many people in response to our research have become intimately woven into the language and understandings shared within this book. What marked our research journey both during our year in the field at Ravine Elementary School alongside children, teachers, families, administrators, and one another, and in co-authoring this book, was a process of trying to stay with the negotiation of relational narrative inquiry, a process both informed by and co-composed by multiple "I"s, both in the living and in the telling of our narrative inquiry (Clandinin and Connelly 2000; Connelly and Clandinin 1990).

Co-composing a relational research text

The collaborative writing in this multiple authored research text challenged our understandings of voice and signature. In the text we wanted to honour the voices of many participants as we heard them in relation with individual researchers. But in writing this research text we also wanted to honour each of our unique voices as researchers at the same time as we composed a collaborative signature. Since our group is scattered across Canada, working in universities, schools, and government, we learned to write in relational, improvisatory ways as we co-composed this research text. We read and reread field texts. We made individual notes. We engaged in taped teleconference conversations where we shared tentative interpretations. We transcribed those conversations, read them, and talked again in a recursive, reflexive cycle. By the time we met for an intensive week-long writing retreat in the summer of 2004, we had a tentative table of contents.

At the writing retreat, we worked side-by-side, in pairs or trios, crafting chapters. In afternoon sessions we shared our writing, reading work-in-progress drafts aloud and receiving response. When a group felt they had done all they could with a particular chapter they moved to new partners or new chapters. By the week's end we had drafts of all chapters but the last.

Still searching for a way to create the elusive collaborative signature, we agreed to circulate the chapters to each team member. We each had two weeks with each chapter, revising, editing, and adding. We then sent the chapter on to another co-author and received a draft of a work-in-progress chapter we had not yet worked with.

The final phase was for each of us to read the whole set of chapters, to each give feedback on each chapter and for one of us to take each chapter, to work with seven sets of comments, and to prepare the final version.

However, because of the multiple layers of authorship at work in narrative inquiries, in both the living and in the telling, research texts are understood as relationally authored texts. It was Neumann (1997) who helped us to better say, to better show, that what we came to know both in the living of our inquiries and in the composing of our research texts, was profoundly relational. She wrote:

> *On others who have written this with me.* In writing this chapter, I learned that in composing autobiography, I do not (and cannot) write only about

myself; I write also about others in whose presence I become my self. But I also learned that I do not (and cannot) write only by myself. I am indebted to those who have read and talked and listened and, literally, written with me ...

(1997: 115)

This process challenged our ideas about what it meant to honour and respect multiple voices and multiple interpretations. It helped us attend to tensions and contradictions without smoothing them over. It awakened us to more deeply notice our own stories to live by as we bumped against the institutional narrative of research as individual and competitive. It scaffolded new identity threads within us as well as new wonders and hopes about ways in which relational narrative inquiry, both in the living and in the telling, holds promise for further understanding interruptions in stories to live by as well as the deeply interwoven lives of teachers, children, families, administrators, and researchers as our lives meet on school landscapes.

Chapter 3

Children's stories to live by

Teachers' stories of children

As Marni walked down the hallway on the first day of school she heard singing coming from Gale's Year 1/2 classroom. Entering the classroom she saw the children gathered around their teacher in the meeting area at the back of the room. Together they were singing and doing the actions to 'If You're Happy and You Know It'. The room was open and uncluttered, the walls waiting for children's work. The desks were arranged in groups of four, each desk decorated with a nametag. As Marni moved toward Gale and the children, one young child, Sadie, caught her attention. Sadie was sitting in the midst of the group of children. She was a step behind her classmates in the actions and singing. She seemed to be unfamiliar with the song, although she was actively trying to participate. As the song was finishing Sadie moved closer to another girl, Seeta, who was sitting at the back of the meeting area. As Sadie sat down beside her friend, she put her head on Seeta's shoulder and fell into a clapping rhythm that more closely matched the rhythm of the other children in the class.

(Interim research text, based on field notes, September 4, 2002)

As shown in the above interim research text, Marni met Sadie at the start of the school year as she, herself, was beginning to learn rhythms of being a researcher alongside the children and Gale, and as Sadie was beginning to learn about life in school. Sadie's experiences in school raised questions for us about the ways children compose their stories to live by in relationship with their teachers.

On this early fall morning, as Gale and the children sang, acted out, and clapped in rhythm to the song, 'If You're Happy and You Know It', Marni noticed that Sadie was out of rhythm. Marni's noticing turned our attention to how children such as Sadie learn to renegotiate and compose their stories to live by as they enter onto school landscapes. Sadie was in Year 1 and the school year was just beginning. As Marni participated in this unfolding moment in the classroom, she noticed that Sadie was the only child who seemed to have visible difficulty with the song. Sadie did not seem to know the lyrics and she seemed unfamiliar with the clapping rhythm. Looking around at her classmates, Sadie seemed to gradually realize she was out of step, out of rhythm with her teacher and classmates in the clapping and actions to the song. Appearing to awaken to this knowing of herself, Sadie moved to sit beside Seeta, a girl with whom Marni sensed Sadie had an already established relationship. Moving next to her friend, Sadie leaned her body into her friend's body and, in this side-by-side way, Sadie's clapping shifted. She began to clap and act out the song, falling into rhythm with her classmates and teacher.

As we returned to this interim research text of this early moment in a Year 1/2 classroom, we did so with questions about the ways in which children's stories to live by were shaped by the stories their teacher lived and told of them. In this chapter we attend to how, over time, Sadie's stories to live by moved to both fit within and to bump against her teacher's story for her in school. We began to see a distinction between Sadie's stories to live by and Gale's story of Sadie. We also began to see how this bumping created tensions for Sadie and for her teacher.

As we awakened to these wonderings with Sadie, our wonderings reverberated across the stories of other children we were also coming to know at Ravine Elementary School. We began attending to the experiences of Erica, a girl in Year 6, and Julie, a girl in Year 1. Stories of them, also shared in this chapter, helped further our inquiries into the ways in which teachers' stories of children shape children's stories to live by in school.

Attending to Sadie's stories to live by as she began school

Returning to Marni's opening interim research text from this first day of school, we noticed Sadie seemed to not yet see her teacher, Gale, as the one who knew or as the one to look to for knowledge of how to live in this classroom. Rather, Sadie looked to another child, Seeta, to learn how to live in this classroom. Seeta was a friend from daycare, and it was Seeta that Sadie looked to for help as she tried to bring herself into the rhythm of the singing, clapping, and acting out of the song. Perhaps this relationship with Seeta helped Sadie feel less frantic in what we imagined was a new and uncomfortable experience. As Sadie momentarily lived through feelings of uncertainty and ambiguity, she reached out to her friend, Seeta, as a way to enter into both the unfolding activity and, we imagined, the classroom context as a child who fits with the rhythms there. Relying on an established relationship with Seeta, Sadie began to renegotiate her stories to live by, her stories of who she was and who she was becoming as a child in school.

As Marni began to hear stories of Sadie, we came to know that Sadie lived a story of relationship with other children, both at home in relation with two older brothers and at a daycare in relation with her brothers, Seeta, and other children. In the moment of the field note, Sadie continued to live out this story of relationship with children as she looked toward a child, Seeta, as the one who knew how to live in school.

As we attended to the ways Sadie renegotiated her stories to live by in these unfolding, uncomfortable moments in the classroom, we had a sense that Sadie already embodied a story of relationships with other children as a way of maintaining her story of herself as a child who fits in. In part, we saw this in the ways Sadie tacitly knew how to move out of tension without calling on her teacher. She called on a child. However, on this first day of school, Sadie did not choose just any child to help her. She chose a girl with whom she shared a relationship in another context to help her to shift into the rhythm of the singing, clapping, and actions. Relational knowing seemed central to how Sadie negotiated this in-classroom moment. As a way of living alongside others, relational knowing is an active construction of knowledge and, therefore, is a knowing within the moment based on a shared history with the other (Hollingsworth 1994).While Sadie was in Year 1 and Seeta was in Year 2 in their shared classroom space, it was the first year either of the girls worked with Gale as teacher. At this early point in the year, Sadie did not yet know Gale. They did not yet have shared history to bind them. Instead, Sadie began to construct a story of who she was going to be in school relying heavily on her knowing of herself in relation with the one person she did know – Seeta. She brought all of her bodily knowing to try and compose who she was going to be in school.

The moment of singing was our first recognition that Sadie seemed uncertain of her stories to live by in this in-classroom place on the school landscape. In part, we understood this moment as one of tension for Sadie, a moment when her stories to live by of being a child who fits in were momentarily interrupted by a new story of becoming a child who does not fit, who does not know the rhythms surrounding her. As Sadie felt the tensions this awakening seemed to shape, she searched for a way to lessen her felt tensions. Joining her friend Seeta at the back of the group was the action she took. It was Sadie's relational knowing with Seeta that, in this moment, seemed to help Sadie continue to be able to live out her story of fitting in.

Later in the morning, on this first day of school, Gale invited the children to take out their snacks to eat as they watched the morning announcements on the in-school news network.

> Sadie started to eat her sandwich during snack time and Gale asked her to keep it for lunch and to take something else out instead. Sadie laughed, burped, and continued eating the sandwich.
>
> (Field note, September 4, 2002)

It was in this moment of snack time that we first began to see the bumping up of Gale's stories to live by as teacher with Sadie's stories to live by. There was no indication that Gale had any particular story of Sadie at this moment. Gale did know the rhythm of a school day and she was trying to help Sadie know the rhythm of what and when to eat in school. We imagined that, for Sadie, eating the sandwich was a way of appeasing her hunger; it was a way to attend to her bodily knowing that she was hungry. That she continued to eat the sandwich suggested that Gale's story of children needing to save their sandwich until lunchtime did not fit with Sadie's stories to live by. Again, Sadie did not seem to be aware of the teacher's position in the story of school as the one who knows in the classroom.

One possible reading of Sadie's response of laughing and burping might be as resistance to the imposition of her teacher's knowledge. Another reading, from the perspective of trying to understand Sadie's experience in terms of her stories to live by in relation with her teacher, might reveal her response to Gale not as an act of resistance but as an expression of wanting to maintain narrative coherence in her stories to live by. Carr (1986) wrote "coherence seems to be a need imposed on us whether we seek it or not. Things need to make sense. We feel the lack of sense when it goes missing" (p. 97). Perhaps Sadie was searching for a way to make sense. We saw her living a story coherent with who she was, that is, that she responded to her bodily knowledge, a knowing which told her it was time to eat. Huber *et al.* (2004) helped us understand how this moment could be understood not as a story of resistance but, rather, as an expression of narrative coherence in a child's story to live by. However, Gale, knowing the rhythms of a day in school, tried to interrupt this expression of Sadie's knowing in order to help her come to know a new bodily rhythm.

As teachers, we know Gale was expressing care (Noddings 1984) in her interaction with Sadie. Gale knew Sadie had only a sandwich, an apple, and a juice box in her paper lunch bag. She knew Sadie would be hungry by lunchtime and would need her sandwich then. We imagined Gale was trying to introduce Sadie to the rhythm of the school day, a rhythm which was different from Sadie's bodily rhythm. We imagined Sadie developed these bodily rhythms both in her home and as she spent time at a daycare, a context where snacks were often provided for children in both the mornings and afternoons. We imagined that at daycare Sadie was used to eating the lunch she brought from home in one sitting.

Inquiring into these two field notes constructed on the first day of school left us wondering about this interrupting of bodily knowing within the rhythms of the school day and in relation with teachers. Teachers also come to embody school rhythms and, in turn, are shaped to live out their stories as teachers in ways that fit with the dominant stories of school which are, at least in part, shaped by school rhythms (Clandinin 1986; Connelly and Clandinin 1988; Davies 1996). In the field note of snack time, Sadie did not seem to understand that in this new place she had to learn to live within the plotlines of school stories and that, in asking her to choose something else from her lunch bag, her teacher was trying to help her come to know a new rhythm of a day. Perhaps because there are no subsequent field notes about eating sandwiches at snack time, Sadie learned to eat her sandwiches at lunch and shifted her stories to live by to fit with the rhythm of eating food at school.

On this first day of Year 1, we saw Sadie living out her bodily knowledge. We imagined she lived a story of herself as a capable child and as a child who relied on relational knowing to help her figure out new rhythms in unfamiliar surroundings. As this story of who she was began momentarily to shift toward a possible new story of herself as a child who did not fit in, Sadie again relied on her embodied knowing to maintain her story of herself. She depended on her relationship with Seeta to help her to continue to negotiate narrative coherence, that is, to figure out the rhythmic singing, clapping, and actions of the song. What Sadie did not seem to learn, on this first day of school, is that Gale, her teacher, was the one who held the knowledge of school. Instead, at least on this first day of school, Sadie seemed to see herself and Seeta as the ones who knew. She seemed to see friends as people who would help her to negotiate who she was in this new place.

In this chapter our inquiries focus on the ways in which children compose their stories to live by in relation with their teachers' stories of them. Our opening notes showed us that, at least in these early morning moments on the first day of school, Sadie did not yet seem to have a story of who her teacher was in the classroom. She and Gale were strangers. As we attended to Sadie's life over time in the Year 1/2 classroom and to Sadie's shifting relationship with her friend Seeta, we began to see the composition of Gale's story of Sadie and how Gale's story shaped Sadie's stories to live by.

Attending to shifts in Sadie's stories to live by as the year unfolds

As the days continued to unfold in this Year 1/2 classroom, still early in the school year, Marni's field notes showed that Sadie's stories to live by did begin to shift. Not only did Sadie begin to recognize Gale, the teacher, as the one who knew but she also began to name Gale as the one she should look to when she realized she was not in rhythm with the stories of school.

> Marni walked into the classroom as Gale was sharing a story from her weekend. Mondays were a day for the children to write in their notebooks and to share stories of their lives. Gale printed her story out on the overhead for the children to read. Her story spoke of a cat so she drew a cat on the overhead. The children were then asked to compose their own stories about their adventures on the weekend. Many children told their story in picture form. Sadie's desk was situated right beside the overhead. Marni noticed immediately that Sadie's picture matched the

one that Gale drew. "I tried hard to be neat … It's just like teacher's," she told Marni as Marni knelt beside her desk.

(Field note, October 30, 2002)

Later that day, the children returned to their desks after gym class to prepare for home time. It was unusual for Marni to spend an entire day at the school and she was feeling tired. She felt like it had been a long day. Sadie was the only one who did not return to her seat when requested. Instead, she moved over to the meeting area at the back of the room and laid down. Several times Marni watched her look toward Gale. When Gale did not respond, Sadie continued to lie on the carpet.

(Field note, October 30, 2002)

In the first of these two moments we had a sense that Sadie did not trust her own knowing in writing about her weekend. While other children wrote and drew moments from their weekend experiences, Sadie copied the cat drawn by her teacher on the overhead. We wondered what Sadie was thinking and feeling as she did this. Perhaps she was unsure of her abilities as a writer, as a printer, or as a drawer. Perhaps she felt her stories of her weekend experiences did not fit nicely alongside her teacher's story or her classmates' stories.

Unlike earlier field notes, we sensed in this field note Sadie's story as someone who fit in was becoming more open to the possibilities of being interrupted by her teacher's story of her and by the story of school. We wondered if Sadie was beginning to not trust her own knowing and to not trust the rhythm of her stories to live by. If we read her actions in this way, we could say that when Sadie merely copied her teacher's cat instead of composing something from her weekend, she was experiencing an interruption in her knowing of herself as fitting in with the classroom rhythms. What also seemed to become interrupted in this moment was Sadie's earlier lived story of reaching out to friends to help her figure out how she could continue to fit in. In this in-classroom moment Sadie did not appear to reach out to a friend as a way to help her to fit with her teacher's story of children sharing stories of their weekend in their notebooks. There was, in this moment, a sense that Sadie may have begun to name herself as "not knowing" (Vinz 1997).

We wondered if Sadie did not trust that what she knew outside of school would be valued in her classroom place. Sadie showed us that she did know, at least in this moment, that knowledge rested with her teacher. Unlike earlier in the school year, Sadie now seemed to know that her teacher's knowledge was the knowledge that counted in the classroom. This was an important shift in her story and an interruption in how she seemed to have lived her life in the classroom as the year began. While we did not know why Sadie's desk was positioned "right beside the overhead" (Field note, October 30, 2002) we did wonder why, unlike before, Sadie did not reach out to Seeta. It was possible Seeta was away from school on this day. It was also possible that Sadie's explanation to Marni, that she "tried hard to be neat," and that her drawing was "just like teacher's," was Sadie's way of fitting in with the classroom story of writing in her notebook on Monday morning. In this second interpretation, Sadie could still be seen as a child who knows in her teacher's eyes.

However, in the field note from the afternoon of the same day, we were less clear if Sadie knew that Gale was the one who held the knowledge in the classroom. Sadie chose, by lying down in the carpet area, to follow her own bodily knowing. She was tired from the long day and from the recent gym class. She did not return to her desk as requested by her teacher, but instead moved to a spot on the carpet in the back of the room. We wondered, in Sadie's glances at Gale, if Sadie knew that Gale's knowledge was the knowledge that counted, but the knowing of her own body was what she needed to attend to in that moment. It was less clear if Sadie was willing to renegotiate her stories to live by to fit with the story of school. We wondered how tiring it was for Sadie to learn this new story of being a student in school, a student who was beginning to not trust her own stories to live by as she constantly attended to the stories that structured school in this classroom. Sadie's stories, as lived out in the classroom, were often in tension with the story of school. One possible way to think about this is that the story of school was shaping Sadie's stories to live by. Another way might be to suggest that Sadie was continually negotiating a place for her stories in the classroom and that she experienced fitting in as a diverse and unfolding process.

Living the tension

As the year unfolded, Sadie's stories, as lived out in the classroom, became in almost constant tension with Gale's story of her.

> It was mid-November and the children were getting ready for morning recess. Sadie was dressed in snow pants that were clearly too small for her. Her feet were bare and when Marni asked her where her socks were, she said she couldn't find them. Trying to be helpful, Marni searched with Sadie, finding the socks under Sadie's desk. Still hesitant to go outside, Sadie told Marni, "I don't want to wear my snow pants ... It's not that cold outside ... I have my favourite shirt to keep me warm. I painted it myself. Pink is my favourite colour so I used lots of pink." As Marni watched, Seeta helped her friend pull her jeans out the bottom of the snow pants to cover her ankles. Putting their arms around each other they went out to play.
>
> After lunch when the children were being sent outside once more, Gale noticed that Sadie was preparing to go without her snow pants and asked her to put them on, saying, "It's cold outside and you need to be wearing your snow pants." Sadie replied, "I'm not cold ... and the pants

don't fit anyways." Turning to Marni, Sadie pleaded, "Don't make me wear them." Gale moved to her desk and reached down into a bag of second-hand clothing she kept aside for Sadie. She pulled out a pair of snow pants several sizes larger than Sadie's pink ones. She told Sadie they were hers to keep. Seeta helped her friend put them on and they laughed together when they noticed how large they were. Sadie said, "I look goofy," as she pulled the snow pants up to her armpits. Seeta helped her pull them down around her waist and Sadie wore them outside.

At the end of the day Sadie wore her too-small pink snow pants home; the second-hand ones from her teacher left behind in her cubby.

(Interim research text, based on field notes, November 13, 2002)

In this interim research text, we saw an expression of Sadie's knowing that her too-small pink snow pants were not acceptable clothing for school. In her words, "the pants don't fit anyways" (Field note, November 13, 2002), we sensed that while she arrived at school wearing these snow pants, she was uncomfortable wearing them around her classmates. Sadie first showed us her knowing, the story she planned to live out, when she resisted going out for recess by losing her socks. Marni, not recognizing Sadie's planned story to live out, went in search of Sadie's socks. In time, Sadie let Marni know that she did not want to wear the snow pants at all. When the plotline in the story she was planning to live out was interrupted, Sadie turned once again to her knowing of a relational plotline. She knew and trusted that her friend, Seeta, would make it possible for her to go outside wearing the too-small snow pants. By wrapping her arms around Seeta, Sadie had a visible way of showing the other children that she fit in, that she had a story that allowed her to fit in during recess. Regardless of how she was dressed, she had a friend.

However, we wondered what happened while Sadie was outside during morning recess. By lunchtime she, again, would not wear the too-small snow pants. She hoped that, by calling on Marni, Marni could intercede with Gale on her behalf. Marni did not help and Gale acted by giving Sadie second-hand snow pants, ones that were too large. In this act, we saw that Gale had a story of Sadie – a story that Sadie was a child who needed care and help. We wondered how this expression of Gale's story of Sadie interrupted Sadie's story of who she was in school.

Again, it was her friendship with Seeta that made it possible for Sadie to stay with the plotline of wearing a second pair of ill-fitting snow pants. While Sadie pulled the too-large snow pants up to her armpits as a way to show Gale the snow pants were inappropriate, it was Seeta who pulled them down to fit at Sadie's waist. The pants were still too large, but now they looked more appropriate.

We saw in this moment that Sadie cared about fitting into the story of school, a story that called for snow pants that fit. When she thought she did not fit in, as evidenced by the snow pants, both too large and too small, Sadie fell back into her relationship with Seeta. It was Seeta who, at both recess times and with both sets of snow pants, helped Sadie know what to do to fit in. In the lunchtime moment, we wondered if Sadie experienced her teacher as not knowing what it meant to go outside with snow pants that did not fit. Sadie experienced Seeta as knowing how to help negotiate a place in relation with classmates in the out-of-classroom place, the recess playground.

As we noticed the snow pants left behind in the cubby at the end of the day, we became aware that Sadie had to negotiate conflicting stories of who she was and who she was becoming: one told by her mother of who Sadie was, a story Sadie needed to live out outside of school; one told by her teacher of who Sadie was that began to shape who Sadie was and was becoming both in- and out-of-school; and one Sadie was trying to compose for herself. By leaving the second-hand snow pants at school and wearing her too-small ones home, we realized Sadie was trying to live out the story her mother was telling of her. By wearing the clothes that Gale had for her in school, we saw Sadie trying to live out the story Gale was telling of her. As these two stories bumped up, they created tension for Sadie, a tension which her friend Seeta helped her negotiate into a story she could live as she moved between conflicting plotlines of home and school. It was the tensions that Sadie experienced as these stories bumped up that created interruptions in her stories to live by.

Sadie learns competing stories of being in school

However, over time, as the year progressed we began to see Sadie move away from Seeta as one who knew. Throughout the year, Seeta was often in trouble with Gale and with supervisors at lunch and recess. She was inattentive during teacher-directed lessons, she wandered around the room at inappropriate times, she typically sat at the back of the space when the class gathered together in the meeting area, and she had few friends other than Sadie.

By the end of the year, Marni's field notes showed Sadie was shifting her attention towards Sarah as a child who knew how to live a life as a good student in school. Like Seeta, Sarah was in Year 2. She had straight brown hair often worn in different styles. She had nice clothes, did well in school, and was popular among her classmates. Sarah was the one who raised her hand whenever a question was asked in the meeting area. She seemed confident in her stories to live by at school. She knew herself as a good student.

> Sadie asked if Marni would come outside with her and Seeta. They planned to shovel snow off the front walks and wanted Marni to watch them. Overhearing the conversation, Sarah asked if she could join them as well. At recess time they led Marni to the front foyer where they picked up snow shovels and carried them outside. They were obviously familiar with this routine. "I like to help at school," Sadie told Marni.

Sarah added, "I'm on student council and it's important that I help out the school too." While Sadie and Sarah seemed to take their job of clearing the sidewalks quite seriously, Seeta tried to turn the activity into a game. When one of the girls would clear a path, Seeta would come from behind and cover it up again. Other times she would throw snow at Sadie or Sarah or hide behind a tree or bush and jump out as the girls passed by. Sadie and Sarah just shrugged their shoulders and kept right on working.

(Field note, February 3, 2003)

"I got a walking card[1] yesterday because Seeta lied and said we were leaving the playground when we weren't," Sadie told Marni. "I wasn't really going to leave the school ... I was just joking," she continued. As a result both girls had to eat their lunch in the office and walk with a supervisor during recess. Sadie was angry with Seeta and blamed her for what happened.

(Field note, February 25, 2003)

Sadie drew a picture of a sunset on the white board at the back of the room during free time this morning. "Sarah showed me how to draw sunsets," she said. She shared how she had seen a sunset last summer and was now drawing this picture for her classmates. "I'm good at sunsets," Sadie told them after the sharing.

(Field note, May 29, 2003)

Sadie's relationship with Seeta became complicated as Sadie came to know other ways of living in school. Sadie knew Seeta from time spent in daycare and time spent at school. But Sadie also came to know there were competing plotlines in the story of school. She knew Seeta as one who often was in trouble, but she also knew Seeta as her friend and someone who could be helpful in school. We saw this as Sadie and Seeta volunteered to shovel the front walk of the school during recess time. They knew that this would be appreciated by teachers and visitors to the school. They were hopeful that Jeanette, the principal, would notice what they did. It was Sadie and Seeta who initiated this activity and invited Sarah to help.

Sadie's story of who she was becoming at school was complex. It was not a smooth story. We wondered if Sadie's knowing of who or what to attend to kept shifting back and forth as she learned to attend to and live competing stories. Sadie continued to get in trouble throughout the year as she negotiated multiple ways of being in school. She was the student who shovelled the sidewalk with her friends; she was also the student who attempted to leave the school grounds at lunchtime, suggesting it was a joke when she was caught; and she was the student who learned to draw sunsets from Sarah, a student who knew how to live the plotline of good student in the story of school. As

Sadie came to know herself as a student in the story of school, she began to lose confidence in Seeta as the one who knew. By sharing how she learned to draw a sunset from Sarah, we wondered if Sadie experienced Sarah as one who knew. By asking her teacher if she could share the sunset with the class we wondered if she was telling her teacher that she knew too. Attending to the places of tension in these moments and these wonderings helped us begin to understand how stories to live by, identities, are negotiated and continually shaped and reshaped in the moments of meeting.

Attending to Erica's stories to live by

Erica was another child who helped us attend to the ways children's stories to live by were shaped by the stories their teachers lived and told of them. Erica, a participant in Shaun's research, was a self-assured girl in Year 6 in Lian's classroom. This was evident in how she carried herself, in how she responded in class, and in her willingness to participate in discussions and ask questions. Erica told Shaun that she enjoyed playing hockey, baseball, and soccer, and described herself as "sporty" and "not girly" (Transcript of individual conversation, November 22, 2002). She preferred to play with boys because she found it more demanding and, in her words, "it's competition" (Transcript of individual conversation, November 22, 2002). In class it was evident Erica aligned herself with her teacher, Lian. Lian often spoke to her students about her own identity as "sporty" and Erica liked to draw attention to this story she shared with her teacher. Erica frequently made this link in class discussions and in research conversations with Shaun.

While Erica was confident and assured during the year we spent at Ravine Elementary School, she had not always felt this way in school. Erica did not begin school at Ravine Elementary School but originally attended a French Immersion program at another school. It was there she experienced difficulty with her school work and peer relationships. She told Shaun, "We really didn't enjoy it. It wasn't a really good school … they didn't treat [me and my family] very nicely" (Transcript of individual conversation, November 22, 2002). Erica talked with Shaun about her previous struggles with her school work and how that changed when she came to Ravine Elementary School. Lian was also Erica's teacher when Erica arrived at Ravine Elementary School for Year 2. It was at that time Erica began to restory herself as a successful student in school. Lian was once again Erica's teacher in Year 5 and Year 6, but there was an important interruption in Erica's stories to live by in Year 5.

At Ravine Elementary School students were grouped in multi-aged classrooms with Kindergarten children comprising one grouping and Years 1/2, 3/4, and 5/6 sharing other classroom spaces. During Erica's year in Year 5 she was teased and bullied by the Year 6 girls in her class. Erica told stories of her experiences in Year 5 during a number of research conversations with Shaun, as did Lian, Erica's teacher. "Erica had a lot of trouble last year"

(Transcript of conversation, March 12, 2003). As Erica's stories to live by as a successful student in the story of school came under threat by the bullying and teasing, Erica turned to Lian for help in sustaining her stories to live by. In order to feel safe at school, Erica gradually made a stronger relationship with Lian. As Erica learned to story herself as similar to Lian, that is, as sporty, she frequently told her story in ways that highlighted the plotlines she shared with Lian. Lian did not discourage this.

On Monday mornings, Lian and the Year 5/6 children often shared a classroom rhythm of telling stories about the things they had done during the weekend. In these conversations Erica always spoke, often twice. The first time she shared, she would tell something she had done and, during her second contribution to the classroom conversation, she talked about something that more closely mirrored Lian's weekend activities. However, as she continued to highlight these shared plotlines, other students in the class began to story Erica as a teacher's pet.

Being storied as teacher's pet created tension for Erica. She did not want to fall out of the plotline of being part of a friendship group, nor did she want to be teased as the teacher's pet. Erica wanted to be included by friends and she wanted to be a good student, both important plotlines in her stories to live by. She somehow needed to attend to who she was and to do so without being teased. Remembering how it felt in Year 5 to be teased, Erica soon stopped pointing out the plotlines she and Lian shared. She stopped participating as frequently in group discussions and she became quieter in class. Perhaps this happened over time, but Shaun and Lian noticed it as a more abrupt change. When Shaun talked with Erica about the changes he had noticed, Erica told him:

> And um you know it's just, it's terrible when you come in every morning and all you do is you get teased and when you do a partner activity nobody wants to be with you and you're always doing things by yourself and it's just, and so I thought if I kept up with, you know, always being everything that I, that would happen to me again and I just, I remember last year I just thought, "OK, I don't need that." So I just, I laid off a bit.
> (Transcript of individual conversation, May 16, 2003)

In Year 6, Erica found a circle of friends within the classroom. Recalling her experiences the year before, she made the decision to visibly align herself with her friendship group and to stop living a story where she made explicit the similarities between herself and her teacher, Lian.

Attending to Erica in school, however, provided only a partial view. We learned Erica had begun to e-mail Lian after school. As Shaun and Lian talked further, Lian described how her Hotmail account had not been active until recently. When she activated it, she learned Erica had been e-mailing her quite a lot.

I reactivated it to do group e-mails this weekend and it said ah, "Miss Elliot, please tell me why you won't e-mail me back. I hope you're having a good weekend. Um if you could pull me aside in class I'd really appreciate it." So I e-mailed her back and I said, "Erica," I said, "have you been e-mailing me? My, my um, my e-mail hasn't been activated. I just reactivated it. I hope you're having a good weekend."

(Transcript of conversation, March 12, 2003)

As Shaun and Lian continued to talk, Lian wondered if Erica was trying to maintain contact in a new way, "to get me a different way" (Transcript of conversation, March 12, 2003). Shaun responded by noting that Erica "sort of went underground with her admiration" (Transcript of conversation, March 12, 2003). Erica was learning to live a cover story in the classroom of who she was in relationship with Lian. At the same time, however, she attended to her own stories to live by as someone who lived a story like her teacher, through improvising a way to continue to maintain close contact with Lian. She moved the expression of her story from an in-classroom place to an out-of-classroom place through e-mail and through asking Lian to pull her aside in class so they could talk, without being in view of the class and opening herself up to teasing. We wondered if the action Erica took in emailing Lian was a creative way to attend to both the stories on the classroom landscape and to her own stories to live by. Carr (1986: 91) wrote that when our reality does not fit with our desires "It is our practical imagination that is involved. … in the matter of coping with reality." Erica coped with the problem of wishing to maintain a relationship with Lian without fear of being teased by finding an alternate form of contact. It was this story of contact that was important to Erica. Lian did not interrupt Erica's stories to live by as she continued to create an e-mail space for Erica to sustain herself.

In Sadie's stories to live by in school, it was evident how her teacher shaped them. This was less obvious for Erica. Lian appeared to do little to influence Erica's choice to align herself with her peers. However, Erica's history with Lian suggested something else. Lian was important in Erica's stories to live by in Year 5 when the older girls in the classroom marginalized Erica, and when she first came to the school in Year 2. Erica's e-mails to Lian suggested Lian's continued importance in Erica's stories to live by. Lian was able to step aside for Erica to maintain her relationships with her peers, taking her cues from Erica. In this way, we saw Lian's actions shaped Erica's stories to live by as much as Gale's actions shaped Sadie's stories to live by. The influence of the stories the teacher told of each child shaped the children's stories to live by in pervasive ways in each situation.

Julie: resisting a school story of who she should be

Julie was another Year 1 student we met on the first day of school in Laura's Year 1/2 classroom. Anne, the researcher in this classroom, noticed Julie almost immediately. Her hair was short, black, and thick, with two small ponytails jutting out from the sides of her head. Her ponytails bounced as she walked across the room. While half of the children in this classroom were in Year 2 and had been in Laura's classroom the year before, the other half were new to the classroom. Julie, the only child of visible Aboriginal descent, was one of the new ones.

> Laura began the day by reading a story to the class. After the book, Julie raised her hand and said, "I have a tummy ache. Mommy said I have to go home every time I have a tummy ache." Laurie asked Julie's assigned Year 2 buddy to take her to get a drink of water. Julie didn't say anything more about feeling sick for the moment.
>
> Soon, it was time for each child to print the alphabet on lined paper. Most children got right to work on this, their first pencil and paper task of the school year. Julie left her desk and walked toward the door, ponytails bouncing. She sat at the table beside the door and announced, "I can't write ABCs." Laura spoke quietly with her and brought her back to her desk where Julie picked up her pencil and printed both her first name and last name quickly and then began to print the upper case alphabet.
>
> After recess, the class gathered on the carpeted meeting area of the classroom. Laura read a funny picture book to the children called *Parts* (Arnold, 2000) about body parts. There was lots of talk and laughter as Laura read the book. Julie wandered away from the group on the carpet, and came over to the side table where Anne sat, and asked Anne what she was writing as she scribbled field notes in her new blue notebook. She stood beside Anne and watched her write until Laura called her back to the carpet. When Julie returned to the carpet Anne noticed her rock herself back and forth. Anne wondered if this was a way of comforting herself in the midst of her new surroundings.
>
> (Interim research text based on field notes, September 4, 2002)

Anne's immediate sense of Julie was that she was a confident child with a strong story of who she was and who she was becoming. Within the first half hour Anne noted how Julie was beginning to live out a different story than the one her teacher seemed to be expecting of her in the classroom. After being asked to sit close together with her classmates and listen quietly to Laura read a story, Julie announced she had a tummy ache and needed to go home. As a group of researchers, we wondered if perhaps Julie came into the Year 1/2 classroom with a story of what the first day of school would be. When the story being lived out in the classroom did not match with the one she imagined, she looked for an exit by explaining that her mommy had said that she needed to go home whenever she had a tummy ache. In this moment, Julie showed us she carried a story of her mother's knowledge counting and how she invoked her mother's knowledge as a way to support her own knowing. However, when Laura, the teacher, responded in a way other than what we imagine Julie expected, Julie said nothing more about feeling sick. Perhaps, in this moment, Julie was somewhat dis-positioned as she gained a sense that her mother's knowledge did not count in this in-classroom place as it did in other places in her life.

In the next moment, when Laura asked the class to write the ABCs, Julie left her desk, walked to a table where Anne was sitting beside the door and announced, "I can't write ABCs." Anne recalled for us that her initial reading of Julie's response was that Julie did not know how to write her ABCs. However, as the moment continued to unfold another reading emerged, a reading more consistent with Julie eventually writing both her first and last names and the alphabet. This reading highlighted that Julie did not want to write her ABCs at that particular time. Perhaps, again, Julie's story of how she imagined her first morning in Year 1 did not match with the events unfolding in the classroom. As we considered this possibility yet another reading of the moment gained plausibility, a reading perhaps more consistent with Julie's move out of her desk and to the table by the door. In this reading Julie did not see Laura as the only one whose knowledge counted in the classroom and, similar to Sadie on her first day in school, perhaps Julie was also living a story of narrative coherence, one where she had choice about including herself in an activity.

After recess, the way Julie wandered over to Anne made us wonder if Julie was beginning to create a story of who she was going to be in the classroom, a story more consistent with who she was and how she lived. Her story of herself as a knower continued to emerge as she left the activity, the other children, and Laura, and came to watch and question Anne. We wondered if Julie was trying to figure out if there were other possible ways to compose a life in this Year 1/2 classroom. We wondered about several possibilities as we watched Julie in these first weeks. Was she was going to interrupt Laura's story of school? Would Laura's stories interrupt Julie's stories to live by? Would Julie's stories to live by be a competing plotline (Clandinin and Connelly 1995), one running parallel to and living in healthy tension with the story of school? It was these wonderings that helped us stop and attend to the ways lives are shaped in moments of meeting.

One of the children in the classroom had a birthday on the weekend and had just turned six. Several children announced that they were six too. James pointed out that Julie was five but shaking her head Julie said, "I am a different kind of old." Julie has the aura of being much older and wiser to Anne in some ways. She can be quiet and then say something that will be exactly right; she is often alone but doesn't seem unhappy.

(Field note, October 21, 2002)

We came to know Julie's stories to live by as ones that lived outside, and yet alongside, the story of school in the classroom. When we shared Julie's expression of herself as a "different kind of old" with Mary Young, a colleague who is Aboriginal, Mary spoke of a few people who carry the wisdom of the ancestors within them (Young 2003). She wondered, as did we, if Julie was indeed one of the old ones.

Another place we saw tension emerge between Julie's stories to live by and school stories was in Julie's attempts to stay at school during lunchtime. One of the school stories at Ravine Elementary School was that children who stayed at school for the lunch hour needed to pay a fee to cover the cost of lunchtime supervision. Julie's parents lived close to the school and she was expected to go home for lunch. Mid-September was the first time Anne noticed Julie's desire to stay at school during the lunch break and that her desires were bumping up against the plotline of a school story and Laura's, her teacher's, story.

In the third week of school Laura told me that the day before, Julie, the only one in the class who regularly went home for lunch, left the school at the beginning of the lunch hour but came back five minutes later saying that no one was at home. Laura, away from the school during the lunch hour, called Julie's home on her return and found that Julie's stepfather was at home wondering why Julie had not come home for lunch.

(Field note, September 20, 2002)

At this early point in the school year Julie, still trusting in her own story of herself as a knower, constructed a story that let her stay at school during the lunch hour and be with her classmates – a story we imagined was probably consistent with Julie's stories to live by. To be able to live out this story of spending her free time playing with friends, Julie told Laura that no one was home during the lunch hour. Julie's story, however, was interrupted when Laura phoned home to check with Julie's stepfather. On the following day, when Laura related the events of the previous lunch hour to Anne, Anne sensed a tension had emerged between Julie and Laura. Anne wondered in this moment if Laura's story of Julie had shifted to include a plotline of needing to check up on Julie. Furthermore, Anne wondered if Julie was coming to see Laura as someone who prevented her from living a story consistent with who she wanted to be, that is, as able to spend her free time playing with her friends.

In mid-October Anne began, on Thursdays, to meet with four children from Laura's Year 1/2 classroom to engage in weekly lunchtime book conversations. She would remind Julie the day before to bring her lunch. The other children in the group and, in fact, all the other children in the class, always stayed at school for lunch so it was not necessary for Anne to remind them. The first few times Anne and the children met, the lunchtime supervisors questioned Anne about Julie staying for lunch. They wondered if Julie's parents should pay for her to stay for lunch even though she was with Anne and did not require additional supervision. Perhaps the lunchtime supervisors, knowing the school story that children who stayed at school during the lunch hour were required to pay a fee, were unsure about who both Anne and Julie were in this school story.

On several occasions, Julie told Anne she was staying for lunch on days other than Thursdays. She told Laura this as well. On these days Laura would check to see if Julie had a lunch in her backpack, and, if not, Laura would call home to check with Julie's stepfather. Except for Thursdays, Julie's stepfather would tell Laura that Julie needed to come home for lunch. Laura, being responsible to the school story that only those children who had parental permission and who had paid the lunch hour supervision fee were allowed to stay at school during lunch time, continued to work toward helping Julie fall into congruence with the school story. Julie, perhaps not fully understanding the school story around lunch hours, seemed to want to stay at school on days other than Thursdays and experience lunch in the classroom. She persistently looked for ways to do this in spite of Laura's insistence on compliance with the school story. Knowing she was allowed to stay for lunch on Thursdays, Julie seemed to look forward to the lunchtime book conversations with Anne and her other three classmates.

> I asked Julie if she had brought her lunch (because today is our lunch group). She smiled and said "yes." Laura told me this morning that Julie had come up to her and said, "I have a secret." She said the secret was that she was having lunch with me in Mrs Smith's room. Laura said Julie was smiling and excited.
>
> (Field note, November 7, 2002)

The lunchtime issues simmered throughout the fall as Julie consistently wanted to stay for lunch but was not allowed, except on Thursdays. One morning in early December, Julie told Anne several times that she was staying for lunch that day. It was not a Thursday, and therefore, the group was not meeting. Anne briefly wondered why Julie was staying but then thought maybe no one was going to be at her home during the lunch hour. Anne did not explore the conversation further with Julie.

> Julie had been saying to Anne all morning that she was staying for lunch today. She told Laura this too, just at lunchtime. Laura asked Anne if she knew anything about this and Anne said that Julie had been

saying this to her a lot today. Laura called home and talked to Julie's dad, who said that sure, Julie could stay. Anne got her coat on and got ready to go, and Laura said, "Aren't you staying for lunch today?" She thought Anne was having a lunchtime group today, Anne realized belatedly. Anne thought that was why she called to see if Julie could stay. Laura called Julie outside the class, and asked her to sit in the pit, a circular gathering area outside the Year 1/2 classrooms. Some of the children came to the door to see what was happening to Julie. Anne felt terrible that this misunderstanding had occurred. Julie was sitting in the pit with her head down; Anne thought she was crying. Laura was talking to Jeanette outside the door, telling her that she didn't know what to do.

(Field notes, December 2, 2002)

This event seemed like a culmination of the accumulating tensions surrounding lunchtime during the time Anne was at Ravine Elementary School. Julie had consistently wanted to stay for lunch but was not allowed. The story she was trying to live bumped up against the school story Laura and others at Ravine Elementary School followed, that children were not allowed to stay for lunch unless they brought a lunch and their parents paid the supervision fee in advance. Julie continued to resist this school story and looked for creative ways to stay for lunch. Laura continued to interrupt Julie's attempts and to teach her that she could not stay for lunch unless she followed the school story. The bumping up of Julie's and Laura's stories eventually led to the moment described in the field notes above.

The day following the field notes of December 2, 2002, Julie was not at school. We wondered how the lunchtime events had shaped Julie's stories to live by. Might she have come to see herself as on the borders of school life, as outside the circle of those who stayed (seemingly effortlessly) for lunch daily, while she worked hard to try to stay for just one day? We know from Anne's later conversations with Julie that the events on December 2 caused Julie unhappiness. We wondered if the happenings of that day shaped her stories of who she was around lunchtimes and around her place in the classroom. Did she become afraid to take risks after this reprimand? Prior to December 2 Anne had seen Julie as a child who was already on the edges of classroom life. After her experience of being questioned, we wondered if it would be even more difficult for Julie to move in from the margins.

Living a competing story

Julie continued to live her stories to live by in some tension with the story Laura told of her, throughout the school year. She resisted turning toward Laura as the one who knew, unlike the shift Sadie made in her stories to live by in another Year 1 classroom.

Anne left the school at lunch and was waiting at the bus stop to catch a bus to the university. As she waited, Anne watched children going home for lunch from Ravine Elementary School. Julie came out of the school, crossed the street and walked toward her house for a minute or two, then slowly turned and walked back toward the school. Julie had not given up trying to stay at school for lunch, apparently. She walked back and forth along the sidewalk across the road from the school, perhaps waiting for Anne to get on the bus before returning to the school grounds. They waved at each other, but Julie did not come over to see Anne.

(Field note, June 12, 2003)

Even at the end of the school year, Julie still seemed to be looking for ways to stay at school for lunch. It appeared she had not been shaped by the school story of the rules around staying for lunch. A book conversation between Anne and Julie provided another way to think about Julie's strong desire to maintain her stories to live by.

Julie chose a book from the selection Anne had brought, entitled *The Wise Woman and Her Secret* (Merriam 1991). As they opened this book and began to read, a big grin spread over Julie's face. Anne had forgotten that the little girl, a main character in the story, had the same name as Julie. Both of them were excited by this. In the book, the character Julie meets a wise woman. Everyone else is trying to force the old woman to reveal to them her secret (the secret of her happiness). They are frustrated and even angry that she will not tell the secret, but instead asks them to look in the barn, in the well, in various places to find it. Julie goes along with the crowd to each of the places the wise woman suggests, but rather than frantically searching for the secret in each place, she enjoys the beauty of what she finds in each place. Finally, the people give up and leave the wise woman in disgust, but Julie remains behind and talks with her. The wise woman tells Julie how she is curious about the world around her and has many questions and wonderings. Continuing to ask and wonder is how the wise woman has found fulfillment. This is her secret. Julie begins to see that it is a good thing to "wonder and wander," although many around her had ridiculed her for this in the past. At the end of the book, the character Julie says, "I have lots of questions." Julie, sitting beside Anne, was quite absorbed as they read this story, and she smiled at Anne and said, "I have lots of questions too," as Anne read this page.

(Field note, June 12, 2003)

Throughout the year, Julie's stories, with her "lots of questions," resonated for Anne with what she thought of as wisdom – quiet inner strength. The wise woman in the book found that her wisdom seemed not to be understood by most others, and so became a secret, though not one she intentionally kept from other people. Julie, too, seemed to us to have a secret strength, one that enabled her to persevere in the face of a powerful school story of what happens at lunchtime at school. Julie's story made us wonder if being wise is a secret story for her and for others who resist the stories their teachers tell of them.

As Julie worked to sustain her stories to live by, Laura responded from within the plotline of a story she had composed of Julie and from within the plotlines of the school stories. Anne, living alongside Julie, attempted to understand what became competing stories between Julie's stories to live by and Laura's story of Julie. These competing plotlines were sustained. They did not, at least in Year 1, become conflicting plotlines which may have reshaped Julie's stories to live by.

Attending to different rhythms in children's stories to live by

Earlier in this chapter, we saw Sadie moving toward fitting into a school story her teacher, Gale, lived and told, a story in keeping with the rhythms of school which teachers know so well. Attending to Sadie's stories over time we saw that her coming to know the stories of school as her teacher told them were filled with moments of tension. We saw Sadie begin to question her stories to live by. Near the end of the year, we watched as Sadie moved towards being part of the school stories and rhythms her teacher Gale lived and told. Sadie's stories to live by, at least on the school landscape, did begin to shift in response to the stories Gale was telling of her.

While Laura attempted to shift Julie's stories to live by, to help her fit in with the rhythms of school that Laura knew, in this case the lunchtime rhythms, Julie resisted with a strength surprising for one so small. She seemed to have a strong sense of her own rhythm, her own knowing of what she needed and desired; a rhythm that was perhaps not recognizable by her teacher. Why was Julie's competing rhythm so strong? Was she able to sustain her rhythm through her off-the-landscape relationships with her family? Perhaps their different narrative histories made it difficult for Julie and Laura to grasp each other's rhythms. We saw in the December 2, 2002 field note that coming to school with a different rhythm was not something Julie was rewarded for. It seemed, in Julie's Year 1 experience, that having one's own rhythm, and resisting a shift to fall into the teacher's or school's rhythm, was not something that was rewarded in school. The glimpses of Seeta we saw in Sadie's story corroborate this idea. Seeta was often in trouble because she did not readily adapt to the rhythms of Gale's classroom.

Erica was able to continue her stories to live by, of being like Lian, because Erica found a space to express her stories to Lian through e-mail. Erica was older and perhaps saw the need to divide her attention in ways that allowed her to be part of the friendship group in the school story on the Year 6 landscape and her own stories to live by as being a person like Lian. It seemed that Erica used her imagination to improvise a way to continue living and telling both stories.

In Sadie's stories to live by, Seeta was important in how Sadie found a way to be in school. In Erica's stories to live by, peers played an equally important role. The difference was the way in which both of these girls accessed their peers to shape their stories to live by in school. Erica experienced tension with her peers in the past. When she found a peer group in which to belong, Lian, recognizing Erica's need to maintain a narrative coherence of belonging in the classroom, stepped back in order for Erica to continue her story of belonging in the class. Erica and Sadie interacted with their peers within the plotlines of their teachers' stories. We wondered about the difference in Erica's, Sadie's, and Julie's interactions with their teachers. We wondered if their teachers' responses reflected the children's different ages; if teachers felt the need to shape children's lives in school in different ways at different ages.

We return once again to the refrain we heard in the first interim research text of the chapter, "If you're happy and you know it, clap your hands." As we think about Sadie, Erica, and Julie composing their lives within the stories of school and school stories their teachers and other children tell of them, we wonder where the spaces are for more than one version of a rhythm, for more than one song to be sung.

Living in the midst of wonderings

As we worked alongside Sadie, Erica, and Julie, attending to their stories to live by and to their teachers' stories of them, we did see competing plotlines begin to conflict. Often, as a result, we saw children begin to shift who they were in order to better fit within the story their teachers told of them.

As we watched closely and saw those shifting, changing stories, we wondered whether children's stories to live by were shaped in more educative ways. We wondered about how to become more attentive, as teachers and researchers, to how our stories of children shaped who they were and were becoming.

As we inquired into our field texts and wrote research texts based on them, we wondered about the place of relational narrative inquiry in shaping more wakeful places (Clandinin and Connelly 2000) about the meeting of children's and teachers' lives in schools. We wondered about the professional knowledge landscape of schools, increasingly shaped by plotlines of accountability, and the gaps and silences, the secret stories and cover stories this dominant story of school shapes for children and teachers.

Chapter 4

Children's fictionalized stories to live by

As the first months of our inquiry at Ravine Elementary School unfolded in the fall of 2002, several of us talked about a concept that seemed linked with the children's stories and stories of children to which we were attending, something we started to call fictionalized stories. This term did not come up for a few months. As we started to attend to children's stories and stories of children at Ravine Elementary School, it was these stories that drew us to wonder about the place fictionalizing plays in stories to live by.

Fictionalizing stories of teachers, teachers' stories

The idea of cover stories (Crites 1971) has been woven in and out of Clandinin and Connelly's work for many years. When they (Clandinin and Connelly 1995) first attended to cover stories they wrote of cover stories as the stories teachers told that allowed them to fit within the plotlines of the accepted stories of school. For example, they wrote that when whole language, as an approach to reading instruction, fell outside the plotline of what was acceptable in reading instruction in some schools and districts, some teachers composed carefully crafted cover stories in which they had phonics books, basal readers, and spelling workbooks in their classrooms to cover or hide their continued use of a more whole language approach. Clandinin and Connelly (1995) played with the idea of cover stories as a way that teachers told stories of who they were and what their practices were that enabled them to continue to live who they were. Cover stories were a kind of deception and could, as Crites (1979) noted, also be a kind of self-deception. We realized that the careful composition of a cover story was a kind of fictionalization of our teacher stories that allowed us a way to continue to live out our stories to live by. The fictionalization was given form, structure, and plotline by what was seen as the acceptable story of school. The fictionalized cover story of a teacher story had to fit within the story of school. Teachers were aware of stories of school. They knew the consequences of falling outside the acceptable story of school: bad evaluations, difficult class assignments, possible transfers, and, for beginning teachers, no renewal of temporary teaching contracts. We had not considered the fictionalizing that children might also engage in.

Learning to attend to children's stories, stories of children

In this research, as well as in the earlier study at City Heights, we shifted our attention from teachers and their stories to live by to also include children and their stories to live by. In particular, we wanted to attend to the bumping up places among teachers' stories to live by and school stories and children's stories to live by. This brought us back to reconsider the fictionalizing we first attended to as cover stories. As we thought about this we realized we needed to attend more closely to the distinction between children's stories and stories of children. We wrote of this in Chapter 3. In this chapter we turn our attention to three children – James, Catrina, and Aaron – to help us understand this distinction in relation to fictionalizing and cover stories. We first turn to James, a child in Year 1 and a participant in Anne's study.

Anne used children's literature as a way of creating spaces for children to tell and retell stories of who they were. James was one of four Year 1 and 2 children who gathered with Anne on a weekly basis for a three-month period. The four children and Anne came together over the lunch hour to share favourite books and to talk about them in relation to their lives both in and out of school. Months later, when the group lunchtime book conversations ended, Anne returned to talk with the children individually in order to share written accounts of her understanding of their shared experiences.

James's stories, stories of James

James's stories, early in Year 1, were not always smoothly aligned with others in his classroom. Anne described how she saw him living in those first days.

> He had a hard time sitting in his desk, and his chair would often fall over. He would quietly pick it up and try again to sit still. When it was time to write or draw, he was often unable to get much down on paper. During free time with his classmates, he often remained on the margins of the activities. Laura [his teacher] shared her concerns with James's mother around how James was not fitting into the story of school being lived out in the classroom.
>
> (Interim research text based on field notes, September, 2002)

As this research text suggests, a story of James as a child who did not fit in started to be told early in the school year. Anne, though, was hearing James tell other stories of who he was, stories of himself as interested in a non-fiction book he wanted to read with Anne.

He was interested in sharks, the pages on electricity, the chemical reactions section. He explained how electricity travelled through the wires, how the shark found its prey by smell, how the chemicals in the photographs combined to make an entirely different substance.

(Interim research text based on field notes, September 2002)

As James told his story as someone interested in how the physical and animal worlds worked, Anne began to tell a story of James as bringing an avid eagerness to his explanations and of making good use of his extensive vocabulary. As September unfolded Anne saw James as a child who lived and told a story of himself as being curious and eager to make sense of the world. Anne continued to note the way James's stories found expression in his actions.

One of the children threw a barely eaten granola bar into the garbage and Laura noticed it and told the children that we shouldn't waste food. She said it would be better to put the granola bar back in your lunch bag if you can't eat it, so your parents would know that you had too much food in your lunch today. She talked about how granola bars cost money and we don't want our parent's money to be wasted. "Money doesn't grow on trees, does it?" Laura remarked. James spoke up: "Actually, money kind of does grow on trees, because money is made of paper, and paper comes from trees."

(Field note, September 25, 2002)

Also in September, Anne's field notes reflected James as living a story of curiosity.

Laura was starting a printing lesson. She drew several upper case Os on the whiteboard too close together, and asked, "What's wrong with these?" James turned to Anne and said, "If you make them too close together, they look like magic rings stuck together." This was not maybe quite the answer Laura was looking for, but it showed James was attending and understanding that you shouldn't make your letters too close together.

(Field note, September 12, 2002)

When the lunchtime book conversations began in October, Anne chose Baylor's (1985) book *Everybody Needs a Rock* as one of their first group read-alouds. She chose this book as she thought it might connect with Bob, another Year 1 child in Anne's study, as he was interested in rocks and minerals. As Anne read, James quickly noted how Baylor integrated numbers into her book with reference to mountains being made out of "a hundred million small shiny beautiful roundish rocks" (p. 7). In the conversation following the reading of the book, James told a future-oriented story of himself as someone who was "going to be a billionaire too. Oh, and a rocket scientist. And then I'm going to catch a star" (Transcript of lunchtime group conversation, November 7, 2002). Later in the same conversation he stated, "Inside myself, I have billions and billions of wires. Oh, did you know that one thousand, five hundred and sixty-three times zero is zero?" (Transcript of lunchtime group conversation, November 7, 2002).

Throughout the lunch hour book conversations, as well as when Anne spent time in the Year 1/2 classroom, James continued to tell stories to Anne that held plotlines of who he was and how he was positioning himself in his world. In November, when Anne read *A Quiet Place* (Wood 2002) in the lunch hour book conversation group, James and Bob became animated as they looked at the scenes in this book. According to Anne's field notes, they had lots to say about the landscape of each quiet scene.

> As we paused on the ocean page, James said, "I love the beach. At the beach, I would go surfing. But it's very, very, very dangerous, because a mudslide could come down. I could surf a hundred waves ... no, 8,063 waves ... that's a record breaker."
> (Transcript of lunchtime group conversation, November 21, 2002)

As Anne interacted with and attended to James, both in and outside the classroom, she began to compose a story of him as a child who entered into books with his whole body, becoming, as in the transcript above for example, a surfer at the ocean. Anne constructed her story of James from fragments of his talk, his responses to books in the lunchtime conversations, and the actions she saw him living at lunchtime and in the classroom. At the same time as Anne was forming a story of who James was, she was also becoming attentive to the story of school being shaped in James's Year 1/2 classroom and to the stories Laura, James's teacher, and James's mother were beginning to tell of James. As she listened, Anne learned about Laura's and James's mother's concerns around James's classroom behaviour and his lack of large and fine motor coordination. The story they were composing of James was one with plotlines of James having difficulty being a good student. Fitting with their story, James was tested at a local hospital clinic, diagnosed with an attention deficit, and medicated by November of that fall. Following that diagnosis, plans began for James to be placed in a program the next year for students with specific learning disabilities.

In mid-November, Anne asked James, during one of their lunch hour book conversations, if she could scribe a story for him. James's choice of subject matter for his scribed story was scary and slightly gory, a choice Anne knew, even as she was scribing, would fall outside the acceptable story of school being lived out in the classroom. Anne knew the stories being told and written during their lunch time together were travelling back to the classroom as the children often wanted to share their responses with others in their Year

1/2 classroom who were not a part of the lunchtime conversations. The story James told to Anne that he wanted her to scribe was one she later discovered drew on his reading of books from the *Goosebumps* (Stine 2000) series, a series of books classified as having thriller themes for young readers.

> James and Anne went into Miss Green's office and sat on cushions on the floor. Anne had pencil and paper ready and asked James if he would like to tell her a story and have her write it down for him. James smiled and began to tell her a "scary story" about digging in the playground and finding a human hand. Anne tried to move him away from the scary story idea and they talked about some other possibilities (which Anne suggested). James politely discussed the other ideas Anne had but then came back to his original idea and continued to tell about the monster he conquered when everyone else had been scared and had run home. He ended the story by saying he was alone on the playground and he was lonely. He asked if Anne and he could read his story to the class.
>
> (Field notes, November 14, 2003)

As we attended to the above field notes what became apparent was that, while Anne continued to hold onto and to support a story of James as a curious child eager to make sense of his world, she also started to live storylines with him of trying to help him learn to fit into the story of school being lived out in his Year 1/2 classroom. Becoming increasingly aware that the story James was living and telling of himself was bumping up against the stories Laura and James's mother were telling of him, Anne felt the need to help James learn to fit more smoothly into acceptable student plotlines. She was, in our narrative terms, trying to help him compose a cover story. But James resisted Anne's attempts. Instead, he continued to live storylines consistent with his own story of who he was and who he was becoming. James, through his enthusiasm and creative engagement with books, ideas, and other texts he encountered, seemed to tell a story of himself as thoughtful, curious, and imaginative.

As Anne spent time with James alone and in large and small group conversations, she noticed he did not talk about the stories his mother and Laura were telling of him. He also did not seem to be letting their stories shape the perceptions he had of himself. Rather, he continued to tell stories of who he was and who he was becoming. As we attended to the gaps between the stories James told of who he was and the stories others told of him, we began to wonder about the fictionalizing James undertook in the stories he told of himself. It was quite a different process than when we composed fictionalized cover stories that allowed us to sustain ourselves by a kind of cover or camouflage. For example, the setting for the scary story was the school playground. James chose this location rather than other, possibly scarier, sites to locate his story, and while he was successful in vanquishing the monster, he was left alone on the playground. We began to wonder about the range of meanings and purposes for which children might fictionalize their stories.

Fictionalization is the act of using what you know of something – your life, a place, events – to create a story around this knowledge that shifts the original story of experience. We wondered if James was doing this as he told that scary story of school, a story of being left alone, albeit triumphant. Had school, by mid-November, become a place where he felt there were monsters and where he felt alone? Perhaps James, in his engagement with children's literature and his encounters with Anne, was scaffolding a broader story of who he was and who he was becoming (Huber *et al.* 2003), one that encompassed his creativity and curiosity. In this broader story, James was able to conquer monsters. Perhaps James noticed, but only on the periphery, the stories being composed for him by his mother and teacher and others in the school. Hoffman (1989: 74) wrote of childhood as a time and place when "we are not yet divided," as a time "to which we gave ourselves wholly, without reservations" (p. 75). Perhaps for James his childhood landscape was intact; fictionalization allowed him to compose stories to live by that attended to his experience without calling upon him to be divided.

Attending to James's stories over time

In the spring of the school year, Anne returned to Ravine Elementary School to engage in additional individual conversations with the four children involved in the lunch hour book conversations where she read the narrative accounts she wrote about the children's experiences. Anne tape-recorded the individual conversations as she wanted to inquire into the ways in which the individual children responded to her writing. Attending closely to the stories James lived and told about who he was and who he was becoming, Anne composed stories of James which she shared with him when she returned. Anne was aware of the school story created of James, a story with a plotline of not fitting in, of attention deficit, and of learning difficulties. James did not tell Anne the school stories being told of him. Instead, he persistently told stories of himself as a strong and capable person.

> In May, when Anne returned to the school, James and Anne spent some time together and he told her he has been reading *Goosebumps* (Stine 2000) chapter books. Anne asked James if he remembered telling her the story of the ghostly hand in the playground in November. He smiled and very animatedly retold part of the story.
>
> (Field note, May 8, 2003)

In June, Anne found that, as she read several pages of what she had written about James to him, he seemed to use this experience as a way to reconsider his stories to live by. In the following example, she read a paragraph about how James knew what to say when Charlene (a child in his classroom) talked about her mother leaving the family. He talked about his pet dying and how sad it was. Anne wrote that she saw James as a caring person who listened to others and responded when appropriate.

When Anne read another paragraph of her writing to James about how he and Justin helped a child in Kindergarten one day at recess, James was quiet for a moment. Then he said slowly, "Yeah, I'm very, very, very kind" (Transcript of individual conversation, June 11, 2003). Anne agreed and James continued, "I think I learned that from a book ... how to make people happy" (Transcript of individual conversation, June 11, 2003). Anne wondered if books were places where James learned other possible ways to tell stories of who he was and who he was becoming.

One of the stories being told of James was that he was a good reader. Laura told Anne in May that James was a strong reader and this was also in Anne's writing about James. When she read this to him he picked it up and said, "Yeah, I'm one of the best, I'm one of the best Year 1 readers because I'm on *Magic Tree House* and that's step books" (Transcript of individual conversation, June 11, 2003). *Magic Tree House* (Osborne 1998) books are a series of beginning chapter books in the adventure and mystery genres.

The next part Anne read to James was her retelling of a story from the previous fall, from a lunchtime book conversation.

> James made a drawing with Bob after they read *Everybody Needs a Rock* (Baylor 1985). As they drew, they talked about how rich they would become by visiting stars and other planets and moons to collect rocks to bring back to Earth to sell. James had talked about going to eighty-five thousand places to find a good rock, and then he mentioned making billions of dollars. He asked Anne, "Oh, do you know that one thousand, five hundred and sixty-three times zero equals zero?" When Anne read this to James in June, nine months later, he responded, "I'm really good at math."
>
> (Interim research text based on field notes, June 11, 2003)

Being a good reader, being good at math, and being very, very kind were plotlines in the stories James told Anne about himself. We wondered if the story of school being lived out in James's classroom might have shaped the stories James told of himself at the end of his first year of school. In November, James resisted Anne's subtle attempts to shift his ghostly hand story to a cover story more acceptable to the story of school. In June, as James paused to reflect on a story previously told to Anne about helping a Kindergarten child, was he realizing gradually that his stories now, unlike the ghostly hand story recounted in November, needed to fall within more acceptable plotlines such as being "very kind" through "reading lots of books?" Perhaps in June, James was responding to the ways Anne was trying to shape a cover story for him. Why did James now tell a story of being a good student in math and reading? We wondered if James began to tell a story of himself as a successful student in these subject areas to craft a cover story that allowed him to continue his competing stories to live by alongside the school stories of him as an unsuccessful student. We see James's stories to live by as an imaginative, thoughtful, and humorous boy as a competing story with the school story of him, and his use of a cover story as a response to the growing tensions he was experiencing. Was James's deeper noticing of school stories beginning to divide him such that a cover story might be necessary to protect him? By dividing we refer to the need for secret and cover stories, the need to learn where we can tell certain stories of ourselves. Hoffman (1989), writing about her experiences of childhood, said, "Later, of course we learn to be more parsimonious; how to parse ourselves into constituent elements, how to be less indiscriminate and foolish in our enthusiasms" (1989: 75). Seeing cover stories as a reflection of this parsing, we wondered if James parsed some of the stories he told enthusiastically in the fall, so that his stories to live by could be reshaped and retold by May and June to fit with plotlines acceptable to the story of school. Were the stories he told at the end of the year a way for him to negotiate the tensions of his life in school?

But Anne's notes kept us perplexed. As she returned to her transcripts and field notes of the November 21, 2002, lunch hour book conversation when they read *A Quiet Place* (Wood 2002), she read how she noted James's excited response to the page that showed a beach scene with big waves breaking on the shore. Her notes revealed how James imagined himself as a surfer. As Anne read this description to James in June, he picked up on the storyline, a possible telling of who he might become, and began to tell another story of how he surfed at the beach and saw dolphins and a whale. He described how he had seen,

> "A big black [whale]. I jumped off my surfboard and went onto it. It took me back to the shore … I thought it could talk, but that was when I was younger … I was four years old. I'll show you what I was doing." …
> James got up and stood swaying as if he was trying to stand on a whale. "I thought I would fall off but then I got up and I was like this. I was hanging ten!"
> (Transcript of individual conversation, June 11, 2003)

In the face of other tellings of him, and in the safe place Anne created for James through her relationship with him, James returned to other imaginative stories of who he might be and who he might become. He began to create a fictional character of himself as a boy who rides whales, a character that enlarges the possibility for James of who he might become. We saw in this return the notion of James scaffolding his stories to live by through the intentional conversation spaces created through encounters with children's literature with Anne (Huber *et al.* 2003). In these moments we did not see James composing cover stories. Instead, we saw these moments of fictionalization as enthusiastic responses to literature as he played with stories in creative and adventurous ways.

Another page in *A Quiet Place* (Wood 2002) has a detailed illustration of a desert landscape. Anne read to James her description about how he had talked with Bob about how the "spikes" on the cactus were a form of protection for that plant. They even acted out a short role play last November with James as the cactus and Bob as an animal trying to eat it. As Anne read this to James he immediately began to spin a story from this paragraph, which he seemed to use as a prompt. "And I've been to the desert and I had to use my knife to open a cactus to get my water. I had to fill my ... what are those things cowboys use?" (Transcript of lunchtime group conversation, June 11, 2003). Anne suggested a canteen, and James continued, "Yeah, and I was riding my horse, and I found a little ghost town ... we had some showdowns there" (Transcript of lunchtime group conversation, June 11, 2003). James went on to say how cowboys needed to have lassos as well as guns, because "they can't shoot when they're on a horse, because they need to hold on. They need to use lassos to catch the bulls" (Transcript of lunchtime group conversation, June 11, 2003). Anne realized James was bringing in many things he knew about the desert and cowboy lore to create a story of himself, a fictional character. Again we saw James enlarging the possibilities of his stories to live by through his engagement with children's literature.

We were struck by the complexity of the storying and restorying as Anne, in her research, tried to sustain what she saw as James's stories to live by in the midst of stories others were telling of him. We saw how the stories of James and James's stories bumped against each other. He stayed silent with Anne about the stories that he was living as the school story moved him into a special education setting. Even though we were told that James did not fit into his Year 1 classroom we saw how his good student stories of being good at math and reading and being very kind did fit in with the story of school. We do not know if James was purposefully reconfiguring some of his stories to cover and protect the stories of who he was and who he was becoming. We also saw James draw on his imaginative encounters with books to begin to fictionalize stories of himself for other purposes. We wondered if James fictionalized stories of himself as strong and clever in order to enlarge the spaces of possibility in his stories to live by. We wondered if this allowed James to sustain a competing story, a story in dynamic tension with school stories told of him. Did his fictionalizing with Anne sustain and scaffold stories of who he was and who he was becoming as he encountered his first year of school? Did fictionalizing stories enable continuity for James in who he was and who he was becoming on school landscapes?

Fictionalizing in Catrina's stories to live by

Throughout our research conversations, we began to understand fictionalization as a recurring theme in the lives of other children at the school. We wondered more about purposes, intentions, and audiences for which children created fictions. Catrina, a child in the Year 5/6 classroom in which Shaun worked, told a story of herself as an expert on fashion in order to fit within the plotline of what she considered to be a popular Year 5/6 student. Catrina's peers, other teachers, and Jeanette, the school principal, told Shaun a story of Catrina as a girl who did not fit in. In the fall Catrina spoke to Shaun about her knowledge of makeovers – makeovers for pets and for people. Was Catrina aware of how she was storied by others at school and was she creating this story as a response to their stories? We wondered if this was a cover story because it allowed her to foreground her knowledge rather than her appearance, which was unkempt and not of the fashion favoured by other Year 6 students. Catrina told this story of makeovers in order to demonstrate that she knew about fashionable appearance even if she was unable to achieve it herself. However, this cover story became a more complex fiction when she began to talk about other girls coming to her for fashion advice. There was no evidence of other girls in the class approaching Catrina for advice on fashion.

Catrina seemed aware of how being popular shaped a student's experience in school. She told Shaun how she was also known for her taste in music and how bringing in a CD was making her popular with her classmates. Because Shaun had not noticed an appreciable improvement in her relationships with other children over time in Catrina's classroom, he questioned her about the stories she was telling of who she was. During one conversation Catrina told Shaun her pet tarantula escaped and was loose in the school. When he finally established that Catrina had created a fiction to impress him, Shaun asked her if the story of her taste in music, which according to Catrina was making her popular, was also one she created. Shaun framed his question to her as one of truth. In this second story she would not be shifted. Shaun backed away from his questions about truth and made a note to ask Catrina's teacher, Lian, if Catrina had brought a CD to class.

> Then Lian told Shaun how Catrina had brought a CD to school that she had made. It had Avril Levigne on it and other singers. She asked Lian to put it on and she did. Eventually the other girls came up and started singing along and they asked Lian if it was her CD and she said no, Catrina had brought it. No comment was really made about this and the girls started dancing to the music at the front. Catrina sat in her desk paying attention but reading. Then she came up and hung out at the edge of the group, but the girls didn't welcome her in. Lian said it wasn't done intentionally, but was a way of life for them … they didn't think to include her so eventually Catrina went back and sat down.
>
> (Field notes, March 26, 2003)

The story captured in the above field notes was not the story Catrina told Shaun. In Catrina's version she joined the girls, dancing among them and even singing along with one of the other girls. As we considered Catrina's and Lian's stories alongside each other, we glimpsed the poignancy of how Catrina was positioned in these contrasting stories of the moment. We wondered how Catrina made sense of these moments. She spoke of herself as popular in the class as a result of bringing the CD. Yet Lian observed her on the margins of the dancing girls. In conversation with Shaun, Catrina seemed to see the moment of the CD story as sustaining the fiction she told of herself as popular with her classmates. We wondered if, for Catrina, like James, this fictionalization enabled her to enlarge the possibilities for her stories to live by. Had this story of being popular allowed her to imagine herself in relationships with other people in the class?

This moment in the research highlighted, for us, the role of fictionalization in maintaining narrative coherence (Carr 1986). Being marginalized on the school landscape created tensions for Catrina. Was Catrina, during the time in which she was a participant in this research, struggling to achieve narrative coherence by composing a fiction of being a popular girl? The makeover story in the fall and the CD story of the spring indicate a temporal quality to her story of being popular. Her fiction of being popular was an ongoing story Catrina lived by in school. Catrina maintained her story to live by of being popular, of being involved in the relational life of the classroom.

In one moment in the research Catrina told Shaun about the ghosts who inhabited the school. She told him that, prior to Ravine Elementary School being built, the property had been a farm yard. She said that the classroom they were currently working in was located on the site of the original farmhouse. In this farmhouse, there had been a murder; the mother of the family had been killed and now her ghost, according to Catrina, haunted the school. Catrina assured Shaun she knew this because there was a book about it in the public library. Shaun looked into this and was never able to find such a book. He wondered why she needed to tell a story about ghosts in the school. She had spoken about ghosts in a previous conversation. In this earlier conversation she spoke about the ghosts in the empty classroom Shaun and she walked through to get to the space where they had their research conversations. Later in the same conversation Shaun discovered this had been Catrina's classroom at the beginning of the year. He wondered if she used the ideas of ghosts to talk about her memories of being in that space. When she began to talk about the ghost of the murdered mother, Shaun wondered at this need for another ghost story. In conversation with other researchers at the school, Shaun learned a photograph that hung in the school foyer was of a mother; a parent and volunteer at the school who had been murdered in her home several years earlier. Students at Ravine Elementary School knew the story of this parent who had died. When we found out about the parent we saw a connection that possibly explained Catrina's story. This example of fiction was not the same as fictionalizing stories to live by. Rather, we saw this as simply a fiction created about an event.

In a later conversation, Catrina drew on her story of ghosts to explain her stories to live by in relation to bullying. An ongoing problem for Catrina at school was her need to deal with bullying. In one incident, Catrina had gone to the mother of a girl who was bullying her in order to get the girl to stop. When Shaun asked Catrina why she was so brave she replied, "I am not brave. I'm afraid of the dark" (Transcript of individual conversation, January 22, 2003). Shaun suggested, in the conversation, that she could be brave about some things and not others. When he asked again why she was so brave she replied she did not know. Eventually she responded, "Probably because I faced ghosts and they are a lot easier to deal with. I have! [in response to Shaun's scepticism] At my old house and in my old school ... Mmmhmm, so I faced ghosts and they can't be much harder than people" (Transcript of individual conversation, January 22, 2003). Was Catrina using this story of ghosts, as she had used her story of being popular, to enlarge the possibilities for her stories to live by? In both fictionalizations she was finding a way to negotiate her stories to live by on the school landscape. Perhaps Catrina used a story of being knowledgeable about music and fashion to create a fiction of being popular and a story of facing ghosts to create a fiction of being brave.

As we attended to Catrina we saw her create fictionalized accounts of herself in order to sustain her stories to live by. Both James and Catrina created and told these fictionalized accounts of who they were in order to sustain themselves as the school stories of them threatened their stories of themselves and who they were becoming. As researchers, we became aware of their fictionalized accounts as we attended to the bumping places between children's stories and stories of children, and of the need to attend more closely to how the children were attempting to sustain the narrative coherence of their stories to live by.

Joining into fictionalizing: stories of Aaron

We saw in our stories of Aaron, a Year 2 student, how we, as researchers, joined Aaron's teacher and principal in composing fictionalized accounts of his life. We saw this particularly as moments of tension arose around his school attendance. It was only by slowing down, stilling our voices, that we began to hear Aaron's stories and his mother's and grandmother's stories of him. As researchers and teachers we attended from our own stories of school to Aaron. In doing so our focus almost blotted out these other stories. We begin with an account of Aaron as the tensions around attendance emerged.

Aaron's stories, stories of Aaron

Aaron's attendance had been sporadic in Kindergarten, averaging about one day a week, until he stopped coming all together five months into the school year. For the next two years, Aaron moved in and out of a few schools. Twice his mother re-enrolled him at Ravine Elementary School but failed to bring him either time.

Although Aaron should have been in Year 3 given his age, he eventually returned to Ravine Elementary School and due to his schooling history was placed in a Year 1/2 classroom. While often late for school, Aaron's attendance improved and he missed no more than a day every few weeks. In early November, Jeanette, the school principal, received a call from Aaron's grandmother telling her that Aaron would be absent for a few weeks. They had plans to visit family in a northern Métis settlement. Jeanette expressed frustration that Aaron was once more experiencing interruptions to his schooling. As Marni, the researcher in Aaron's classroom, listened to Jeanette share her concerns with Gale, Aaron's teacher, wonders arose in all of them about how to prevent Aaron from continuing to fall further behind. Maybe Aaron could stay at home with his aunt and uncle? Gale then puzzled aloud about the possibility of having Aaron stay with her. Marni offered to help by keeping Aaron on the weekends. At the time, they saw this as a caring response to Aaron. Jeanette was beginning to worry that she might have to involve the district's truancy officer if old patterns re-surfaced for Aaron.

(Interim research text created from field notes, October 24, 2002; November 7, 2002)

In this interim research text, Marni captured some of the history of Aaron's schooling and attendance issues. Tensions around attending various schools and inconsistent attendance at Ravine Elementary School surfaced in the text. We also saw the beginnings of the creation of a fiction around Aaron's schooling. As Marni and Gale imagined what they could do to assist Aaron in his attendance at school, they did not take into account what Aaron or his family might have wanted for him. Jeanette saw this newest absence from school as part of older patterns and began to think about what she might need to do as a result. Gale and Marni decided to ask if it was possible for Aaron to stay with them while his family went on this visit. They contacted the grandmother to make their suggestion and then they spoke to Aaron.

Although Aaron's grandmother was cautiously open to this idea, she wanted Aaron to have a say in the decision. "He doesn't like to stay with strangers," she told Gale on the phone, "… you need to talk to him about it." "But I'm not a stranger. I've seen him every day for the past two months," Gale replied.

Gale and Marni met with Aaron in the nook behind the classroom. Aaron never once made eye contact with Gale as she invited him to stay with her while his grandmother went to the Métis settlement. He glanced up at Marni once or twice as if to see where she stood on the matter. Marni remained surprisingly silent as she noticed Aaron's legs beating a steady rhythm beneath the table. "I'm not going with my grandma. I'm going to stay with my dad and my sister," he told them in a whisper, head bowed low. Gale and Marni glanced at each other. They didn't know there was another sister. What else didn't they know about Aaron?

(Field notes, November 7, 2002)

In this story of Aaron, the adults began to compose a fictionalized account as they imagined how they might support him in school. Initially their thoughts of keeping Aaron in school were based on conjecture. He could stay at their homes and they would be responsible for bringing him to school. A shift occurred, however, when they approached Aaron's grandmother and then Aaron with their idea. Interestingly, Aaron's grandmother named them as strangers, a title to which they reacted, one perhaps the grandmother was using to suggest a place in Aaron's stories to live by outside of school.

A profound tension in fictionalized stories to live by occurs when the fictionalized story moves beyond making sense of our stories to live by or creating possibilities, to interact with other's stories to live by, particularly when the individual has become a character in the fictionalized story. This can also be seen as an interruption in a person's stories to live by. In Marni's interim research text, three interruptions occurred. Gale and Marni experienced an interruption in their fictionalized story of caring for Aaron and Aaron experienced an interruption in how he positioned himself in his family as well as an interruption in his story of attendance at Ravine Elementary School.

Fictionalization as arrogant perception

Aaron's life as a son and grandson was intertwined with his life as a student. Because he was a member of the Ravine Elementary School community, the school story of Aaron was shaped, in part, by his interrupted attendance. This story of Aaron was mainly told by the school staff and by us as researchers. As we became increasingly aware of Aaron's life experiences, however, we became troubled. Marni's research alongside Aaron began as she inquired into Aaron's stories of school; she found these stories continually interwoven with his life outside of school. The story of Aaron's attendance could be understood by seeing his life as a student and as a member of a family.

Aaron's desk sat empty the first day after Christmas holidays. Marni phoned Aaron's home trying to reach his mother Karen, but instead reached Karen's older sister, Claire, who was in town from her home in the Métis settlement. She told Marni how Aaron's mother and stepfather had recently separated. Karen had moved to the settlement with Aaron and his younger siblings. "I'm glad they split up," Claire told Marni. "Evan just keeps coming and going and leaving her pregnant ... She needs to be with her family now especially since she's pregnant. She has nobody left here."

(Field notes, January 6, 2003)

Regular attendance was one of the plotlines used to understand a successful story of school. Gale and others at Ravine Elementary School, including us as researchers, saw Aaron's record of poor attendance as an interruption in a coherent story of school for him. Marni and Gale stepped into a fictionalization when they suggested that they could care for Aaron during his grandmother's visit to family in the Métis settlement, and that Aaron would be okay with this. Marni and Gale did not see their act of caring as privileging the story of school and interrupting the narrative coherence of the stories Aaron lived by with his family. Through his silence and body language, Aaron told Marni and Gale that he did not experience their invitation as caring. His grandmother had referred to Gale as a stranger. It was only in reflection that we began to understand that Aaron would feel a stranger in Gale's and Marni's homes. In their offer they were viewing Aaron and his family with a kind of arrogant perception (Lugones 1987) that privileged their story of Aaron but failed to attend to Aaron's stories of himself and his stories of Gale and Marni.

Multiple fictions

Aaron often found himself caught between the stories others were trying to shape for him. His mother, Karen, shaped the fictionalization of Aaron as a member of Ravine Elementary School by continuing a story of Aaron as a member of the school community. Karen sustained the story of Aaron as a student at Ravine Elementary School through her conversations with Marni about the importance of school in her story of Aaron's future and her ongoing plans to have her son return to the school.

> Aaron had not been attending school since leaving Ravine Elementary School but Karen shared she had "been helping him keep up with his homework . . We practice spelling ... He can do lots of words. And I give him math problems. I write them down for him to do – almost every day," she said. Karen asked if Marni would bring out some more homework for Aaron. She wanted Marni to tell Jeanette and Gale that Aaron would be back at Ravine Elementary School after Christmas. "I

know he needs stability in his life and moving schools often isn't helping him," Karen shared.

(Field note, December 8, 2002

But this fiction began to break down over time, particularly for Marni, who began to see other narrative threads in Aaron's stories to live by. As she experienced Aaron's life on and off the school landscape, she experienced shifting stories of Aaron as she moved between the landscapes alongside him. Encountering Aaron as a son and grandson increased her recognition of the multiplicity of his life. By sharing her research story with her research community she began to see that Aaron's life had narrative coherence as a boy who moved in and out of school and community landscapes. This movement in and out of school was, at least in part, his story of school. The story worked for him because when he did go to Ravine Elementary School he was welcomed, cared for, accepted, and found he still had a desk and a name tag and was kept alive in people's memories. He was storied as a valuable class member.

> Aaron immediately headed for his classroom and found his desk. It still held his nametag. The rest of his classmates were outside for recess but Aaron began to put his new school supplies away. Then he folded his hands on top of his desk and waited for the bell. "Aaron's here!" the children shouted as they crowded around him and began to rub his newly shaved head. Unselfconsciously Aaron shared, "My mom shaved my hair 'cause I had lice." His classmates just smiled and chatted to him as they continued to rub his head.
>
> (Field notes, February 14, 2003)

Karen, Aaron's mom, also had a narratively coherent story for Aaron. She continued to play her part in the fiction that one of his narrative threads was a school story. She told this story to Marni and also to Aaron.

> Karen told [Marni] that she's definitely planning on coming back for Aaron to finish his year at Ravine Elementary School. "I don't want him missing too much more school," Karen said. "Look at how good he's doing," she reported as she instructed Aaron to show [Marni] a piece of his homework that had been taped to the fridge.
>
> (Field notes, March 20, 2003)

Aaron did not return to Ravine Elementary School. A tension was introduced into this story of attendance when Jeanette, the principal, suggested she might need to involve the truancy officer. Jeanette threatened to invoke the story of school that is the dominant story of school and the one that, legally, the school must follow. Jeanette hesitated though, as with

Aaron's teacher, Gale, she continued to wonder what it meant to care for Aaron. As researchers, we wondered if the larger story of school, one that involved truancy officers and attendance board hearings, was a way of caring for Aaron. Gale and Jeanette wondered if they needed to report that Aaron was not in school. We all experienced the ethical tensions that these conversations brought up. All year, Aaron's teacher maintained a place for Aaron in her classroom through the continued presence of his nametag on his empty desk and then on her filing cabinet. By keeping an empty desk and a nametag, she held onto the fiction that Aaron remained a student in her classroom. Keeping his desk, placing his nametag on the side of the filing cabinet, and keeping Aaron alive in the memories of the children in the classroom allowed Gale to continue her story to live by; that is, as a caring teacher who was open to the multiplicity of children's lives. This helped keep Ravine Elementary School a welcoming place for Aaron as he continued to move on and off the school landscape. The truancy officer was never called.

Lingering thoughts on fictionalizing

Aaron's stories to live by were shaped by the life he lived in transition alongside his family. The landscape on which he lived with his family was continually shifting. Aaron's stories to live by as a student at Ravine Elementary School were shaped by his interrupted attendance. The story of school, of regular attendance as critical to student success, was a dominant story. If we imagined regular attendance as a way of maintaining narrative coherence in a student's stories to live by, we saw how Aaron fractured our understanding of a narratively coherent story of school. Aaron helped us begin to imagine what might be otherwise if the school story of attendance was more fluid, embracing the complexity and multiplicity of a student's life. When Gale, Jeanette, and Marni shared their concerns over Aaron's story of interrupted attendance they began to entangle the story of school with the story of Aaron. They wondered together about what it meant to care for Aaron and moved through moments of tension together with Aaron, his mother, his grandmother, and each other. Opening up this conversation put them on uncertain ground where they began to explore other ways to understand Aaron's stories to live by.

We did not see Aaron as creating a fiction. Rather his mother's fictionalization about his homework and his imminent return to school provided a cover story which maintained a space for him in the classroom and in the school stories of him. Marni, Jeanette, and Gale sustained this story of Aaron, entering into the fiction being shaped around his attendance at school.

James and Catrina, however, were authors of their own fictionalizations. We saw these fictionalizations working in two ways. Sometimes their fictionalizations appeared as cover stories protecting them from school stories being told of them. James began to tell stories of himself as successful in math, reading, and writing, perhaps as a way to compose a cover story that would allow him to appear to fit within the plotlines of being an acceptable student. Catrina created a fiction of being a popular girl who knew much about fashion and makeovers. This fiction seemed to serve as a cover story for Catrina that allowed her to imagine a space where she fit within the plotlines of popularity in the classroom. These fictionalizations were brave attempts, but struck us as fragile and tenuous, as we did not observe the fictions having the power to reposition James or Catrina on the school landscape. Both James and Catrina remained marginalized in their classrooms: James as a struggling student and Catrina outside the circle of popular girls.

We also saw James and Catrina fictionalizing for what seemed a different purpose. When James told how he could ride whales, conquer monsters, and have adventures we realized these were not operating as cover stories. We wondered if these stories enabled him to enlarge possibilities of who he might be and might become as he composed his stories to live by. James became a powerful character in the fictions he created alongside the literature he read with Anne. Perhaps this helped him imagine stories to live by as a strong and able boy, one who could shape his own stories to live by.

In her story of having fought ghosts, Catrina was able to imagine a way of dealing with bullies. This fictionalization gave her the possibility of stories to live by as a brave girl who could confront bullies and their parents. As with James, fictionalizing a story helped Catrina compose stories to live by with increased possibilities of who she might be and who she might be becoming. We had not previously considered the different types of fictionalizing of their stories in which children might engage. In attending to the stories of these three children we became aware that fictions may be created by and for children in school for different purposes and we began to realize the complexities of how fictions are intertwined with stories to live by.

Chapter 5

Children's and teachers' stories to live by in a school story of character education

We first began to attend to the plotlines of school stories of character education at City Heights, the urban school where we met Melissa and Lia. There was no mandated or planned program of character education at City Heights School. Rather, the curriculum of character education seemed more tacit, more interwoven within the story of school; it was a more hidden kind of curriculum (Jackson 1992). As Jackson drew attention to this kind of curriculum he wrote that there are "two separate curricula in every school: one explicitly endorsed, the other not" (p. 8). Naming this second, unofficial, unwritten curriculum as a hidden curriculum, Jackson explored how both curricula are simultaneously enacted in schools. It was, in part, due to this more hidden nature of the curriculum of character education that weeks slipped by at City Heights before we gradually began to attend to what was being taught in the school-wide morning announcements. Each morning, as part of the morning announcement, a recurring message suggested that the children should have a day of high-quality, productive learning. This message, loudly spoken to the children and teachers each and every morning of our year at City Heights School, was derived from a business model of education, a model focused on high productivity and high quality. Attending to this morning message as a more hidden aspect of character education, we began to awaken to ways in which this morning message was woven into a story of school in which schools were places of business, places of production. Emerging from this story of school were school rules and routines consistent with the business model; that is, the shaping influence of this business model was seen in its emphasis on punctuality and on being responsible for a prompt arrival at school, of being self-disciplined with good work ethics, and of completing assigned tasks diligently and on time, and so on. When broken, these rules had consequences such as going to the office and asking for a late slip or being held indoors during recesses or lunch hours to complete unfinished tasks or to make up for missed minutes. The consequences were designed to evoke in children a sense of shame and a desire to become more responsible, more self-disciplined, and so on.

At first we only attended in a peripheral way to how character education was interwoven into the story of school at City Heights. We saw it as a competing story to the stories Emily, the teacher, was living alongside Lia, Melissa, and the other children in the Year 3/4 classroom. While the children, Emily, Janice, and Jean were constructing in-classroom storylines where the particularities and diversity of the children's and families' lives mattered, the school story of character education was perpetuating plotlines where all children needed to adhere to specific and singularly defined notions of what it meant to be responsible, self-disciplined, honest, hard-working, and so on. It was not until we came to know something of the lived stories of the children and families in the Year 3/4 classroom that we began to notice the competing story of character education bumping against their, and our, stories to live by.

Lia's story, described in Chapter 1, was one story which caught our attention. Her late arrival at school, understood in the context of her unfolding stories to live by, was a story of familial duty, of responsibility for her brothers before herself. Looked at in the context of her life, Lia was acting responsibly. It was only when her late arrival was understood from within the plotline of the interwoven character education story of school that it could be read as a story of irresponsibility. Lia's late arrival at the school, and her even later arrival in the Year 3/4 classroom, was not an irresponsible act from within Lia's plotline. However, viewed from the story of school composed around a business model, Lia was acting irresponsibly. Becoming aware of how the curriculum of character education, subtly woven into the story of City Heights School, was bumping against children's and families' stories to live by, we began to attend to it much more directly. Focusing on the bumps it shaped in children's experiences in the school as the plotline of character education bumped up against their and their family's stories to live by, we came to understand the interwoven plotlines of character education not only as a competing story but, at times, as a conflicting story depending on the particularities of a child's and a family's life stories.

The curriculum of character education becoming explicit

Even though there was not a formal character education program while we were at City Heights School, we knew many schools in the local school districts were implementing formal programs. Many of the character education programs in these schools seemed to be grounded in philosophies that understood "moral education – the training of heart and mind toward the good … [as] involv[ing] rules … as well as explicit instruction, exhortation, and training" (Bennett 1993: 11). The character education programs were often surrounded by conversations about how children "must achieve at least a minimal level of moral [education to] … enable them to make sense of what they see in life and ... [to] help them live ... [life] well" (p. 11). In these ways, the programs were aimed at teaching children to possess specific character traits such as responsibility, caring, honesty, loyalty, perseverance, and so on. They seemed to rely on Bennett's belief that "the vast majority of Americans [and Canadians] share a respect for certain fundamental traits of character: honesty, compassion, courage, and perseverance" (p. 12); traits Bennett named as "virtues." These virtues-based character education programs popping up in schools across local districts also seemed to be encouraging a plotline similar to Bennett in that virtues such as responsibility, honesty, patience, courage, loyalty, and so on were "the basics" and could be taught without "complexities and controversies" (p. 13). For example, one's behaviour was either responsible or not; honesty was always expressed by eye contact and so on. Virtues were expressed in a certain range of pre-determined behaviours, regardless of context or what we saw as cultural and institutional narratives. Cultural and institutional narratives did not seem to be relevant in how these virtues-based programs were designed.

Over time, and as an increasing number of schools implemented more explicit, formal character education programs, we wondered about such modernist understandings of character education. We also wondered if changing the curriculum of character education from hidden to official would shift how children, families, teachers, and administrators experienced it. By character education programs becoming explicit, would they also be more open to inquiry? Would the ways in which virtues were understood within schools such as City Heights School become more complex as they opened up to questions around context and the multicultural, multi-family, multi-religious, multi-sexual, multi-language, multi-political, multi-economic realities of public schools? These wonderings and our experiences with Lia and other children at City Heights School shaped a background for our attending to the school story of character education unfolding at Ravine Elementary School.

A school story of character education at Ravine Elementary School

As a growing number of schools within local school districts began to pilot virtues-based character education programs, Jeanette, the school principal, and Suzanne, the teacher-librarian, sensed that the implementation of formal character education programs would soon be a mandate for all district schools. Both lovers of literature and both committed to helping children learn to love stories, Jeanette and Suzanne chose to build Ravine Elementary School's character education program using various forms of children's literature. Rather than implementing the already popular pre-packaged materials that provided definitions of virtues and had children complete worksheets and engage in pre-determined group activities, Suzanne and Jeanette organized

Ravine Elementary School's character education program around a series of twenty values, with two values being introduced each month through the sharing of children's literature at the weekly assemblies. The weekly assemblies were organized according to year levels: primary (Kindergarten to Year 2), junior (Years 3 and 4), and senior (Years 5 and 6). Values focused on during our time in the school included responsibility, care and concern for others, respect, tolerance, sharing gifts, perseverance, and honesty. The following interim research text provides a sense of the school-wide assemblies:

The weekly assembly as a school story

Each week children and teachers gathered in the music room located in the school loft. Parents, volunteering in the school, often accompanied the children. While the children sat cross-legged on the floor, parents and teachers sat on chairs or bleachers at the sides or back of the room. Suzanne and Jeanette typically stood at the front of the room playing clapping games to focus the children and to keep them from distracting one another until all of the children, teachers, and parents were gathered and the assembly was ready to begin. After a few words of welcome from Jeanette, either Suzanne or Jeanette would introduce the pre-selected value by first reading, playing, or acting out a piece of children's literature that seemed to portray the value. Then children, parents, and teachers would share examples of how they thought the value could be lived out. The assembly concluded with Jeanette or Suzanne asking teachers to share comments on their observations of the children, events, and activities of the past week. Comments were typically directed to the children and often referred to behaviours they had witnessed. For example, while one teacher made reference to a creative game he noticed children playing during recess, another noted how the boot room had not been kept tidy and organized. Although the formal teaching of character education occurred primarily during assembly time, values were also often part of daily school announcements, classroom conversations, and library displays. The monthly values were also displayed on the large notice board positioned on the lawn outside the school's front doors.

(Interim research text, April 2003)

Improvising a competing story

Before we arrived at Ravine Elementary School, and as Jeanette and Suzanne had suspected would happen, a school board directive was sent to all elementary schools requiring them to implement a character education program similar to the one we had glimpsed a couple of years earlier at City Heights. Unlike City Heights School where the curriculum of character education was more hidden, it was now officially part of the formal curriculum at Ravine Elementary School. While as a research team we all felt somewhat uncomfortable with a program focused on the direct teaching of values, we appreciated that teachers, administrators, children, and families at Ravine Elementary School were caught within a district mandate. We recognized that Jeanette was particularly vulnerable in this mandate as it was her responsibility as the principal to ensure the program was in place. Jeanette knew that when district superintendents and other district personnel visited the school they would expect to see the program operating and that she would be held accountable to address inquiries and questions raised.

Jeanette and Suzanne, acting before the officially mandated program was required, designed a program that fit with their love of children's literature. Although they had improvised a competing story to the dominant plotlines in the district, Jeanette knew she could point to the innovative literature-based character education program as fulfilling the district mandate. The literature-based program was also coherent with Jeanette's story of herself as an innovator, someone who always pushed against dominant stories of school within the school district. It was an example of Jeanette's story to live by as someone who could show others how things could be lived differently in schools. We explore Jeanette's stories to live by more fully in Chapters 6 and 9.

As a research team who also loved children's literature, when Suzanne rushed into Jeanette's office minutes before assembly asking for titles of books that illustrated a certain value, we were willing helpers. We suggested titles and helped to search through the shelves of children's books which lined the perimeter of Jeanette's office. We also attended the assemblies as often as we could. While we were not comfortable offering suggestions during the assemblies about how to live out values or ways we had seen values demonstrated in the school or on the playground over the past week, we also did not enter into school conversations with teachers, children, and families about the direct teaching of values.

Beginning to trouble the Ravine Elementary School story of character education

As earlier described, when we arrived at Ravine Elementary School we brought research puzzles with us around how children's, teachers', administrators', and families' stories to live by are shifted or interrupted as they bump against each other and against stories of school. We did not arrive at Ravine Elementary School with research puzzles that directly inquired into the Ravine Elementary School's story of character education. However, the school story of character education began to catch our attention when we started to share our experiences of the assemblies and to tell stories of children, families, administrators, and teachers we were coming to know in our research. In the following field texts and our unpacking of them we give a sense of our waking up to and working to understand moments when the story of character education at Ravine Elementary School interrupted children's, families', and teachers' stories to live by.

Shelby and responsibility

Today a story about responsibility was read in primary assembly. Jeanette talked about choices that reflect responsible action. Marni watched Shelby, a Year 1 child in Gale's class. Shelby listened intently, smiled at the pictures, and raised her hand when a question was asked.

As Marni watched Shelby, she reflected on the stories she was beginning to tell of Shelby: stories of a quiet child who gets along well with other children but prefers to be on her own or in the company of adults; stories of a child who has difficulty with attendance.

(Field notes, January 9, 2003)

Shelby was often storied in Marni's field notes. At first our research team listened, but without a sense of tension, as Marni began to tell stories of Shelby alongside stories of life in the Year 1/2 classroom and of the primary assemblies. However, as we heard Marni's field texts over time and as the stories within them became more layered, feelings of tension emerged within us.

Shelby was absent from school today. Gale expressed concern to Marni not only with the amount of school Shelby was missing but the numerous occasions when she was late for school.

(Field notes, January 22, 2003)

As Marni shared these stories of Shelby's absences from, and lateness to, school with the research team, she also shared stories of her conversations with Shelby's mother. For the most part, Marni's conversations with Shelby's mother occurred when she came to the school to volunteer in Shelby's Year 1/2 classroom. The field notes Marni wrote about her conversations with Shelby's mother reflected stories of her struggle with depression (Field notes, January 27, 2003). They also revealed moments when Shelby's mother told Marni stories of tensions at home emerging from her marriage, the learning difficulties Shelby's older sibling was experiencing, her experiences of taking high school upgrading courses, and her future plans to attend a local college (Field notes, May 15, 2003). Marni's conversations with both Gale, Shelby's teacher, and with Shelby's mother began to awaken Marni, as well as the rest of our research team, to the complexities of Shelby's life.

A few days after the assembly on responsibility Marni and Gale talked about Shelby's attendance. Gale wondered if Shelby's lack of attendance was related to her mother's emotional health. Gale spoke of how Shelby needed to become a more responsible student and how Shelby's mother needed to support this goal. For Gale this meant having regular attendance and arriving at school on time ready to attend to her daily work.

(Field notes, January 27, 2003)

As Marni shared her and Gale's conversation with the group of researchers, we saw the interconnectedness between Gale's story of what it meant to be a responsible student and the way being responsible was defined in the school's character education program. We began to wonder what we could make of Shelby's intent listening, smiles, and eagerness to answer questions at the primary assembly which focused on the value of being responsible. Was Shelby able to see herself within the school story of responsibility being told to her during the assembly in ways Gale, her teacher, was not able to see in Shelby's actions? Did Shelby not yet have a sense that the story her teacher told of her was that she "needed to become a more responsible student"? We considered again how cultural and institutional narratives seemed to be living outside Ravine Elementary School's story of character education.

Marni's field notes continued to provide us with an in-depth look at who Shelby was and who she was becoming.

Shelby told Marni "her mother was kind of sick and [she] needed to stay home and take care of her."

(Field note, January 30, 2003)

As Marni talked about her conversation with Shelby to the research group, she spoke about how living responsibly to Shelby meant helping to care for her mother. Marni's story made visible a place of tension between Shelby's stories to live by and the school story of character education. For Shelby, a child in Year 1, living a story of responsibility meant helping to care for her mother who was "kind of sick," whereas being a responsible student in the school story meant coming to school regularly, on time, and remaining on task. As we tried to understand who Shelby was and who she was becoming we began to see her as caught in a place of tension, a place where her stories to live by were in conflict with her teacher's story and the school's story of responsibility. Shelby could not live a story of responsibility to her mother at the same time as living the school's and her teacher's story of being a responsible student. As we reflected on this tension within the plotlines of Shelby's life, we recalled stories of other children we had known both from our childhoods and as teachers. We remembered how, when these children had been forced to choose, their first responsibilities had been to home rather than to being a responsible school student. We also told stories of moments when, as teachers, we, too, had failed to recognize these conflicting responsibilities in children's lives.

Attending closely to Shelby's life helped us understand how, seen from within one plotline, that is from within the plotlines of Shelby's stories to live by, Shelby was living out the value of responsibility. Seen from within another plotline, that is, being a responsible student in the school story, she was not living out the value of responsibility. As we thought about who Shelby was and who she was becoming in these plotlines, we were reminded of Greene's (1995) work around multiplicity. Seeing something of the multiplicity Shelby was living by we wondered if possibilities existed within formal character education programs that are attentive to children's unfolding stories to live by, spaces where children, such as Shelby, might figure out what it means to live responsibly as they attend to the multiplicity of their lives.

Erica's inclusion of others

Two Year 5/6 students, Erica and Catrina, helped us to further understand the complexities of children's stories to live by as they bumped against plotlines in Ravine Elementary School's story of character education.

> While Lian and Shaun talked in a research conversation, Shaun questioned whether or not Lian felt there was a hierarchy to the ways experiences and epistemological shifts happened in the classroom. Shaun wondered whether or not children and teachers were equally important in scaffolding others' shifts and if children caused shifts for teachers. In response to Shaun's questions, Lian and Shaun talked about Catrina and how they saw her on the margins of the class. Lian wondered if Catrina was afraid of her. Lian also told Shaun how Catrina had recently asked Erica to be her writing partner for a review of a standardized writing exam and that Erica had agreed. Shaun was surprised Erica accepted because Erica was typically very socially conscious in the class and Catrina was not a girl she had worked with before or one who belonged to Erica's social group. Lian explained she thought Erica had agreed to work with Catrina because Erica thought Catrina was a strong writer and because Erica wanted to be inclusive of Catrina in response to the senior assembly about including others on the previous day.
>
> (Interim research text based on transcript from individual conversation, May 15, 2003)

Intrigued by what Lian storied about Erica agreeing to work with Catrina, Shaun picked up on it in his one-on-one research conversation with Erica the following day.

When Shaun asked Erica she replied, "Well because um, um well she asked me and I thought, 'You know it's not very nice to turn down somebody,' and yeah and then another thing was um I noticed that I can, I can be a pretty mean person sometimes. And I thought, 'You know, I could actually take a step up and be more nice to them.' And I mean at that point I just thought about it and didn't really care what my friends thought so like ..." When Shaun asked Erica later in the conversation if the senior assembly had influenced her she told him it had and that Lian had continued the conversation in the class and that it had also reminded her of what she had learned in D.A.R.E. (Drug Abuse Resistance Education).

(Interim research text based on transcript from
individual conversation, May 16, 2003)

When Shaun shared these field texts in one of our research team conversations, we initially wondered if the senior assembly caused Erica to shift the stories she was living by. In Chapter 3 we showed something of the stories Erica lived by. In that inquiry we pulled forward identity threads of Erica as self-assured and confident, as enjoying sports and being competitive, as conscious of her popularity and attentive to being accepted by her peers (particularly those who were seen as popular), as a successful student, and as previously bullied and teased by older students. Understanding Erica's response to the senior assembly as shaping her decision to work with Catrina seemed to reinforce the effectiveness of the character education curriculum at Ravine Elementary School. In understanding Erica's decision in this way we could say Erica chose to "be more nice" and to work with Catrina after attending the senior assembly which focused on the value of being inclusive of others as well as the follow-up conversation in the classroom. In this way, then, Erica decided not to worry about what her friends thought, a storyline she had not usually turned away from. Perhaps the senior assembly and follow-up classroom conversation gave Erica the necessary courage to start to shift the stories she had been living by in relation to others, particularly peers who were seen as less popular and more marginal, peers such as Catrina. We wondered if the senior assembly created a space for Erica to engage in travelling to Catrina's world. Lugones (1987: 17) explored "world travel" as a possible way to move beyond viewing others arrogantly. She wrote that "travelling to someone's 'world' is a way of identifying with them ... because by travelling to their 'world' we can understand *what it is to be them and what it is to be ourselves in their eyes*" (emphasis in original) (p. 17). Had the senior assembly drawn forward for Erica memories of her Year 5 experiences at Ravine Elementary School, a year in which she was bullied and teased by Year 6 students? As Erica remembered these experiences we wondered if she traveled to Catrina's world and identified with the ways in which Catrina was marginalized in their current classroom.

Yet, as we continued to think about Lugones's (1987) notion of arrogant perception in relation to the above field texts we were struck by the possibility that the senior assembly and the following classroom conversation might have shaped new stories to live by for Erica, stories in which she was, through the character education curriculum, being subtly shaped to view Catrina with borders of arrogance. Lugones reminded us that "[those] who are perceived arrogantly can perceive other[s] arrogantly in their turn" (1987: 5). Might Erica have interpreted the senior assembly and class discussion as an experience where adults with authority were arrogantly perceiving her alongside other students at Ravine Elementary School? If Erica felt arrogantly perceived as being non-inclusive toward others, was she then, in turn, now arrogantly seeing Catrina as someone who was in need of being included? Could Erica have understood her inclusion of Catrina as a way for Erica to be seen by others, particularly Jeanette, Suzanne, and Lian, as having achieved the value, that is, as having lived out the value of inclusion? Understanding Erica's acceptance of Catrina's invitation for them to work together in this way led us to wonder how Catrina might have experienced Erica's positive response. On one hand, Catrina could have understood Erica's response as authentic. On the other hand, might Catrina have learned that she was now seen by others, in particular Erica, as needing to be included.

While we do not know how Catrina experienced Erica's inclusion of her, we wondered how, caught within this powerful plotline, Erica and Catrina could find a space where they might explore inclusion in the context of their unfolding lives. In raising these kinds of wonderings we were drawn toward questions of how children and teachers begin to live out the plotline of inclusion in ways that smooth out the multiple and layered ways in which inclusion is a deeply contextual and never-ending process. Now that the value of inclusion had been covered at the senior assembly and in class, what kinds of possibilities still existed for the continued negotiation of, and inquiry into, the complexities of living lives attentive to inclusion? Without this ongoing negotiation and inquiry, "the basics" were being taught without "complexities and controversies" (Bennett 1993: 13).

Continuing to inquire into children becoming characters in the school story

As we continued to puzzle over whether the school story of character education might perpetuate plotlines of children desiring or feeling the need to be seen as virtuous characters, we were drawn to another moment lived in the Year 5/6 classroom.

> Catrina told Lian and some of the girls in class that she was Leo's girlfriend and they were going to a nearby convenience store after school was over. When Lian talked to Leo about this he denied the whole story.

Lian was concerned that Catrina was opening herself to teasing from the girls. When Lian talked to Catrina about it she told Catrina that she shouldn't be making stories up that could result in her getting teased by other students in the class. Catrina told Shaun later that while she wasn't really Leo's girlfriend, she and Leo had planned to go to the store together after school. Catrina was bothered that Leo hadn't been honest about this with Lian and that Lian thought she was the one who wasn't telling the truth. Lian was troubled when she found out what had really happened.

(Field notes, February 5, 2003)

As we attended closely to the unfolding events in the above field notes we became intrigued by the stories Lian, as teacher, seemed to be living in relation to the school character education story and the value of honesty. Lian, relying on her knowing that Catrina, at times, created fictions of who she was (something we explored further in the previous chapter), tried to warn Catrina about the dangers of making up stories. Lian did not want Catrina to make herself vulnerable to being teased and being seen by other children in the class as someone who did not live by the value of honesty. However, as the events in these field notes unfolded, Lian learned Catrina had not been fictionalizing this story. Rather, it was Leo, when directly asked by Lian, who had not disclosed his and Catrina's after school plans to go to the store together. As Lian discovered she had been wrong about who Catrina was in this moment, she felt troubled. We wondered what was shaping Lian's feelings of tension. Might her felt tensions have emerged from recognizing that she had been so preoccupied with the school story of needing to teach children to adhere to plotlines of living virtuously that she had arrogantly perceived Catrina? In this way, was the only plausible possibility Lian had seen of why Leo's and Catrina's stories did not match that Catrina had not been honest? Did Lian's feelings of tension come forward as she traveled to Catrina's world and imagined how Catrina might have experienced the story Lian told of her? We know from the time Shaun spent in the Year 5/6 classroom and the conversations he and Lian engaged in that Lian cared deeply for the children with whom she worked. We also know that the children with whom Shaun engaged in ongoing research conversations saw Lian as caring about them. We wondered if this moment of tension shifted Lian's understanding of the complexities of teaching virtues.

Continuing to inquire into teachers becoming characters

We, as a group of researchers, were not the only ones who expressed tensions over the plotlines of Ravine Elementary School's story of character education. Teachers at Ravine Elementary School also voiced their struggles with the complexities they experienced in the direct teaching of values. For example, during a one-on-one research conversation between Suzanne, the teacher-librarian, and Marilyn, Suzanne shared her uncertainty about teaching the value of honesty outside of context and relationship. The following transcript segment highlighted Suzanne's dilemma:

> I'm in a real quandary about the honesty [value] too.... It's such a hard thing and it's at the forefront of my mind.... There is a book I used before for a book talk and it fits in with honesty but I don't know how much. It's called *The Skull of Truth: A Magic Shop Book* (Coville 1997) and the boy gets hooked up with this skull and it compels him to tell the truth. So he is having dinner and his aunt says, "Do you like the rhubarb casserole I made?" He says, "No it tastes like old socks." And the skull compels him and he says these things and so he gets in all this trouble for telling the truth. So I don't know, I don't know if that's my job to teach the kids values. Okay, well what I do is try to be as honest as I can unless I lie and it's not for my personal gain but so not to hurt somebody else's feelings. That's probably my understanding of honesty in a nutshell. But that's maybe not the value that other parents want their kids to [learn].... It's a gray area and so what do I tell kids? It is dishonest to steal a library book. I mean that's black and white but maybe if [the librarian] isn't there and the computer [to sign out books] is not working and you need the book for a book report and you know you're going to bring it back tomorrow. I don't know. I've got to figure it out.
>
> (Transcript from individual conversation, March 7, 2003)

Suzanne engaged in this conversation with Marilyn just prior to the upcoming school assemblies focused on the value of honesty; assemblies she and Jeanette were responsible for organizing and leading. In the above transcript fragment we saw Suzanne trying to figure out the "gray area" of teaching values. She knew she was responsible for finding children's literature to share at the primary, junior, and senior assemblies focused on the value of honesty, yet she was uncertain what understanding the literature should present. Should it, she wondered, portray a message such as the one represented in *The Skull of Truth* (Coville 1997) or should she find other pieces of literature that more closely matched her own understandings of honesty, that is, "to be as honest as I can unless I lie and it's not for my personal gain but so not to hurt somebody else's feelings" (Transcript from individual conversation, March 7, 2003).

As Suzanne shared her tensions, we saw how the school story of character education was, at least in relation to the value of honesty, a conflicting story for her. In the research conversation with Marilyn, Suzanne made visible Veugelers and Veddar's thoughts that "values ... get their real meaning within a context" (2003: 379). While in part Suzanne's struggle emerged from needing to teach values void of context, her tensions also came from not knowing what understanding of the value of honesty parents wanted their children to learn. Given the diversity of children's lives at Ravine Elementary School, Suzanne struggled with knowing from within which cultural and institutional narratives the value of honesty should be taught.

Noddings (1984: 184) raised a similar argument that "in order to engage in true dialogue with our students, we educators will first have to engage in true dialogue with their parents." Although Suzanne and Jeanette had worked together to improvise a competing story to the more dominant story of character education in the school district, Suzanne was still caught within contradictory plotlines. Plotlines mandated from the district that required all elementary schools to engage in the direct teaching of values bumped up against the plotlines of Suzanne's stories to live by of wanting to honour the diverse knowing and histories of the children and families with whom she worked. We wondered if Suzanne might have experienced the story of character education differently if the district mandate had not required the direct teaching of virtues but, rather, focused on the active participation of students, where together students and teachers "acquire the skills to learn to reflect on values and to give their own interpretation of them" (Veugelers and Veddar 2003: 385). Unfortunately, since 2003 the school district mandates surrounding character education programs have become even more prescriptive and restrictive. Schools in the district in which Ravine Elementary School is situated are now expected to offer a character education curriculum which focuses on twelve virtues, each of which has been given specific district definitions.

Engaging in conversation about values

As we thought about Shelby's experiences and how she was storied in Ravine Elementary School's character education story of responsibility, questions came forward for us around how narrative contexts seemed to be living outside the school story of teaching a character education curriculum. We wondered if explicit, formal character education programs could include possibilities where children engaged in making meaning of values in relation with their unfolding, multiple identities. Exploring Erica's, Catrina's, and Lian's experiences and who they might have been becoming in the school story of character education raised more questions for us. We puzzled over how teaching values in this pre-defined, "basic" way (Bennett 1993) might be perpetuating borders of arrogance among children and between children and teachers. Might these perceptions of arrogance hold children and teachers within plotlines of desiring to see themselves and to be seen by others as virtuous characters while closing down possibilities for exploring values in personal, relational, multiple, and contextual ways? Catrina's and Erica's experiences helped us to think through what it might mean to be arrogantly perceived by others, in particular by peers and by adults in positions of authority. Questions also emerged for us about Suzanne's experiences as a teacher responsible for co-planning and co-leading assemblies focused on the direct teaching of values. We were curious about how the plotlines within formal character education programs might shift as they moved away from the direct teaching of values and toward engaging children, families, and teachers in processes where, together, they inquired into who they were and who they were becoming in relation to diverse values. What we began to imagine was a process where values could be storied, restoried, and relived.

As we thought further about what it might mean for children, teachers, and families to engage in these processes, we were drawn to another moment in the Year 5/6 classroom when Lian, the teacher, and the children were involved in a class meeting. Class meetings were not a regular rhythm in the Year 5/6 classroom but, rather, it seemed to Shaun that they arose when there was a need. The following interim research text reflects one class meeting:

> Lian called a class meeting with the Year 5/6 children to discuss problems occurring on the playground and in the classroom. To shape a beginning place for the meeting, Lian reminded the children of the recent senior assembly and that the two values of the month were tolerance and respect. Lian asked the children to identify both in- and out-of-classroom problems. One child suggested, "In the classroom people are kind of not respecting." When Lian asked the children to say more about how they were not respecting each other, the list they generated in conversation included: being loud, teasing, name calling, making fun of each other, getting frustrated with each other, and not giving others chances to participate. Lian suggested to the children they were not being patient with each other and then made more connections to the two values of the month. When Lian asked the children what could be done to solve the problems some children came up with ways Lian could monitor their behaviour. Lian made it clear she did not want to be responsible for a behaviour modification system but, rather, saw the children as needing to be responsible for themselves. She said, "I think that you are old enough and you know what your job is and you know how it feels to be doing the right things and how it feels to be doing the wrong things and I think that you can make that choice for yourself. It's something that has to come from you, right. Not because I'm going to give you points to do it."

> Throughout the class meeting children repeatedly suggested Lian step in and solve problems among them. At times, Lian fell into the plotline of being the one in charge by generating rules and providing solutions. At other times, she turned ownership back to the children, asking them to talk about where the problems were coming from and how they might

respond to them in respectful ways. As the meeting unfolded, children gave lived examples of what it looked like when they were not respecting and being tolerant of each other and how they felt when they were not being respected by others. One child said, "Well you know the saying that you treat people the way you would want to be treated? Well I know some people who treat other people really nice and just because they aren't the best ones, they don't get along very well. Like sometimes you can treat someone really nice and then they can just be, you know, mean to you even though you treat them with respect." As the meeting drew to a close the children and Lian discussed respectful and contextual ways they might respond to each other when they were feeling angry or disrespected.

(Interim research text based on transcript from
a group conversation, November 20, 2002)

In this class meeting Lian involved the children in a process of thinking about the values of respect and tolerance in relation to their lived experiences. Rather than becoming responsible for the actions of the children and imposing a structure on them which was designed to manage their behaviour, Lian engaged the children in a conversation where together they were encouraged to identify problems, to think about why the problems were emerging, and how they might respond to each other in more tolerant and respectful ways. Within this space of conversation the Year 5/6 children had opportunities to talk about their feelings and why, at times, they had reacted disrespectfully and intolerantly to others. Noddings (1992: 22–3), exploring dialogue as a necessary component of moral education, suggested:

Dialogue is open-ended; that is, … neither party knows at the outset what the outcome or decision will be. As parents and teachers, we cannot enter into dialogue with children when we know that our decision is already made. It is maddening to young people (or any people) to engage in "dialogue" with a sweetly reasonable adult who cannot be persuaded and who, in the end, will say, "Here's how it's going to be. I tried to reason with you"… . Dialogue is a common search for understanding, empathy, or appreciation. It can be playful or serious, logical or imaginative, goal or process oriented, but it is always a genuine quest for something undetermined at the beginning… . It gives learners opportunities to question "why," and it helps both parties to arrive at well-informed decisions… . It connects us to each other and helps to maintain caring relations. It also provides us with the knowledge of each other that forms a foundation for response in caring… . Continuing dialogue builds up a substantial knowledge of one another that serves to guide our responses.

As the class meeting unfolded, Lian moved in and out of the role of telling children rules and solutions. We imagined, at times, her falling into this role came from children's repeated requests that she take it up, while at other times she sought it when the discussion became too messy or tension-filled. However, sometimes Lian also intentionally pushed against being the one with the answers. By responding in this way Lian opened up possibilities for children to see themselves as in charge of their own behaviours and actions. As teachers and teacher educators we related to Lian's movement in and out of the position of authority. We, too, know the pervasiveness of the dominant story of school that demands teachers demonstrate their competence by being the one in control, that is, by taking their traditional, hierarchical position of being the singular authority in the classroom. We also know that living within this dominant story can create a sense of comfort for both children and teachers as the roles of teacher and learner become distinctly separate and boundaries are clear and established. These roles, shaped by the dominant story of teachers and of students in schools were, we imagined, well known not only by Lian but, as well, by the students. Yet, as became visible in the field texts in these moments and in slipping into these roles, the children and Lian could not engage in the kind of dialogue encouraged by Noddings (1992). In no longer questioning why the problems were arising and what stories they were living by in relation with them, neither the children nor Lian could continue to hear the voices of each other and, in this way, they could no longer work toward making well-informed decisions for the future. However, in the moments when this scripted story gave way, the children and Lian, alongside each other, did experience moments when they could inquire into how the values of respect and tolerance might be restored and relived in each of their lives in more personal, relational, and contextual ways. Like Bateson (2004: 342–52), we, too, see that:

> participation precedes learning, not vice versa, and ambiguity potentiates learning... . Children need to ... [have opportunities] to *work with* ambiguous materials, not just reject them: to watch something, to critique it, to puzzle it out... . We should regard responding to ambiguity and living with it as a skill. A kind of literacy, for which we need a new word.

Chapter 6

Living alongside children shapes an administrator's stories to live by

One of the people we all came to know well at Ravine Elementary School was Jeanette, the school principal. Jeanette and the members of our research group knew each other from within multiple and different storylines. For example, Jean knew Jeanette from working on earlier research projects in her school, from serving as her graduate supervisor, and from working together on various alternative teacher education programs and committees. Marilyn knew Jeanette from working together on research projects and from her work as a teacher in the same school board. Pam knew Jeanette from past and present research projects and from spending many hours in conversations with Jeanette at the school over seven years. Each of us had lived stories with, and told stories of, Jeanette. She, in turn, had lived and told stories of each of us.

As we arrived at Ravine Elementary School, we often checked in with Jeanette who would welcome us into her cozy office. She would clear the children's books, files, folders, yellow stickies, and papers off the small table in the centre of her office and invite us to sit and talk. Sometimes conversation arose from our own questions but the relational space we created with Jeanette meant she too had a place to inquire and wonder about things that were on her mind.

Jeanette as principal often improvised ways to widen spaces in the school for inquiry conversations. The traditional role for principal as manager and monitor for policies leaves little room for a principal to express and continue authoring stories to live by in a school. "Walking with someone, as in narrative inquiry, might help keep present a belonging place, when there seems to be none" (Steeves 2000: 233). Perhaps it is in walking with someone that we learn to walk in a good way (Young 2003). Might our presence as relational narrative inquirers in the school have enabled an inquiry place for her, for school participants, and for us?

Often when we engaged in conversations with Jeanette in her office, she would leave her door open and teachers, secretaries, parents, and children would interrupt our dialogue with her. Jeanette would turn toward the person and, with a smile, greet them, deal with their concerns, and say goodbye before turning back to us to continue the conversation. It was in one such conversation that a story of Amit, an 8-year-old girl in the Year 3/4 learning strategies classroom at Ravine Elementary School, began to be told. Jeanette, we realized, as we compared field notes and talked to each other at research meetings, was telling many of us fragments of her stories of Amit. Our own interactions with Amit occurred at a distance, in hallways, in the library, and in other out-of-classroom places. While some of the research team recognized her, she was not a child in a classroom where any of us worked regularly. As we began to listen more closely to Jeanette's tellings, we began to piece together Amit's stories, carefully stitching fragments together. As we stitched, telling the stories of Amit over and over, adding details that one or another of us had heard from Jeanette or from other teachers' stories of Amit, we began to realize that Jeanette's intense interest in Amit told us a great deal about Jeanette and the ways Jeanette's stories to live by were shaped by Amit and other children.

Amit: stitched-together second-hand stories

Jeanette knew stories of all of the children who went to Ravine Elementary School. Whenever one of us asked about a child, Jeanette could tell us a story of that child, something of the child's family stories, stories of who the child was becoming. We marvelled at her knowledge of the children. She came to know these stories from living day-to-day alongside the children at school. She listened carefully to the stories teachers, parents, and other children told her about each child and she pieced together stories from these accounts. She also listened to each child's stories and it was the stories that Amit told her as well as the stories Amit's parents told that helped Jeanette frame her story of Amit. Jeanette's stories of Amit were shaped by stories that occurred both on and off the school landscape.

Usually we went to Jeanette asking about particular children who were participants in our research studies but Jeanette began, on her own, to tell us stories of Amit some time in the fall of 2002. Her tellings did not emerge from our questions but rather from the relational spaces Jeanette shared with us for dialogue. Buber (1947) argued that the heart of education is the inclusive community that comes through dialogical relation. The trusting space created amongst us enabled Jeanette, a school principal, along with ourselves, a place where we could speak openly and honestly; where we could be vulnerable to try to figure out and learn from unfolding events on the school landscape. As Jeanette told us story fragments related to Amit we began to notice her concern, her feelings of being upset. The story began to unfold after she heard some news at a November meeting with Amit's parents.

Jeanette told us Amit was born in Canada but that her parents emigrated from India. Amit's parents, she said, longed for a son and, after many failed attempts to conceive a boy, the mother had finally become pregnant with a baby boy. Jeanette told us she knew that in many Indian families it was the male children who inherited possessions and wealth. When she raised this with Amit's parents, they told her that this was indeed what would happen. Their male child would inherit wealth from both maternal and paternal sides of the family. Jeanette knew that many of Amit's extended family continued to live in India.

As November days passed, Jeanette continued to tell different members of the research group fragments of her stories of Amit, pieces that we gradually fit together. Jeanette told us of Amit's academic difficulties. She told us how she watched Amit struggle in the regular program at Ravine Elementary School and how she arranged, with the parents' consent, for Amit to be tested as a possible candidate for a special learning class placement. When Amit had been assessed as having difficulties with non-verbal learning, Jeanette arranged, again with the parents' consent, for Amit to be placed in the Year 3/4 learning strategies classroom at Ravine Elementary School. Amit was one of only two girls in this small class of fewer than 15 students.

Jeanette continued to be involved in educational programming for Amit and she participated in regular meetings with Amit's teacher and parents. As Jeanette recounted these conversations with Amit's parents to us, we gained a sense of how Jeanette and the teacher had spoken frequently of Amit's gentle nature, her enthusiasm with her school work, and her loving and caring relations with others.

The meeting with Amit's parents that prompted Jeanette to begin to tell us Amit's stories occurred at the November Celebration of Learning,[1] the first formal parent meeting focused on students' academic progress of the school year. The teacher and Jeanette, according to Jeanette, came to the Celebration of Learning prepared to share Amit's progress. They were pleased with how Amit was doing. However, for Jeanette, the parents came with shocking news. Along with the news of the impending birth of a male child was an announcement that Amit would soon be moving to live with her grandparents in India where she would no longer attend school. The parents let Jeanette know they recognized Amit would always struggle with school, as Jeanette and the Ravine Elementary School teachers had made clear to them in previous meetings. Amit's parents spoke of how they made the decision to have their daughter learn to be a wife and mother in preparation for an Indian marriage. Jeanette was surprised to learn that Amit would be married at age 13.

Jeanette added details as she spoke with different members of the research team. She told us she expressed to the parents her concern about Amit and what this move would mean to her life. She told us she tried to explore possibilities for how Amit might remain at Ravine Elementary School. She told of having shared with Amit's parents that their daughter had many gifts that would continue to grow and be recognized in school. Despite

Jeanette's attempts to have Amit's parents reconsider, they would not alter their decision.

Jeanette told us these story fragments over the days and weeks following the November Celebration of Learning. From her tellings we all sensed how worried and anxious Jeanette was about Amit's impending move to India. Many of us shared Jeanette's concern for Amit and her life but because we had a different relationship with Amit we did not have Jeanette's increasingly passionate sense that something needed to be done. Unlike Jeanette who was living the unfolding events in Amit's life in deep and personal ways because of her relationship with Amit, we were coming to know the particularities of Amit's life through Jeanette. We did not have a first-hand relationship with Amit. We wondered at this difference and considered how when we do not experience school landscapes and the experiences of those who live on them first-hand, we can write research, shape initiatives and policies in more removed, and therefore less meaningful and contextual, ways.

The time between the parents' announcement and Amit's departure was short and Jeanette described how on Amit's last day in the school, she hung around during the after-school staff meeting. Jeanette described Amit as terribly sad and troubled by the unfolding events in her life. Jeanette spoke to us about how she too was struggling to understand what was happening in Amit's life. As a way to hold onto the relationship, Jeanette told us that she wrote her home and school phone numbers on a piece of paper for Amit and told her to call collect at any time.

We heard these story fragments as Jeanette met one or another of us in her office or in the hallways. The urgency with which Jeanette was telling us the stories led us to recognize how distraught she was about the turn of events and how desperate she felt about not being able to intervene in the unfolding story. She told us that Amit did call the school the day following her last day at Ravine Elementary School. She said that Amit began the long-distance phone call explaining she had told her mother she was going to the bathroom and had instead found a pay phone and called Jeanette. Amit described how she had flown to Toronto that morning with her mother. From Toronto she was originally to travel the remainder of her journey to India with another Indian family but plans had changed. Instead, she would be continuing her flight to India alone. Sensing Amit's fears, Jeanette described how she tried to comfort her by assuring Amit that the flight attendants would look after her during the flight and that someone would be meeting her at the airport in India. In trying to allay Amit's fears, we sensed Jeanette was also trying to calm her own. Feeling helpless, Jeanette told us how she had said goodbye after reminding Amit she could call collect again anytime. At the time of this writing, Jeanette has yet to hear from Amit.

These stitched-together stories are powerful ones. As a research team we told these stories frequently for they made us think a great deal about who we are as teachers in the lives of children and we wondered what each of us might have done. We thought about how cultural narratives shaped our own lives and how different cultural narratives often shape the lives of the children with whom we work.

Our reason for telling this story here is to help us understand how Jeanette's stories to live by shaped who she was in the unfolding story with Amit and her parents. We wondered about how Jeanette came to compose her stories to live by that brought her to this moment with Amit. As Jeanette lived out her stories to live by in relation with Amit, had she sensed the bumping places between her stories of who Amit was as a girl child and the stories Jeanette composed for girl children? Had she sensed the bumping places between her stories to live by as a mother and the stories Amit's parents were living by in the unfolding events of our stitched together stories? As she lived out her stories to live by as a principal, had she sensed the bumping places between her knowing of being the one with authority in the story of school and the parents' knowing of their authority to shape their daughter's story?

Attending to Jeanette's stories to live by

To begin to explore these questions, we returned to the many field texts of conversations with Jeanette where we asked her to tell some of her stories of growing up, stories of her experiences at home and in school, stories of her teacher education and beginning teaching and administering, as well as stories from her current work at Ravine Elementary School. These one-on-one conversations generated pages of transcripts. In addition to these transcripts, we had other transcripts of ongoing conversations with Jeanette independently and Jeanette with other teachers at Ravine Elementary School where they talked about their ongoing work. We also had field notes from our time in the school at meetings, at school events, and on a daily basis as we interacted with Jeanette in out-of-classroom places. Many of us also had field notes from our work at the school when other teachers, parents, and children spoke of Jeanette. We returned to all of these field texts as we composed a telling of Jeanette's stories to live by, stories woven together from her tellings of who she was and who she was becoming. We wanted to create a temporal sense of the way Jeanette storied herself. We created the following narrative account through selecting words taken from these field texts. Jeanette's words created a kind of word image. We used word images to evoke a more vivid rendering of the moment. Creating word images is a highly interpretive process and we realize we may have portrayed a unidimensional account of Jeanette's unfolding stories over time. We realize that in this one telling there are multiple other possible tellings. This particular telling was created as we tried to make sense of how Jeanette's stories to live by bumped against the stories of Amit and her parents. Her stories, as all of our stories, continue to unfold over time and place.

My early years were very peaceful
But few memories.

My mom saying
You all need to be different.
You need to have exposure to lots of different things
Find what you really want to be.

Growing up we all had something different
That we were good at
Not a competition between siblings
She let us all be different.

Find something beyond school
Not TV, not friends
You have to do it [you have to practice]
Mom – Recognizing everybody's different.

Living in a family
Where we all were different
All celebrated for what we could do.
Didn't make connections
With people different from me.

Started teaching dancing
When I was about 12
First as a helper
Then as an assistant.

School just happened – White, middle class
I was there.
Did what was asked of me
Wasn't engaged.

Group of kids traveled
From elementary
To junior high
Through high school
All together.

Don't remember school in terms of diversity
Other than [brother and sister]
Had trouble at school

Wanted to do things differently
Be more creative.

Took sides of the under-dog
Got in trouble with teachers
Attending to injustices.

I was the student
Who didn't ever cause trouble
Who did what she was told.

[No] major memories of school
Nothing to do with learning in school.
Always a reader.

In this beginning segment of the word image, the narrative threads that seemed to connect across Jeanette's recollections of her stories to live by began with strong threads around the importance of acknowledging and celebrating each child's uniqueness and the importance of creating spaces where children's gifts were nurtured. Her mother's story of parenting shaped a space where Jeanette focused on her dancing rather than on school experiences. Diversity, whether socio-economic, cultural, racial, or ability, seemed unnoticed within a family narrative where uniqueness was celebrated. Opportunities for girls, including a career in dancing, were everywhere. She felt secure in knowing she would be supported whatever her choices.

As a child Jeanette realized her brother and sister saw situations differently than she did. They attended to the difficulties of underdogs, to a desire for social justice, to the desire to be more creative. But for Jeanette this was just the way they were. She saw them as unique, different, but then her family narrative was storied around each child's uniqueness and each child needing to find things that they were good at and enjoyed.

Bringing forward Jeanette's stories to live by that all children were unique and had special gifts we saw how she continued to live this storyline with Amit and her parents. As principal, Jeanette responded to Amit's non-verbal learning difficulties by gaining permission from Amit's parents to place Amit into a learning strategies classroom at Ravine Elementary School. This program was a place where Amit's academic struggles would be more fully supported; where her gifts of being gentle natured and her enthusiasm about her school work as well as living in loving and caring ways with others would be nurtured. Similar to how Jeanette's mother tried to shape storylines for Jeanette and her siblings where they could see themselves as special and unique, Jeanette wanted to shape school stories for Amit where she, and others, recognized her gifts. Enrolling Amit in the learning strategies program, where the class size was much smaller and children received more specialized attention, Jeanette wanted to expand Amit's in-school experiences and future opportunities.

Continuing with the word image, the complexity of interwoven stories revealed the multifaceted, shifting, and contradictory ways her stories to live by unfolded.

University was expected
Assumption we would go on
Education was really important.
Dancing was more important to me than school.

I'll do what you want me to do
Whether I believe it or not.
I have this other agenda
I am okay if I only get 65%.

My whole orientation to university
Get through the bureaucracy
Whatever I have to do.

First year – All arts
At that point not thinking education.
Somewhere made a different decision
Dancing or teaching
Worked into being a teacher.

Tried to keep the dance connection
Didn't have time
Couldn't do both
Stopped dancing.

Just doing what I had to do
To get the degree done.

So that I could be a teacher.

Student teaching
Back to my elementary school
With teacher who taught me in junior high
[And] kids not that different from me.

Upper, middle class area
I still don't notice
The cultural diversity.

Every child's different
That's my mom.

A beginning teacher
I had the privilege
Trying lots of things -
Team teaching
Working together with different age levels
Parents coming in.

But I think I just taught them
The kids I remember were White kids and poor.
Really poor.
Not seeing colour.

[School board] consulting
I remember
Very consciously saying
"I can make a difference
Working with more than one class of children
It's working with teachers
Thinking about teachers and teaching
Where I can make a difference with children."

Being principal
I remember thinking
"I can make a difference
I need to be with kids
A way to have lots of families
Lots of children
Lots of teachers
To try to think about something different
But not power."

As we continued to unwind the storied tellings of Jeanette's university student life we noticed a fraying of Jeanette's imagined story of becoming a dancer. Jeanette danced through her school years. When she was 12 years old she became an assistant dance instructor. We saw Jeanette continuing to compose stories of practicing and doing something different, part of her Mom's stories of the importance of developing a unique gift. Jeanette told of her beliefs in dancing, not school. But as Jeanette grew she encountered family narrative expectations that she would go to university. Threads from stories of early childhood where she "caused no trouble in school," where she "did what she was told" drew her toward living a similar story as university student. We saw Jeanette's acceptance of her parents' knowing that they would play a part in shaping her stories. Although she was disinterested in marks, disinterested in school, and talked of dancing as "this other agenda" that was "more important" to her than school, a White middle class cultural narrative of "going to university" shaped Jeanette's stories to live by. Jeanette tried to continue dancing but found herself "working into being a teacher" eventually realizing she could no longer do both. Jeanette's story of becoming a teacher left no space for her story of becoming a dancer.

But as a beginning teacher we saw how she awakened to the possibility that her stories of teaching could be more than narrow scripts. Although as a student teacher Jeanette returned to the place and stories of her elementary school where the children were "not that different from me," it was her early teaching experiences with children who were "really poor" that scaffolded a new story of teaching as a creative act, perhaps like dancing is a creative act. She had the "privilege of trying lots of things" such as team teaching, having children of different ages and grades working together, and parents participating in classroom activities.

Becoming a consultant, her teaching stories of what might be expanded further. Jeanette's experiences of working with teachers in consulting, and then working with "lots of families, lots of children, and lots of teachers" as a principal scaffolded even wider stories of what an educator could be and do. Jeanette's childhood desires to do something different were continuing to be lived out in the way she desired to create a story of principal that would be "about something different but not power."

Laying threads from these tellings by Jeanette alongside Amit's stories we saw how an interruption of Amit's stories of being and becoming a student resonated with interruptions of Jeanette's stories of being and becoming a dancer. Jeanette's heart was set on becoming a dancer but parental expectations for their daughter to attend university shifted Jeanette toward constructing herself as a university student and a teacher. As Jeanette told of her passion for dancing we were reminded of how Amit, too, had desires to be in school, yet for both Jeanette and Amit, parental expectations, drawn from cultural narratives, shaped alternative stories for them.

Returning to the word image, we saw Jeanette giving up her story of becoming a dancer because her story of teaching at the time left no room for both. But her experiences with "really poor children" as a beginning teacher included opportunities to scaffold and shape more creative stories of teaching. Her teaching stories picked up dropped threads from childhood; threads of doing something different and being creative as she had been when she was a dancer. As Jeanette told a story of being a principal who would "try to think of something different," had she been imagining creating a new world for students like Amit? Might she have been imagining expanding Amit's parents' world through her conversations with them?

Continuing with the word image we learned of Robbie, Jeanette's son, whose stories both sustained Jeanette as principal and scaffolded her thinking in ongoing ways about her work as an educator.

When Robbie [my son] happened
I became more attentive
To children's perceptions
To see a bit more through their lens
As opposed to a teacher's lens
Or a parent's lens.

I remember thinking,
"You know isn't that interesting
What was really important
To us as teachers
Was of non-importance to him.
It wasn't even a memory cell for him.
Yet things he thought were important we kind of glossed over."

As principal
I used Robbie stories
To help parents who are struggling
With understanding how their kids were doing
That it was ok what they were doing
That they could change.

Using Robbie stories as a way of saying
"Here's another way."
Lots of conversations
Not positioning myself as a principal
[Rather as a parent].

In this segment of the word image as Jeanette continued to explore who she was and who she was becoming with us, she showed how her narratives of being a teacher and a principal shifted when she became a mother. As she attended to Robbie, she noticed more carefully who she was becoming as a teacher and principal. She could not see Robbie's experiences with a kind of arrogant perception (Lugones 1987: 4), a perception that comes from "failure to identify with persons that one views arrogantly." Lugones described both loving and arrogant perception as she reflected on her relationship with her mother. She wrote:

Loving my mother also required that I see with her eyes, that I go into my mother's world, that I see both of us as we are constructed in her world, that I witness her own sense of herself from within her world. Only through this traveling to her "world" could I identify with her.

(Lugones 1987: 8)

Jeanette attended to her stories of Robbie's experience, her stories of her own experience and, by travelling to Robbie's world, she attended to his stories as well. As she did so, her stories of who she was as a teacher shifted. Seeing through Robbie's eyes created a new way of seeing for Jeanette, a way to see children of diversity with loving perception. As she said, "When Robbie happened I became more attentive to children's perceptions of what we as adults do" (Transcript from individual conversation, January 31, 2003). While she still saw herself as teacher and principal, she also tried to see herself as teacher and principal through Robbie's eyes. Living in this way, she began to question what she thought was important as a teacher and principal and she began to attend more closely to what he saw as important. Becoming a mother scaffolded a shift in Jeanette's stories to live by as she became more attentive to children's experiences of what was important in school. We saw Jeanette living out these stories to live by as we attended to how she knew and could tell stories of each child at Ravine Elementary School. Her tellings were multi-perspectival and always included the child's vantage point as well as those of the teachers and parents.

As Jeanette shared stories of Amit and the events unfolding in Amit's life with us, she included how Amit wanted to stay at Ravine Elementary School and that she did not want to be sent away from her parents to live with her grandparents in India. As we listened to and thought hard about Jeanette's stories of Amit, we began to recognize how Jeanette was experiencing contradictions in her stories to live by with the events unfolding in Amit's life. Being attentive to her story that Amit's perspectives and desires mattered, Jeanette tried to interrupt Amit's parents' story and help them see alternatives for how Amit could continue to be a student at Ravine Elementary School.

We also saw that Jeanette's knowing of herself as a parent was often part of the conversations she had with parents where she was "not positioning herself as principal." Jeanette tried to use her perspective of being a mother when she had conversations with parents of children in school. But, we wondered, might Jeanette have been seeing from a White, middle-class Canadian perspective? Jeanette was upset with Amit's parents' decision to send Amit to India to become a wife and mother instead of finishing school. Were Jeanette's stories to live by as a mother in her culture bumping up against the cultural stories Amit's parents were living by in theirs?

In this final segment of the word image we saw how Jeanette's stories to live by expanded again as her relationship to a new school landscape was created.

A new school
Involving parents in decisions.
He was the only East Indian person
Helping and interviewing and [picking] teachers
What the [parents] wanted to be in their school
The beginning I think of the multicultural things that developed.

I just asked for volunteers
I just wanted any parent who wanted to come and help.
What would I have done had everyone been white
If everyone had been female
Would I have noted it?

So I don't know
How consciously aware I was
Of some things at that point.
But what I did note
Was it was the other way.

I think by the third year
I had gotten to know lots of East Indian families.
They wanted some very definite things for the kids
Not always what I was envisioning for the school.

We had lots of conversations
They wanted marks to send back to India.
Lots of conversations about
"Well how can we send things back to India without using marks?
How can we do that?"
I wrote lots and lots of letters
To send home to India.

I think when I say I don't see colour
I'm meaning it doesn't make any difference,
It doesn't matter
East Indian
Spanish
El Salvadorian
Native
Or White.

How I work with them is as honouring and as valuing as I can make it.
Learn some of the traditions and their backgrounds
So I can understand
Before [I] react.

To say "You're celebrating Ramadan right now,
I know you can't have a cookie when you come for our birthday
   celebration.
But you know what I've got just for you?
I've got this special glass and I know you can have water
And would you like to use this glass?"

I think of being able to get to the same point
But knowing that different people have to get there differently.
I don't ever want any one of them to feel ashamed.

Working with families
Became what I did
And families began to ask me
To be involved
In some of their lives outside.

Being invited to speak
At a Sikh funeral
Being invited to be part
Of a baptism for a Hindu family.

In this part of the word image, we told of Jeanette's experiences at a brand new school where she found herself needing to work closely with parents, involving them in decision-making around architecture, staff hiring, curriculum, school governance, and school policies. The word image revealed another moment where a shift in her stories to live by were scaffolded. She described how, in an unexpected and unnoticed way, a father, a parent of East Indian heritage, volunteered to work closely with her on the school decision-making as the school was still in the development phase. Jeanette, busy with her professional work in another school, did not attend with heightened awareness to which parents were volunteering or not volunteering to be part of the decision-making process. Within her family narrative, people who were interested or had particular talents came forward. She had not consciously invited volunteers who would represent the multicultural nature or gender balance of the school community. Indeed she wondered, "how consciously aware of some things [I was] at that point" (Transcript from individual conversation, February 14, 2003). However, when it happened that a father of East Indian heritage became involved, a shift in Jeanette's story of who she was becoming was scaffolded. She began to live stories in which she was far more attentive to what parents of diverse cultural heritage were "envisioning for the school" (Transcript from individual conversation, February 14, 2003). Attending in this way shifted how Jeanette lived out her stories of teaching. For example, while still not comfortable with assigning marks for student performance, she realized through "lots of conversations" that marks played an important part in many East Indian parents' stories of school. She realized as her stories to live by shifted that she needed to negotiate a space for a new story of school that honoured her stories as well as the parents' cultural stories of school. Her improvisatory act of writing letters describing students' school performance that parents could send back to India instead of marks scaffolded a new school story mindful of both stories.

Jeanette told us she continued to "learn some of the traditions and their backgrounds so [she could] can understand before [she] reacts" (Transcript from individual conversation, February 14, 2003). In this conversational way Jeanette continued to add more threads to her stories to live by as she imagined ways to thoughtfully negotiate differences she encountered at her new school.

Multiple colliding stories

For Amit, there was more at stake. Jeanette's knowing of the place of women in Canadian culture, a story she had known since childhood, a story in which she could be educated to become anything she wanted, bumped up with a cultural narrative shaping stories for girls such as Amit to leave school and become wives and mothers at a young age. As we attended to who Jeanette was and who she was becoming in this story, we saw her becoming increasingly distraught by her inability to interrupt the cultural narrative and shape a new school story for Amit, perhaps in similar ways to how she had written letters to be sent back to India.

As revealed earlier in the word image, Jeanette told us that, as a principal, she wanted "to think about something different but not power" (Transcript from individual conversation, February 14, 2003). In Jeanette's encounters with East Indian culture at her previous school she was able to sustain her storyline of not using power, but, rather of finding the space with parents and children to try "something different" as she negotiated and improvised new stories of reporting student progress, stories that were both responsive to her own stories to live by and to those on her multicultural school landscape. But now with Amit, Jeanette could not do this. There was no time. As we are reminded in the word image, Jeanette said she needed "lots of conversations" with parents to get to know "some of the traditions and their backgrounds" before reacting. With Amit, her parents had decided and travel plans for Amit were already in place.

Jeanette's stories to live by of not living the position of principal as a position of power bumped against her desire to have Amit stay at school in Canada. Caught in this contradiction, Jeanette tried to use her position as principal in the story of school to interrupt the story Amit's parents were composing for Amit. She expressed concerns to Amit's parents about what Amit's departure might mean in Amit's life. She explored possibilities for how

Amit might remain at Ravine Elementary School. But Jeanette was powerless to make a difference. She could not stop Amit's parents from sending her to India. Jeanette's knowing of the shaping place of principal in the story of school bumped against the parents' knowing of who was to shape their daughter's story.

Jeanette was shaken. Jeanette's stories to live by, as a principal who tried to shape a place to support children in their learning, was interrupted. We were left to wonder if the story earlier scaffolded to support Amit in her learning by placing her in a learning strategies classroom of primarily boys, scaffolded a second story for her parents, a story that led to their decision to send Amit back to India. Perhaps Jeanette wondered this too and her stories to live by as principal were interrupted. However, within the cultural narrative of Canadian schools, this is often how we support children to learn the skills they need in order to be successful students. In this story of one girl child and one principal, Jeanette was unable to interrupt Amit's parents' story to return Amit to India. For Jeanette it was important to interrupt this story. What, however, is an interruption in a child's story to live by?

When Amit slipped away from her mother in the airport to call Jeanette long distance, it was possible that Amit was interrupting her story of obedient child to ask for help. Perhaps interruptions can be subtle. Neither Jeanette nor this group of researchers knows what effect this has had on Amit's stories to live by. For a small girl travelling to a far away place, the knowledge that she may call her principal collect at any time, regardless of how remote this possibility is in reality, may be a strong thread to hold onto and compose a story to live by around. We do not know what will become of Amit. With her departure from the Toronto airport contact with her was gone.

In reflection

At the beginning of this chapter we wondered how living alongside children might shape an administrator's stories to live by. We learned of Jeanette's stories to live by through our many research conversations, expressed in some of the word images found in this chapter. It was through our conversations with Jeanette that we came to know the stories of Amit, of whom Jeanette spoke often. As Jeanette came to live alongside Amit and her parents we learned that, while Jeanette may not have been able to interrupt Amit's parents' stories to live by, interruptions certainly occurred for Amit and Jeanette.

We wondered how the interruptions Jeanette experienced in relation to Amit will continue to shape other stories Jeanette will live alongside children and families at Ravine Elementary School. We wondered how the interruptions both Amit and Jeanette experienced will continue to shape our lives as narrative inquirers in increasingly culturally diverse schools alongside principals, teachers, children, and families. Might Jeanette, along with ourselves, for example, explore further the cultural understandings parents bring to having their children placed into special programs such as learning strategies classes? In a similar way to how Jeanette worked toward creating newly improvised school stories around marks, might the stories she lived with Amit and Amit's parents shape openings to scaffold wider school stories being lived out at Ravine Elementary School?

Clandinin and Connelly (1998) wrote that shaping new school stories is complex due to issues around the ever-shifting school landscape, narrative histories of school participants and epistemological differences amongst practitioner knowledge. Considering the narrative histories of school participants which include their cultural histories, possibilities for Jeanette to negotiate and scaffold a wider story attentive to both Amit's parents' stories to live by and her own could take a long time.

Relationships take time to build. School landscapes shape more or less educative possibilities for building the relational places out of which new school stories mindful of families, children, teachers, and principals, can be negotiated and lived out. Considering this particular school landscape at this particular time we noticed that with Amit's parents, Jeanette had no time. Considering the conduit (Clandinin and Connelly 1995), rampant with prescriptions for how things should be in school and funnelled into the out-of-classroom place, a place where the principal lives, we wondered how time to create relational spaces was also squeezed out as district and government initiatives pressed down upon school landscapes in the name of saving time, in the name of efficiency.

For Amit, perhaps, there was at least time enough for Jeanette to help shape new stories in Amit's life, because Amit, a small girl, had the courage to leave her mother at the Toronto airport for a few minutes and phone Jeanette at Ravine Elementary School. As Jeanette's and Amit's stories to live by became interwoven, our stories as researchers became interwoven too. We wondered how Amit's stories, for us as researchers, for Amit, for Amit's parents, for Jeanette, and for those we do not know, will reverberate over time for all of us in unknown and unexpected ways.

Chapter 7

Shifting stories to live by

Interweaving the personal and professional in teachers' lives

In this chapter, we focused on three teachers – Jim, Sally, and Suzanne – whom we lived alongside at Ravine Elementary School. We attended to their stories of their teaching careers and lives. Connelly and Clandinin's (1988: 25) conceptualization of "personal practical knowledge" highlighted the ways a teacher's knowledge is interwoven with a teacher's life. Teacher knowledge can be seen "in terms of narrative life history, as storied life compositions. These stories, these narratives of experience, are both personal – reflecting a person's life history – and social – reflecting the milieu, the contexts in which teachers live" (Connelly and Clandinin 1999: 2). The stories Jim, Sally, and Suzanne shared with us expressed the personal practical knowledge each of them brought to their teaching just as Jeanette's stories in the previous chapter helped us understand her practice as an administrator as a storied life composition, lived amidst and indelibly affected by the multiple contexts in which she found herself.

Narratively linking teachers' knowledge, contexts, and identity

Attending narratively to a teacher's personal practical knowledge, composed and lived out across the temporal span of a teacher's life, drew Connelly and Clandinin (1999) to consider questions of teacher identity. A teacher's identity is understood as a unique embodiment of his/her stories to live by – stories shaped by the landscapes past and present in which s/he lives and works. While one reading of what we mean by stories to live by might suggest a unitary smooth identity, this is not what we intend. Considering Geertz's (1995) forty-year retrospective on change as a parade we participate in led Connelly and Clandinin to consider how stories to live by may be multiple, evolving, shifting, and contradictory. They wrote:

> Just as the parade changes – the things, the people, the relationships, the parade itself – as it passes, so, too, do teachers' and researchers' identities need to change. It is not so much that teachers and researchers,

professionals on the landscape, need new identities, new stories to live by: they need shifting, changing identities; shifting, changing stories to live by as the parade offers up new possibilities and cancels out others.
(Connelly and Clandinin 1999: 131)

A focus on teachers' stories to live by within an ever-changing parade drew our attention to changing possibilities which have been offered up on teachers' landscapes in- and out-of-school. One possibility the parade has to offer teachers is the diverse nature of students' lives. It was the diversity of the children we worked with that, in part, provided the opportunity for us to be drawn into the parade alongside teachers.

An emerging research puzzle

As we began to compose interim research texts during our work at Ravine Elementary School, we attended to moments and places of tension in people's experiences: teachers', children's, and administrators' experiences. Diversity was one of the concepts around which we attended to the stories told by those involved in the research. As we thought about diversity, in conversations around the Center table and at the school, we did not begin with formalistic categories of diversity based on culture, economics, religions, languages, abilities, sexual orientations, or family structures. As Trinh (1989) noted, categories leak. We were curious about knowing diversity as it was lived, told, retold, and relived in stories, while being mindful of the cultural heritages, cognitive ability ranges, socio-economic statuses, genders, physical abilities, religious beliefs, and so on that shape children's, teachers', and administrators' lives.

We wanted to understand more about how teachers come to live lives which make them attentive to children whose life story lines are different from their own. We were interested to see how teachers' experience with diversity in their own lives shaped their work with children's experiences of curriculum in schools. As we reflected on our own experiences, we saw that our stories of who we were had shifted partly because of the contexts in which we found ourselves and the people with whom we came to live in relation.

Inquiring into our own stories of early childhood, schooling, and teaching experiences we saw ourselves as learning to live and tell different stories of who we were. Attending from our own personal practical knowledge shaped and reshaped by our experiences both on and off school landscapes, we became curious about the intertwining of the personal and the professional in our teaching lives.

Attentive to our lives as a process of becoming (Greene 1995) within the personal and professional spaces in which we live and teach brought us again to puzzle over how we have come to know who we are as teachers of children of diversity. Our wonders led us to consider the teachers we met and lived alongside at Ravine Elementary School. How might teachers at Ravine Elementary School tell stories of how they have come to know themselves as teachers of children of diversity?

Composing field texts

Three teachers, Jim, Sally, and Suzanne, were interested in sharing our inquiry into the ways their stories to live by shifted over their careers. They were interested in exploring the interwoven nature of the personal and the professional in their stories. The main field texts for this chapter were the transcripts of a series of conversations with each teacher. These audio-recorded conversations allowed us to explore the complexity, the multiplicity, and the reflexive nature of our lives as teachers and researchers within the three-dimensional narrative inquiry space.

Working within the space allowed us to travel with the three teachers back to their early childhood, school, and teacher education experiences, slip toward their early teaching experiences, and then slide forward to moments lived during our inquiry at Ravine Elementary School. We travelled inward with them to feelings and responses and outward to remembered events. We moved from their home places to school places as a way to show something of how their evolving stories to live by were shaped and reshaped as their lives met with the diverse life stories of children.

Composing research texts

Research text 1: word images of stories to live by

Not only did we use the three-dimensional narrative inquiry space to guide our conversations with the teachers, we also used the space to consider multiple readings of the field texts. Initially we read the texts to create a temporal sense of the way each teacher storied themselves in recollected moments from early childhood, school, teacher education, and as beginning teachers. Just as we selected words from transcripts to construct word images of Jeanette's stories to live by in Chapter 6, we composed word images for each of the three teachers highlighted in this chapter. Again, we recognized the word images may create a unidimensional account of each teacher; a partial view of their teacher lives so far.

Research text 2: shifting stories to live by

We were mindful of Lyons and LaBoskey's (2003) work with scaffolding through the use of portfolios and also Huber and Clandinin's study (2004: 147) where they revealed scaffolding to be "an unfolding process that enables a child to move from living his or her stories to telling and retelling his or her stories with new insights. In these teaching-learning situations, teachers, too, are learning to tell and retell their stories." Emerging from what we learned from these authors' inquiries was a second way of reading the field texts. In this reading we selected moments where the teacher signalled an instance of heightened awareness, perhaps a moment of tension where s/he was awakened to bumping up against some new possibility offered by the passing parade. These moments of bumping scaffolded a shift in the stories the teacher was living by in relation to children of diversity. As we engaged in inquiring alongside these teachers, we found that sometimes bumps arose in relation to an encounter with a child or situation on the school landscape, other times they drew on storied experiences from off the school landscape to affirm a story to live by or to scaffold a shift in their story to live by.

For each of the teachers, we created word images of their early stories to live by and then showed how their stories to live by were shifting. We began with Jim, a Year 1/2 teacher.

Jim: word images of stories to live by

Middle to upper class White families
Living on expensive acreages
Most of the houses quite large
Ours an ordinary bungalow.

Don't remember what happened in school
Can't picture anybody that wasn't White
Mostly White Protestant and White Catholic
Not that tension a lot of junior highs have now
Nice not to go through that.

Very shy and quiet
Teacher's pet
Goody goody
Didn't get into trouble
Scared to get into trouble
My parents said,
"If we get any news from school,
You are going to get it twice as bad at home."
That's how they raised their family
Traditional.

My parents were old country
Pretty strict upbringing
Father the head of the household

You don't talk back
You don't lip off
Do what you're told
Do it quietly
Do it properly
When you're done you can go play.
I admire the job they did raising us
I think they did the right thing.

Spoke German at home
Didn't speak English until I started to play
With the neighborhood kids
Around 3 or something.
[No] recollection of ever having trouble [speaking English when
    I began school].

Elementary school
I don't think anybody knew [I spoke German]
It never came up.

First time I really remember was in high school
I started taking
German 10, 20, 30
Everyone took the language they knew
All the German kids took German
All the French kids took French
All the Spanish kids took Spanish.
First time I remember
Seeing other kids who might have had similar traditions
The same kind of upbringing.

A lot of things I do
At home, on holidays
Still based in German traditions
And the way things were
When I grew up.
Like Christmas wouldn't be Christmas
If I didn't have certain things that I did
Or certain music that I listened to
Or food that I ate
You know it wouldn't be the same.

Teacher education
Programming for individual kids

Individual needs
Each child treated as an individual
Never really told what a real classroom is like.

Individual differences, to me, meant
Some boys will like soccer
Some boys won't
Some girls will like art
Some girls won't.

Never made clear what kind of difference
Not just academic differences
But social and family differences.
Kids coming to school not being able to speak English
Kids don't speak English at home
Barely just get by in school
Kids who don't have breakfast in the morning
Falling asleep halfway through the morning
That was never made clear
All that was ever said was you need to plan
Each child is an individual.

Student teaching
Didn't even consider where these kids were coming from
I wasn't thinking that deep yet.

Daycare ... beginning work
Half the staff was male
I think kids get an overload of female role models
Especially kids from single parent families
Need that male role model.
Daycare parents
University educated
More open to different kinds of things
Different ways of doing things
More liberal.

Ten years I worked there
Never one problem with a parent
Questioning why I was working
With little kids
People assume
A man working with little kids
Must be a pervert or a pedophile
A hidden agenda.

I was full time with the little ones
Just blew some people away
Not friends
Family was pretty accepting.

The daycare helped
Seeing what kind of differences there are.

The narrative thread that seemed most evident as we talked with Jim about his early childhood, school experiences, teacher education, and his work experience in a daycare setting prior to beginning his first teaching assignment was one of learning to belong in school and in his community. While he recognized that he was different because he spoke another language, he kept this difference invisible as he learned to fit in at school. His parents lived a story of school in which children were to learn, to obey, and to respect their teachers and to do well. This was the family narrative for children at home and at school. Jim lived this story and, as he did so, he quietly fit in without making his German language and German traditions visible outside the home. Only in high school did he become aware that other students may have shared his German language and cultural upbringing. While he learned the rhetoric of treating children as individuals in teacher education, he had not experienced how he might teach in this way. With his own school experience of fitting in to whatever the dominant story of school was, he knew only that there might be superficial differences with respect to student preferences. It was not until he began work in a daycare and in teaching that he began to question his stories to live by and to wonder about the diversity of children's lives and what that might mean for him as a teacher. It was then that he began to attend to diversity in a deeper way. It was also within these contexts that he awakened to how others might story him as a male primary school teacher and daycare worker. He highlighted that it was the support of friends and family that sustained him as he struggled to live on a professional knowledge landscape that questioned who he was as a male teacher of little kids. We wondered if Jim, confronted by this unspoken question, began to attend to diversity in new ways.

Shifting stories to live by: Jim

We drew on two stories from our field texts with Jim where we learned something of how his stories to live by shifted. The first transcript segment is one in which Jim told of his experiences with young children who spoke a first language other than English.

I know ⸻ ⸻ Indian kids in my classroom they'll
hang ou⸻ ⸻ then when it comes
to Cele⸻ , "Well how are
they do⸻ you know what?
They're⸻ o it at home and
then h⸻

⸻ :ember 16, 2002)

As we ⸻ awn back to Jim's
stories as⸻ :out his childhood
experien⸻ :e went outside to
play with⸻ e in which German
languag⸻ me, another family
narrativ⸻ : a child he had to
do well⸻ e must have learned
and pri⸻ s stories to live by to
fit in, ⸻ ;erman language and
heritag⸻ rk for the students of
East I⸻ :, the children of East
India⸻ i together" (Transcript
of inc⸻ n asked by parents how
their⸻ Jim foregrounded the
plot⸻ :s to have their children
spea⸻ es to live by of children
nee⸻ ral practices in the home
col⸻ its, that is, that they need
to Jean Cla⸻

⸻ ed how different families'
cu⸻ liversity.

⸻ i Soup with Rice and every
⸻ with rice. We have chicken
⸻ ith just for fun you know. It
⸻ -pot and then we have it for
⸻ a poem that goes with it and
⸻ all of this stuff. It is just sort
⸻ ist Indian kids don't eat meat
⸻ :n soup so they can't have the
⸻ ut they are sort of left out and
⸻ l for them too because like I'm
⸻ and they know they can't have
⸻ that" but they probably don't
understand really wha⸻   f it is for them. They just know

Welcome to Edge Hill

Customer name: HEARN, VALERIE

Title: Composing diverse identities : narrative
inquiries into the interwoven lives of children
and teacher
ID: 700836
Due: 01-11-12

Total items: 1
11/10/2012 12:26
Checked out: 3

Items that you already have on loan

Title: Succeeding with your master's
dissertation : a step-by-step handbook / John
ID: 792226
Due: 17-10-12

Title: Shaping a professional identity : stories of
educational practice / F. Michael Connelly, D.
ID: 791564
Due: 25-10-12

Please retain this receipt for Your Records

that they are not getting it and all the other kids are. But I feel sort of bad for them because they are missing out.

(Transcript of individual conversation, May 5, 2003)

In this transcript fragment Jim tried to make sense of his stories to live by as a teacher of children of diversity when their cultural and religious beliefs bumped up against school stories, stories he was organizing and promoting as a teacher. In Jim's childhood school experiences, his cultural understandings and differences lived smoothly alongside the dominant school stories and, at times, created places of belonging. In this moment, the Chicken Soup with Rice activities, activities designed to be fun and to build community in the primary grades, were causing some children of diversity to be excluded. As we attended to the narrative thread of learning to belong that was woven throughout Jim's stories to live by, we saw how he was trying to live out this thread with the children of East Indian heritage by including them in the song and poem activities and by offering them the crackers. He wanted to show the children possibilities for how they could live stories of belonging even though they could not participate fully in all of the activities. In this way we saw Jim trying to scaffold a shift in the children's stories to live by in school, a shift that encouraged them to learn to negotiate school stories and search for openings where they could belong. But, this experience was also scaffolding a shift in Jim's stories to live by as teacher. Repeatedly, Jim explored how the exclusion of the children caused him to "feel bad" and linked his feelings both to not knowing if the children really understood why they were not allowed to participate and to how the children were "missing out" (Transcript of individual conversation, May 5, 2003). We knew from Jim's stories how strongly he believed school should be a place where children felt they belonged and we knew from stories of his childhood that his sense of belonging as a student came from fitting into the school stories that surrounded him. Jim's tension in this story showed us that he was not expecting the children of East Indian heritage to fit into the school story of Chicken Soup with Rice. He did not, however, abandon the Chicken Soup with Rice activity in his classroom. Jim was able to stay with these tensions he experienced by searching for ways to widen the school story so it could become a story where all children could fully belong.

Another teacher in our inquiry was Sally, a vice-principal and Year 5/6 teacher.

Sally: word images of stories to live by

Elementary school – All White kids
Junior high – All White
High school
Went to school

With someone who wasn't White
Didn't phase me in the least.

I was Ukrainian
That was different than anybody else
That was what I knew.

[My parents] both Ukrainian
Did our Ukrainian background.
Dad was a teacher
Taught in [inner city schools]
Never a conversation around the dinner table.

Mom talked a lot about the ladies who worked for her
[East Indian and Chinese]
I met them
Saw saris and all these different things
Staff parties
Potluck
Every kind of food under the sun.

My brother
Best friend was Pakistani
Was just my brother's best friend
A non-issue in my family.

[Our community] was pretty White
My experience
Only as far as I could ride my bike.

The farm my dad grew up on
One side was a Scotsman
Other side was a Hutterite colony
And then on the other side was a Polish family.

I remember going to the farm
To the Hutterite colony
They looked different
It's not like I never saw anybody different
It just never occurred to me.

High school
Had a close group of two or three friends
Started to get really involved in Ukrainian dancing

Spent most of my time dancing.
Went to school and left
Really didn't participate
Went to classes and left
Dancing
That's where my social life was.

University same thing
Little fish in a big pond
Never was diversity talked about
It was never anything brought to my attention.
Elementary generalist. Minor was counseling
Even in counseling they didn't talk about diversity
Talked about kids with emotional difficulties
Academic difficulties
Just touched on that
That was it.

Student teaching
[First] practicum in [a] White neighbourhood
Middle class, upper middle class
No problems
Little clones walking around.

Second practicum
It wasn't all little White kids
From middle class
The classroom that I did my practicum in
Was all White kids
The thing that stood out
I'm not Catholic
I'm Ukrainian Orthodox.

Strong belief that religion has no place in schools
Would not teach the religion class
At first, they were threatening to withdraw my practicum.

Learning, it needs to be global
It needs to be everything
If you're just teaching Catholicism
When you have other religions in the world
You're not teaching
You're not educating on a global scale.

If I'm going to talk about religion
I want to have everybody represented
Which is where we're living
That was my issue
I don't like one way is the right way.

As we attended to stories Sally shared with us about her childhood, school, and teacher education experiences, we were drawn to the important place culture held in her stories. As a child, Sally's Ukrainian heritage was a central focal point in both her immediate and extended family. Not only was it something to be celebrated within her family but it was also what made her "different from anyone else in her community." For Sally, the plotline of celebrating cultural diversity extended beyond her family and was also lived out at her mother's place of work. Their staff parties included "every kind of food under the sun" and women of East Indian and Chinese heritage dressed in their cultural clothing. While Sally grew up with an understanding that cultural diversity was something to be celebrated, she also experienced ethnic diversity as a "non-issue." Perhaps it was for this reason Sally was not attentive to the lack of ethnic diversity in her elementary and junior high schools and in her community or why she was not "phase[d]" by it when she saw youth from other ethnic backgrounds in her high school.

Sally's teacher education program did little to help her learn to attend more closely to the experiences of children of diversity. Here, diversity equalled children with emotional or academic difficulties and even that was "just touched on" in her university courses. It was not until Sally's second student teaching experience that she encountered a story of difference that conflicted with her own story. Within this Catholic school setting, Sally's different religious beliefs were neither a place of celebration nor a non-issue. Rather, she was expected to silence her beliefs, her difference, and to teach the children a singular perspective of religion. As Sally told how she bumped up against this story of school, she made visible a narrative thread that she was unwilling to conform to storylines that suggested there was "one right way." She wanted to live a story where "learning [was] global" and "everybody [was] represented." As we attended closely to Sally's telling that, as a pre-service teacher, she was willing to teach religion if she was able to teach it in a way that represented everyone's religious beliefs, we wondered about the rhetoric surrounding diversity and difference that she may have learned within her university courses and if her desire to teach everyone's religion might have been shaped in this rhetoric. Like we wondered with Jim, we wondered what it meant for Sally to confront personal difference on a school landscape. What did it mean for teachers when they experienced difference in their own lives in school settings rather than in off-school contexts?

Shifting stories to live by: Sally

Sally also shared many stories that suggested possibilities where her stories to live by shifted. The first occurred when she was in her first year teaching in a Grade 1 classroom in an elementary school with an ethnically diverse population. In the following transcript segment she spoke of a moment of awakening:

> I was hired during the summer. I walked into [the multicultural school], and that first day got my class list. I will never forget, first name on my class list, Ananth Bandura or something like that. And there was Ami and Pav and Preet and Whammy; these wonderful names I couldn't pronounce worth beans. And all I remember is having so much fun meeting these kids. I could care less about anything other than they came in with big, huge hugs. We had so much fun together and they laughed at me trying to pronounce names because this is the first time that I had to go through a class list that didn't have your basic names on it. I was so excited to have my own class I could really care less what they looked like and who they were or anything like that. I started to meet some of the parents and it was [my] instinct to immediately talk to the mother first, just a natural instinct. And so as the parents would come in I'd introduce myself and immediately [I would] talk to the mom and I noticed lots of grandmas were coming in and dropping off their little ones. I'm not really paying attention to any of this. And then my first conference in November, Ananth's family came in. Mom and Dad came in, sat down, so again I started talking to them and naturally started addressing Mom. And every time I asked a question Dad would respond. Not Mom. Dad would always answer it. Okay fine I just kept on talking mostly to Mom but Dad kept on responding. Then I finally clued in. Okay, this is a pretty patriarchal family. So finally the light bulb dawned and it was probably half way through the conference but finally the light bulb dawned. And I thought, "Okay I have to kind of shift a little bit here." So that's when I finally started to address more of my conversation to Dad. And what was really interesting was Mom visibly relaxed. And I didn't clue in. She was obviously feeling a little bit awkward because she wasn't responding to me. Dad kept on doing it and so when I finally shifted my conversation she kind of relaxed into her role and I had my conversation with Dad. The whole conversation kind of shifted. All of a sudden, okay now I realized I'm addressing the right person, I'm doing the right thing, I'm in the right situation. He was extremely respectful, probably one of the most respectful parents I had in all the conferences. Just a wonderful man. But it was one of those things that I just didn't think about. That was probably the first time that I realized that okay there are some cultural differences in the world and I'm in a situation where I need to start to learn some of these things.
>
> (Transcript of individual conversation, March 24, 2003)

In this transcript segment, Sally described her first teaching position. She was excitedly looking forward to meeting the class and was initially startled when she got the class list. The names of the children, mostly of South Asian origin, were unknown to her. They were not what she called "basic names" (Transcript of individual conversation, March 24, 2003). However, she knew the story of school, knew there were class lists and when she met the children, they seemed like all children "with big, huge hugs" (Transcript of individual conversation, March 24, 2003). She could proceed with her enthusiastic story of who she was as a teacher and the children worked to help her understand how to pronounce their names. Nothing in who she was as a teacher needed to shift except she needed to learn to pronounce names shaped within another language and culture. She continued to live out her stories to live by, stories in which both parents shared equally in parental and professional jobs. Her stories to live by were ones in which she, as a young woman, assumed that mothers played the most central part in children's early years. She also lived a story in which the family that lived together was not an extended family so she did not attend to the parts grandmothers played in schooling. She continued to live what she knew from her own family narrative until the first conference with parents. It was in the moment of meeting parents that she began to awaken to another cultural and family narrative. As she at first enacted her stories to live by, she sensed tension as her stories bumped into the parents' stories to live by. She noted the tension and, in the moment, struggled to shift, at first naming the tension as a result of a "patriarchal" (Transcript of individual conversation, March 24, 2003) family structure. She continued to search for a way to be "respectful" (Transcript of individual conversation, March 24, 2003) and eventually began to live new stories with the parents. This moment of tension, this heightened awareness, scaffolded the beginning of new stories to live by as she realized "there are some cultural differences in the world and I'm in a situation where I need to start to learn some of these things" (Transcript of individual conversation, March 24, 2003).

In the second story, Sally told of her experiences in a second school. Drawing on her experiences in her first school as well as her personal experiences within her family and cultural narrative, she awakened to ways her stories to live by had shifted. It was the intersection of experiences from her personal and professional landscapes that began to scaffold a shift in her stories to live by.

> If you want to think about diversity, look at our kids here. We've got everything from the mom and the dad and the two bikes in the garage and the minivan to a restraining order on dad's second cousin's uncle and we've got family flow charts that will boggle your mind. At my last school it was more consistent. It wasn't high socioeconomic, it was very middle class but it was consistently middle class and we maybe had three, three families in the whole school who stayed at the apartment buildings

way far away whereas here we've got low income housing complexes over here, apartment complexes over there, and a whole Aboriginal complex that an [Aboriginal] Band bought. In terms of transiency this is probably the most that I have ever seen. Our Aboriginal kids are here for two weeks, and then they are on the reservation for three weeks, and then are back here for a month and then they decide to go to Saskatchewan (the neighbouring province) to visit their uncle's cousin. This is the first place where I have had to deal with Aboriginal cultures which is very different than East Indian. In my last school, I got used to my East Indian families going to India for three months and okay I had figured out how to deal with that and that was fine. Now here, like I said, this is my first experience with Aboriginal cultures and that's a whole different culture and that was another learning curve for me.

(Transcript of individual conversation, March 24, 2003)

As we listened to Sally tell of her experiences in two different schools over her first few years of teaching, we saw her waking up to deeper understandings of diversity. In her first school, her story of school collided with the story of school of children and families of East Indian heritage. For her, learning about another culture, language, and ethnic heritage was a "learning curve" (Transcript of individual conversation, March 24, 2003). When we looked back to her stories of growing up where her cultural heritage was important and was a central plot line in her story, she recognized the centrality of children's cultural heritage. She used her experience of growing up in a middle class community with two parents and her sibling to understand the children's lives in this first school. She used her stories to live by as a way to find similarities with the children's lives. While she was at first uncertain about what an absence from school for three months meant in the life of a child, she came to understand it as a kind of family vacation to visit extended family. In her own life she storied how she would go to the farm to visit her grandparents. In the children's lives, they would go to India with their families to visit grandparents and other extended family members.

When Sally arrived at her second school she felt, in some ways, she understood cultural diversity in children's lives. However, she discovered that children could come from very different family structures and socio-economic situations. While she tried to learn these diversities, she faced another difference from her own life. Now she struggled to figure out the cultural narrative in families of children of Aboriginal heritage. Their absences from school, unlike the ones of children of East Indian heritage, did not follow a pattern, did not happen just once a year as a special family vacation, were not just about visiting grandparents but rather were uneven, frequent, unannounced, and unexpected departures. Her stories to live by, shaped in her own history, were not helpful to her coming to know these children. As we engaged in research alongside Sally, she made visible for us how she was still in the midst of a "learning curve" (Transcript of individual conversation, March 24, 2003) as she tried to learn to teach children of diversity.

In both school settings, her stories to live by bumped sharply into the children's and families' stories to live by. In her first school, however, she could draw on plotlines and threads from her own stories to scaffold a way to make sense of the children's stories. In the second, she had no threads from her stories to live by to help her scaffold an understanding of these children's and families' lives, yet she wanted to attend to these new stories. Because it was outside her stories to live by both in terms of economic and cultural narratives, she was in the midst of creating a new narratively coherent story of who she was as teacher (Carr 1986).

Our third participant was Suzanne, a teacher librarian.

Suzanne: word images of stories to live by

Golden childhood
Apple of my parents' eyes
Wonderful time
Older siblings
Never sibling rivalry
Pretty spoiled.

Leave it to Beaver neighbourhood
Tract houses
Suburbia
Full of kids
Grew up together
Didn't worry
Candy store
Baby boomer community.

Best friend went to the Protestant school
I went to the Catholic school
Didn't seem to be a problem.

Good student
Goody two shoes
Happy sitting in rows
My handwriting on the wall
Because it was neat
Good experience
Played school
Neighbourhood kids
Wanted to be the teacher.

Friend
Really struggled [in school]
Felt ashamed for her
Used to think of myself as smart
Kind of us and them
Felt sorry for them
Never occurred to me to help them
Unless a teacher said.

Bring home report cards
Mom and Dad would say
"You're so smart"
They were into self esteem.

Where I did get my humiliation
Was picking the baseball teams
I would be near the end all the time
Talk about shame.

High school
Fun
Crowd of girls I hung out with
Met my husband in Grade 12.

When I grew up
A teacher or a nurse
That was the only choice
I knew I didn't want to be a nurse.

Teacher education
Don't really recall
Very content driven.

Started off teaching
Interested in class control
Sign of a good teacher
Kids in rows
Being really quiet
Top grade fives
Screened that way
Diversity, I got the top
[Other teacher] got the rest.

Kids do the same page in the workbook

Dead silence
Sit at my desk
I'd think
I have nothing to do
No behaviour problems
Never occurred to me to challenge them academically.
A parent saying
"How are you enriching the program?"
Never occurred to me.

As we read across transcripts of our conversations with Suzanne about her childhood, school experiences, and beginnings as a teacher, narrative threads seemed to emerge of wanting to get along with and please others and to be seen by them as being "good." Storying herself as having a golden childhood, Suzanne made visible how the responses she received from others were important to her and shaped how she saw herself. Growing up in a close-knit community where the residents shared many life commonalities, Suzanne felt a strong sense of belonging. She attended schools where she quickly learned the stories of school and who she needed to be within these contexts to be viewed as a good student, a storyline that was important to both her and her parents. Plotlines of difference "did not seem to be a problem" in Suzanne's school or community experiences. While she associated deeper emotions with her lower skills in baseball and her friend's academic struggles in school she was not particularly attentive to them.

The narrative threads that shaped Suzanne's childhood also wove across her stories to live by as a beginning teacher. Adhering to the dominant story of the time, that is, a time when women either became teachers or nurses, Suzanne became a teacher because she did not want to be a nurse. Similar to how Suzanne lived stories as a child of wanting to be seen as a good student, she also worked hard to been seen as a good teacher. This meant children were silent and conformed to what the teacher expected. Differences in ability were still not something Suzanne readily attended to but, rather, the students all worked on the same page in workbooks. As we listened to Suzanne's beginning teacher stories we were reminded of how the dominant stories of schools during this timeframe were shaped by children working at the same pace through progressively more difficult workbook activities.

Shifting stories to live by: Suzanne

We pulled forward only one of Suzanne's stories from our research conversations. In Suzanne's story she recalled moments from her fourth year of teaching and then slid forward to her present-day understandings of teaching. As we moved across time and place with Suzanne we saw how her stories to live by have shifted.

I taught for three years at Mount Royal. The fourth year I had a tough class. It was tough for me at that point. Probably with this much experience now it would just be a regular class. But there was Angie who was quite emotionally disturbed and I remember just thinking, "I can't teach any more." Like I hated it.

They were just, in my world, horrendous compared to what I had taught before. And Angie would just do things like, you know, the desks were in rows and you'd pass out paper to the first person and then they'd pass it back. And she would take hers, look at me and then crumple it up and throw it on the floor and go like, "What are you going to do?" I think now at our school, we have kids that do that and we defuse it or you figure out what to do, but back then it was just a huge kind of power thing. I remember coming home, I was making spaghetti sauce one night and I was crying into the sauce and my husband came home and I said, "I just hate it, I just hate my job, I can't do it." I look back at it now; I probably could have handled it a lot better. I didn't have the experience then. It was just behaviour, it was dealing with behaviour all the time where I didn't have to do it before.

Well actually I had more luck with Angie than many other teachers because I'm not confrontational myself. Well what I would do was I would take her out and I'd say, "What's wrong?" [She would say,] "Everybody hates me." I felt like saying, "Well of course they do because you're acting like such an idiot." But of course I didn't. [I would say,] "No, everybody doesn't hate you." But it was a bit hypocritical because I was very angry with her myself and yet I put on this sort of sweet face. I think I just got through it the only way I could. I think I got tougher on everybody because by God it was my room and I was going to be the boss. And I tended to be pretty strict anyway. I probably became much more strict that year and maybe those kids would have benefited from getting cut a little slack.

Now I certainly would do so many things differently if I was at that school with my experience. I could take Angie and talk to her or find a kinaesthetic activity or somehow give her some success so that she wouldn't feel so wretched about herself. That never occurred to me because every kid was doing worksheet page 19, didn't matter if you could do it, didn't matter if it's too easy, too hard, blah, blah, blah. But now I think, if you could channel her and give her a neat kind of study project or something and maybe get her out of the kids' hair, do something fun, and make her feel wonderful and she could come and present it to the class, there'd be a whole bunch of things I'd do differently.

(Transcript of individual conversation, April 16, 2003)

In this transcript fragment, Suzanne travelled backward across time and place to her fourth year of teaching and described it as a "tough" experience where the children were "horrendous compared to what [she] had taught before" (Transcript of individual conversation, April 16, 2003). Focusing her storytelling around one child, Suzanne provided us with a sense of the frustration this child brought forward in her and how the child's behaviour had not followed a recognizable plotline. In Suzanne's story, Angie did not seem to live by similar narrative threads that Suzanne had as a student. She did not seem to want to get along with or please her teachers nor did she seem to care, as Suzanne had, about being viewed by others and herself as good. Instead, she lived storylines of open defiance, not getting along with others, and not wanting to fit into the stories of school shaping this school context. Unable to use her stories to live by as a way to understand Angie, Suzanne struggled with her own identity as a teacher. Seeing herself as unable to teach or connect with Angie in ways she had with former students, Suzanne tried to sustain her story of being a good teacher by becoming even stricter.

Now, several years later, Suzanne looked back to her interactions with Angie and other students during this time period and recognized how her stories to live by as a teacher have shifted. She attributed these shifts to having more experience, to having learned through her years as a teacher to "do so many things differently." Rather than live her beginning teacher stories of engaging in a power struggle with Angie and having children complete the same work all in the same way, her stories to live by as a teacher had shifted to become ones of finding ways to defuse situations, of pulling forward children's strengths and engaging them in activities where they can be successful, and of honouring children's diversity.

Insights into the interweaving of the personal and professional in teachers' becoming

These teachers' accounts of their experiences of learning to attend to the diverse lives of children helped us see again the interweaving of the personal and the professional in teachers' lives. Who they were becoming as people was intertwined with who they were becoming as teachers. In each of three teachers' lives, we saw this intertwining. We saw this as we heard Sally draw on her childhood experiences to make sense of who she was becoming as a teacher. We saw this as Suzanne told of how her frustration with teaching spilled over into her home life. We saw Jim's need to belong at school in childhood enacted in ensuring that all his primary children could take part in the school activity around Chicken Soup with Rice (Sendak 1986).

Perhaps what was most interesting as Suzanne, Jim, and Sally told of their lives of learning to teach children of diversity were the ways they drew on who they were, their stories to live by as they encountered diversity on their school landscapes. Sometimes they drew forward threads situated more closely with who they were off the school landscape, sometimes they drew forward threads shaped by experiences on school landscapes. Always the personal and the professional were entwined. As Bateson (1994: 108) reminded us "life is not made up of separate pieces." The stories we, as teachers, learn to live, tell, retell, and relive interlap (Huber *et al.* 2004) as we move back and forth among the multiple contexts of our lives.

Several things stood out as we attended to how stories to live by shifted and changed in Jim's, Suzanne's, and Sally's accounts and as we thought about our own lives. A notion of identity scaffolding was helpful to think about how those shifts occurred in stories to live by.

We noticed that change did not happen in an all-transforming kind of way. Rather, change happened as each teacher encountered a situation, met a child, heard a story, and began to use that moment as a trigger to restory who they were in shifting, evolving ways. For example, Sally used the experience of meeting children from different cultural heritages, which she initially attended to because of their different sounding names, to begin to shift who she saw herself becoming as a teacher. At first she assumed she needed only to learn to pronounce their names and she could proceed to live out her stories to live by. She then awakened, as she interacted with the parents of one of the children, to knowing that the child's family narrative was also a cultural narrative. She needed to learn more about the family's story of school. As she awakened, she began to scaffold new stories to live by; ones in which all children were not the same but were shaped by family and cultural narratives. She was in the midst of restorying who she was as a teacher of children of diversity, a restorying that occurred from the "overlapping of lives, the resonance between stories" (Bateson 2000: 243).

Something similar happened as Jim began to wonder about who he was as a teacher around a previously unquestioned practice, the sharing of a classroom activity with chicken soup. While at first he saw this as a community-building, fun activity, it became a moment for him to question who he was as a teacher of children of diversity. His initial wonderings about the activity began a process of restorying who he was as a teacher. This process of shifting was not smooth and quick but was slow, uneven, and a gradual evolving of shifted stories to live by, stories that drew forward some things from the past even as new understandings were added. It was, as Bateson (1994) suggested, a process of improvisation in composing a life.

It was most often in moments of tension that the possibility of a shift in stories to live by was possible. We heard stories of tension that suggested that when something did not fit, did not slide seamlessly into who we were, we were most able to awaken to other possibilities. It was as Jim noticed that some children could not have chicken soup that he felt the dis-ease, the tension that helped him see he needed to shift his practice. At first he gave crackers so the children of East Indian heritage did not feel excluded. Even then he felt uncertain, the tension not quite dissipated. He experienced an ongoing awareness that something was not quite right. The something was something that led to a gradual shift. He awakened to some aspects and then realized that there was more that needed to shift in who he was and who he was becoming as a teacher. It was in the moments of tension that we could perhaps become most attentive to the contradictions in who we were and who we are becoming.

Jim, Sally, and Suzanne drew on their childhood and school experiences as they tried to make sense of who they were and who they were becoming. As they did, there was a recognition that, as Greene (1995: 75) wrote, "the narratives we shape out of the materials of our lived lives must somehow take account of our original landscapes if we are to be truly present to ourselves and to partake in an authentic relationship with the young." Sally first looked to her childhood experiences with her mother's colleagues for what it meant to be of a different cultural heritage. Diversity initially meant saris and different food. She felt comfortable with the "wonderful names" she encountered on her first day as a beginning teacher in a multicultural school. But encountering parents at conference time shifted a broader knowing for Sally. Her tension built as she realized that she was in unfamiliar territory. Perhaps familiar threads from her knowing of difference as a child helped her stay with the tension to "finally [start to] address more of my conversation to Dad." Her comfortable stories from childhood may have locked her into certain stories to live by. However, when her old stories to live by became unstable we saw how her experiences with difference in childhood may have provided the thread to scaffold a deeper and wider shift in her stories of what it meant to teach ethnically diverse children.

We also saw how being comfortable in our stories to live by might mean we become stuck in a story. Tension was felt as our stories were challenged. We might dismiss the tension or we might stay with it, scaffolding a new story to live by. What might make a difference we wondered? One way to think about this was that threads from familiar childhood stories might prove helpful in scaffolding new, wider stories to live by, as we saw with Jim and Sally. Perhaps new stories to live by might be scaffolded from our encounters and relationships with one another at the time. Perhaps finding relational threads to scaffold a new story of really looking at children might, as Clandinin *et al.* (1993: 218) suggested, shape a "sustained conversation in which we need many responses to our stories to be able to tell and retell them with added possibility."

Sometimes it was only as we looked back at our practices that we realized that who we were as a teacher had shifted. The scaffolding that enabled a shifted practice had occurred almost without our conscious attention to it. Suzanne helped us see this through her stories, when she looked back on her experiences with a child in her early years of teaching. It was only as she looked back that she could see how the experience with that child began a shift in who she was becoming as a teacher. As Greene (1995: 86) wrote of her experiences, "the narratives I have encountered in my journey have made it possible for me to conceive patterns of being as my life among others has expanded." Some of the patterns of being in Suzanne's life as a teacher emerged through the research conversations as she retold some of the narratives of her teaching career.

The sense of stories to live by as the interweaving of the personal and the professional, and as evolving, fluid, and multiple, reminded us that when we attended to teachers' lives in school we learned about the complex ways teachers' personal practical knowledge was shaped and reshaped. When we attended to teachers' stories of themselves as teachers of children of diversity, we discovered threads through teachers' stories to live by.

Where are the spaces, we wondered, for telling our stories as teachers, for the kind of questioning that enables each of us to imagine other stories we might live by as we learn to live in relation with children of diversity? Are there spaces in schools for the kinds of conversations to which Jim might lead us? How can his experience with the children's experiences with Chicken Soup with Rice (Sendak 1986) create a space for a conversation about diversity? In her work with South African teachers, Pillay (2003: 217) wrote "these teachers experience their lives in a state of homelessness, constantly shifting and changing in the stance they adopt in the new situations in which they find themselves." As we reflected on the shifting stories Jim, Suzanne, and Sally experienced as they shifted from their certain stories to live by forged in their early years, their schooling and their teacher education to stories to live by reshaped by encounters with children of diversity, we too wondered about the feelings of homelessness that they might have felt. One response was to stay fixed in who they were as teachers, secure that their stories to live by were the only ones. These teachers, however, were in the midst of shifting, changing who they were becoming as they tried to stay awake to the tensions they encountered, to their sense that it could always be otherwise. We are called to reconsider the kinds of learning spaces we need to create for teachers, children, and ourselves in schools, spaces for imagining and beginning to live and tell our shifting changing stories to live by as we dance along in the parade.

Chapter 8

Living in tension
Negotiating a curriculum of lives

In the year-long narrative inquiry in the Year 3/4 classroom at City Heights School, Jean and Janice attended to the children's and teachers' lives as the curriculum was negotiated. One of the places that lives meet in schools is in curriculum making. As we noted in Chapter 1, our view of curriculum making draws on the work of Clandinin and Connelly who wrote that curriculum "might be viewed as an account of teachers' and children's lives together in schools and classrooms" (1992: 392). Their view pointed to the centrality of lives in the negotiation of curriculum. We share their "vision of curriculum as a course of life" (1992: 393), perhaps a curriculum of lives. A curriculum of lives is shaped as children's and teachers' diverse lives meet in schools, in in- and out-of-classroom places. As children's and teachers' stories to live by bump against stories of school and school stories, a curriculum of lives is, in part, shaped. In this chapter we focused on three moments in different classrooms, one at City Heights School and two at Ravine Elementary School, where school stories and stories of school influenced the curriculum of lives children and teachers were shaping.

The first field note we inquired into was from the Year 3/4 classroom at City Heights School. It was one moment of curriculum making where we sensed the possibility of negotiating a curriculum of lives. As we tried to make sense of who we and the children were in that negotiation we identified tensions around the difficulties of making a curriculum attentive to the children's diverse lives. Later in this chapter we focused on our subsequent inquiry at Ravine Elementary School where we inquired into more intentional moments in two classrooms to explore what it meant in children's, teachers', and our own stories to live by as we negotiated a curriculum of lives. The first of these moments at Ravine Elementary School focused on our exploration of a moment of curriculum making involving the students in writing found poetry of their report cards where the telling and retelling of children's stories to live by shaped openings to explore new possible identity threads. The second inquiry moment at Ravine Elementary School focused on our exploration of a moment of curriculum making involving a group of children taking photographs and composing visual narratives of the meanings of community in their stories to live by.

Exploring a moment of curriculum making at City Heights

We begin by drawing on a field note of a City Heights trip to a local fort museum. Puzzled by our inability to live the story we were starting to tell of trying to negotiate a curriculum of lives in the classroom, we redirected our attention to the professional knowledge landscape and to the stories that were shaping that landscape; stories with plotlines of productive days of high-quality learning, of achievement as measured by test scores, of schools as ranked against one another by achievement, of curriculum as mandated outcomes measured by achievement test scores.

We worked in the Year 3/4 classroom for a school year. We had, at year's end, a great many field texts: pages of field notes, conversation transcripts, artefacts of student work, planning documents, and school documents. When we began to analyze our field texts to understand the curriculum making in the classroom, we took different approaches, pulling on different threads that would allow us to understand teachers' and children's stories to live by. As we began this work, we were looking for moments where there was the possibility of making a curriculum of lives. We selected the following moment because it was filled with tension both in the living of the moment and in our interpretation of this field text. It was a moment which allowed us to make problematic the complexity and difficulty in negotiating a curriculum of lives on current professional knowledge landscapes.

In the following field note, a particular topic in the social studies subject matter was being lived out, both in and out of the classroom context.

> We arrived at the school around 8.30 a.m.... . By this time the children were arriving. They were very excited. The bus was to leave at 9:00 a.m. for the fort museum... . As we drove up to the fort the first thing we and the children saw was a group of tepees just outside the wooden fort wall. The children were excited and some of them told stories of having been in family tepees. Others asked questions of how they were made. Some noticed the decorations and lacing. When the children asked if they could go inside we said we were sure that at some point in the morning we would be visiting them.
>
> When the bus dropped us off inside the fort we were met by June and George. They were going to work with us in the three activities – games, beading, and bannock making. George spoke first in a large room where there were two fires going. He explained that the children needed to raise their hands to speak, one person at a time. He was the leader and they were to follow. He wanted to talk first about the fur trade. He asked

what they knew. The teacher explained that they were just coming to the fur trade. She said they had been doing research on the Woodland and Plains Cree lifestyles.

George got the kids to line up and we went to look at pelts in the trading room (very cold). He explained [the processing of fur pelts] and asked the children a few questions about the process. He used Damien and Dustin in a bit of a role play, casting them in the role of Natives bringing furs in to trade. He used Sam as a regular trader with whom he had long traded. As Jean listened with her arms around Brittney and Corina and Van to help keep them warm, she realized that many of the children's ancestors would have been the "Natives" to whom George was referring. He seemed to have the sense of the fur trade as progress and settlement. He did not ask the children what sense they made of it…. . It was very cold in the room and the children were moving about. George had some trouble with this… . We then went up to the factor's house which was heated. George had the children guess how many people lived in the huge house – there were five. The children got to ask a few questions about the objects on the walls, etc. They were very curious about the rest of the house and had many more questions but George took us back to the first room where he had the children sit in groups.

When we moved to the cook house we were divided into groups. Jean went outside with one group to play double ball, the teacher went with the bannock making group, and Janice went with the beading group… . When Jean's group got to the bannock making activity George explained how to wrap the bannock dough around the sticks. He did not ask the children about bannock but many of them were telling Jean that they knew how to make bannock with their grandmas. Earlier Shawna, Darwin's mom, said she did not know how to make bannock. She did not like to cook but her mom made bannock and she loved it…. George did not pick up on any of that. As George slapped the dough on the stick, Lui asked if he could wash his hands. George said, "No." Shawna and Jean helped the children wrap the dough and then they began to cook it on the fires… . There were problems with the cooking, the sticks catching fire and the dough burning… . At one point, Lui asked George a question, calling him Craig. George stopped him and said, "That is the third time you called me Craig. Learn that my name is George." Lui was startled by the harshness of the reprimand and Jean intervened and said that Lui was new to our school and was learning a lot of names… .

We got back to the school after 1.00 p.m. Janice and Jean went to get the lunch food for the children. When they got to the office Shawna was there and they talked about the field trip because the school secretary asked how we enjoyed it. We all said that we thought that George and June had not been good. Jean wondered what Shawna, who was

Aboriginal, thought about the way the fur trade was explained. Shawna said that she, too, had been troubled.

(Field notes, November 19, 1999)

We began with this moment of curriculum making as it was a moment that raised questions about how children and teachers negotiate a curriculum of diverse lives. In the field notes we saw this curriculum as it slowly unfolded in a particular place with particular people in relation. We saw the meeting of the lives of the Year 3/4 children, their teacher's life, the lives of two researchers, the life of a mother, and the lives of two instructors at the local fort museum. In this moment these lives first met at school, then at the museum, and, again, back at school. Curriculum was at the heart of the meeting (Connelly and Clandinin 1988).

As we inquired into this moment, we attended to tension and uncertainty in the making of a curriculum of lives. The explicit subject matter of the museum instructors was connected to the mandated curriculum focus on the early history of Aboriginal peoples currently being taught in the Year 3/4 classroom. The children arrived at the fort in the midst of a unit with this focus. As we experienced the curriculum at the fort there was a continuity of topic between the mandated unit being taught in the classroom and the fort instructors' interpretation of the mandated curriculum. George checked this out with the classroom teacher and she described where the class was in relation to the mandated curriculum. The way we observed the unit being taught at the fort was coherent with what we knew the end of year standardized provincial achievement tests would measure. In the classroom we observed the unit being taught through inquiry approaches, giving children the opportunity to enter into and shape a curriculum through their questioning and through the sharing of their experiences.

In both our living and telling of the moment we felt tensions. The first tension emerged around the instructor's use of the term "Native." George seemed to assume that the children knew nothing about what he saw as an exotic aspect of Native life. In this moment Jean realized the instructor was referring to the ancestors of many of the children. While she experienced tension she did not speak. Jean also noticed the instructor's subject matter plotline was Eurocentric in its description of progress and settlement. While she felt tension about how that plotline was positioning the children, she again, did not speak, did not question.

Another tension surrounded the children's expression of curiosity, an expression that fit with the inquiry that was part of their in-classroom curriculum making. The children were interested in the tepees, their decoration, and how they were made. They were intrigued with the factor's house and had many questions. However, George, as instructor, had questions for the children, to test their knowledge, but he did not welcome the children's questioning. Still, another tension emerged through George's lack of attention to allow the children to bring their knowledge to the bannock making. Children's knowledge and questions were honoured in the curriculum-making approaches in their classroom but as Shawna, Darwin's mother, and Jean moved with the children going to bannock making, Shawna and Jean visibly expressed their tensions when they tried to start a conversation about Shawna's knowing of bannock making. Shawna tried to bring her life to the curriculum being made as she talked about liking bannock and memories of her mother making bannock. Shawna worked alongside Jean to try to interrupt the story George was telling of bannock making. In the moment of bannock making Jean and Shawna both knew that some of the children's lives carried memories of bannock. They wanted this knowing to be the starting point of the activity. What Shawna and Jean attempted in this moment was to shift the curriculum being made at the fort to a curriculum more coherent with the inquiry and life focus of the in-classroom curriculum making. The children joined in trying to shift the curriculum as they storied their knowledge of bannock making in the context of their home lives. George did not seem to listen. Jean felt tensions as George ignored their attempts to reshape the curriculum he was living.

There was another tension as Lui asked to live out a home story of washing his hands before he handled food and was told he could not. Still another tension emerged when Lui called George an incorrect name. Jean intervened at this point and shared a bit of Lui's story. She knew that for George to understand what Lui brought to this moment he needed to know something of the many narratives of experience living within Lui. George, however, did not respond.

Back at the school, in conversation with Shawna, she revealed her concern with the content of the field trip as well as the lack of respect George showed the children. Jean and Janice shared similar concerns. However, later in the day we learned that our and Shawna's lack of enthusiasm created tension for Emily, the classroom teacher, who was asked by someone in the office "if we liked anything" (Field note, November 19, 1999) about the field trip.

As we inquired into this field trip moment we became aware of the continuities, discontinuities, and silences in the meeting of the children's and our lives with the mandated curriculum as it found expression in George's practices. We saw the continuity between the mandated curriculum and the fort curriculum, the unquestioned cultural narrative, the story of instructor as expert, the story of the children as received knowers. At the same time the discontinuity in our stories to live by was marked by the tensions felt but not expressed as we tried to live a curriculum of lives. The silence in the field text was pervasive in our silence about the cultural narrative, about who the children were in relation to the cultural narrative, about the instructor's lack of respect of the children's and Shawna's knowing, and of the instructor's lack of respect for the children's inquiries.

As we returned to the school we were filled with questions of what happened, perplexed at how a situation filled with such possibility unfolded as it did. Like the tepees situated just outside the fort walls that we and the children wanted to visit but were not allowed to, we felt that our trip to the fort had left our lives and the children's lives outside the curriculum that happened there. As we worked through our perplexity we wondered how we could reimagine this field trip as more attentive to the lives of the children, ourselves as teachers, and the subject matter being taught.

Storying and restorying a curriculum of lives at Ravine Elementary School

In our subsequent year-long narrative inquiry at Ravine Elementary School we began to more intentionally negotiate a curriculum of lives attentive to the children's lives. This occurred as researchers worked alongside teachers and began to wonder about how a curriculum of lives might be shaped. In conversation with the teachers they were working alongside, Shaun and Vera wondered how the teachers and children were shaping curriculum in relationship with each other. In the next section of the chapter, we draw on field texts of this negotiation in two classrooms, one a Year 5/6 classroom and another, in a Year 2/3 learning strategies classroom.

Found poetry as a way to negotiate a curriculum of lives

We begin with an interim research text of Shaun's participation alongside Lian and the children and their in-classroom negotiation of a curriculum of lives through working with the children's report cards.

It was the first week of November and Shaun began to notice Lian was spending increasing amounts of time at her desk writing the report cards due out that month. She told Shaun how much time she was spending on the report cards and the tensions she was experiencing around writing them. As Lian recounted her tensions to Shaun, he learned that they were two-fold. In part, Lian storied her tensions as related to time. For example, Lian storied how she tried to work on the report cards one lunch hour and all the lunchtime kids were brought into her room and she had to stop. Secondly, the report cards had to be written at school because they were created by a school system server-based computer report card template which was not accessible from home.

Shaun learned that one of Lian's sources of information about the children was a sheet, "Skills for School Success," that all the children completed at the end of October. At the top of the sheet were the words "What you say is Important!!!!" Shaun learned that Lian included this message at the top of the sheet because she planned to include what the children wrote about themselves when she wrote their report cards. As Lian shared these sheets with Shaun, he was drawn to Kerry's sheet. Kerry was a boy in Year 6 who described himself as a "learner, [and as] funny." On his sheet, Kerry wrote, "I stay on task most of the time. I get distracted really easy so I'm sometimes focused." In response to the question on the Skills for School Success sheet: "Do you work well independently? (do you work well without someone watching over you?)" Kerry responded by writing, "I prefer to work independently because I sometimes say to myself and say, 'Oh, no, I have to do my best work because somebody is watching me.'" It was evident that Kerry had a sense of someone watching him and making judgments about him. He drew attention to his dislike of being watched; aware it was part of school. Lian later used Kerry's words in his report card to describe his work at school in a section of the report card also called "Skills for School Success." When Lian finally finished all of the report cards, she was tired. The report cards went home later in November at a date decided upon by all the Year 5/6 teachers.

After the report cards went home, Shaun suggested to Lian that it would be interesting to find out what the children thought of themselves in relation to the report cards. In order to shape this space, Lian and Shaun asked the children to write found poetry based on the report cards. Lian and Shaun led a lesson where they built a found poem based on a story book. Shaun's first attempt using the book *An Angel for Solomon Singer* (Rylant 1992) was less than successful and, after the students tried to create found poetry from folk tales, they became very frustrated. Shaun and Lian ended this lesson. On a following day Lian used the book *A Christmas Tapestry* (Polacco 2002) to write a found poem. Interestingly, this was a book used in the senior assembly to talk about responsibility and how the senior students in the school were leaders and expected to set an example for the younger children. Lian then had the children return to the folk tales and create found poems based on them. This time, the students were not frustrated as they composed the found poems.

On a subsequent day Lian and Shaun told the children that they would like them to use their report cards to make found poetry. By this time, the report cards had been taken home and returned to the school by the children, and the children had experiences with found poetry to draw upon. Shaun and Lian made copies of the report cards so the children could write on them and highlight phrases and words that interested them. Kerry used a yellow highlighter to mark phrases and words across all subject areas and categories on the report card. In contrast with some of the other children, Kerry did not attend to the marks he received but focused more on Lian's comments.

(Interim research text based on field notes,
November–December 2002)

Kerry
Able to jot down ideas, observations, memories, and reflection.
  Easy to get distracted.

Compares experimental and theoretical results.
  Easy to get distracted.

Sharing ideas and cooperating while working.
  Easy to get distracted.

Gather notes effectively.
  Easy to get distracted.

Enjoyment of our cooperative games and volleyball units.
  Easy to get distracted.

Recognize, and analyze, and create abstract works of art.
(Student work, December 2002)

Later in the school year, in the spring, Lian and Shaun repeated the process of creating found poetry based on the March report cards. In Kerry's poetry there were significant shifts in how he represented himself.

Kerry
Funny member of our classroom and is responsible for his choices.
  Enjoys reading.

Finds multiples and factors and still working on problem solving.
  Enjoys reading.

Can record observations accurately with good detail.
  Enjoys reading.

We have an artist in the room and puts good effort into his projects.
  Enjoys reading.

Participates in dance and on his skills in basketball.
  Enjoys reading.
(Student work, April 2003)

In the unfolding of these moments in the Year 5/6 classroom, we saw the meeting of a child's life, Kerry's, with the lives of Lian, his teacher, and Shaun, a researcher living for a school year in a classroom at Ravine

Elementary School. In the above curriculum-making moments, their lives bumped against a dominant school story of report cards.

As Shaun and Lian worked alongside one another and the Year 5/6 children in the fall and as the school story of report cards began to bump with Lian's stories to live by, she started to share some of her felt tensions with Shaun. She expressed these tensions as interruptions to rhythms of time, relationships, and space. In her recounting of her experiences to Shaun, Lian told of trying to find a space in the day and in the school where she could work on the report cards. Her feelings of tension seemed to come forward in response to the interruptions she experienced in her stories to live by as teacher as she felt her practices being shaped by pressures of living within the school story of report cards as a one-size-fits-all standardized form. In the interim research text there was a sense that, as Lian worked on the report cards, she struggled with feeling that she needed to shift out of her stories to live by as teacher; that is, shifting from stories of living and being responsive to children into a scripted story of report card maker, a story which positioned her as needing to judge children. One way Lian negotiated these tensions was by hanging onto her stories to live by as teacher by inviting children to write about themselves on the "Skills for School Success" sheet. Lian did not dismiss her felt tensions by choosing a story of school over her stories to live by. Instead, staying with this tension, Lian tried to shape a space for children and herself to maintain narrative coherence (Carr 1986) with the curriculum they were negotiating, a curriculum in which children's diverse lives were central.

One way we saw narrative coherence as shaped for the children and Lian was through the negotiation that occurred when the children storied themselves on the Skills for School Success sheet and Lian made a space for the children's stories and her relationships with them on the formal report card. For example, when Kerry responded to the question: "Are you respectful to your classmates and teachers? Are you kind and polite to others?" he wrote, "Yes, I'm [respectful] because I play with them and we both have fun." In the Skills for School Success section of Kerry's report card, Lian wrote, "He [Kerry] shows respect for classmates and teachers." We were struck by how Lian continued to live a story of honouring children's voices. On Kerry's "Skills for School Success" sheet, his response to the question: "Are you responsible for your behaviour at lunch and recess time?" was: "Yes I do because I play kickball and every body has fun." On Kerry's report card in the section for Physical Education, Lian wrote: "Kerry showed an interest in and enjoyment of our cooperative games and volleyball units. He displayed good skills and demonstrated a positive attitude while participating in activities." In both of these instances, we saw Lian giving Kerry back his story of himself as a cooperative, inclusive member of his school community.

Later, as the children worked with their report cards to write found poetry, Kerry seemed to recognize himself in the words Lian used to story him and included them in his poem: "Sharing ideas and cooperating while working.... Enjoyment of our cooperative games and volleyball units." As the children created found poems, they threaded together their stories to live by with Lian's telling of them as we saw above in Kerry's work.

In Kerry's December found poem, as he attended to both who he was and what he knew, he juxtaposed threads of subject matter and threads of himself as a learner. His story of himself, "Easy to get distracted," was always in relation to other statements about his success with subject matter. He also seemed to know that who he was and who he might become in relation with his teacher mattered deeply.

We saw this most profoundly in the shifts in the found poems Kerry wrote of himself between December and April. As mentioned above, in December, Kerry seemed to be juxtaposing himself as a learner with subject matter. In April, Kerry seemed to be intertwining himself as learner, Lian as teacher, the subject matters, and the classroom milieu in stories he told of himself living in his Year 5/6 classroom. For example, Kerry pulled forward Lian's story of him as "funny" and "responsible" and restoried himself as a "funny member of our classroom and is responsible for his choices." As Kerry, Lian, and Shaun negotiated a curriculum of lives through the found poetry, it seemed to shape openings for Kerry to bring forward his life as an artist in the classroom. Following an introduction to the work of Van Gogh and Littlechild, Kerry also began to story himself as an artist. This was a thread picked up by Lian and written in Kerry's report card. Lian showed Kerry one way of looking at his life. Kerry obviously found this thread important and picked it up and carried it forward into his found poem, as he wrote, "We have an artist in the room" (Student work, April 2003). We wondered if the relational support Lian found with Shaun provided a space for imagining a competing story of report cards. What we were drawn to in this unfolding process among Lian, Shaun, and the children were the ways in which this negotiation pushed against a more dominant story of school in which report cards are seen as one way to measure a teacher's accountability to parents, the government, tax payers, school board policies, and so on. By trying to stay with the negotiation of a curriculum of lives in relation with the standardized report cards, Lian, Shaun, and the children composed a competing story to the dominant school story of accountability through report cards. We see this as a way of staying with the negotiation of a curriculum of lives, allowing both children and teachers to live out competing stories to dominant school stories of report cards. It is also a way of shaping a curriculum of lives within the communal space of the classroom.

Vulnerability was a thread woven throughout this unfolding process. In the negotiation of lives, children's and teachers' lives become open to shifting, to becoming restoried.

Visual narrative inquiry as a way to negotiate a curriculum of lives

In Chapter 2 we introduced Vera Caine and her work alongside Kristi, the teacher, and the 14 boys in the Year 2/3 learning strategies class. As Vera entered into the Year· 2/3 learning strategies classroom, Kristi was in the midst of a mandated Social Studies curriculum unit on community. As we described in Chapter 2, Vera eventually gave the children cameras and asked them to take them home and take photographs of community in their lives. When the children brought their cameras and film back to school, Vera sent the film out to be developed.

> Jean had a particular interest in Vera's and the children's visual narrative inquiry work and often stopped down to talk with Kristi, Vera, and the children in the classroom when she was in the school. As soon as Jean knew the children's photographs were back from the developers, Jean stopped down to speak with Kristi and to ask to see the children's photographs. Jean asked to see Josh's. As Kristi searched for the photographs she told Jean she thought Josh had "not understood the task. He must just have taken pictures of the first things he saw." Jean understood Kristi's comment to mean that Josh had misunderstood the meaning of the task as he did not understand he was to take photographs of community. Kristi understood community in the way it was outlined in the curriculum guide, that is, as goods and services, as resources, as dependence and interdependence. As Kristi flipped through the photographs she and Jean looked at photographs of schools, churches, supermarkets, gas stations, and hospitals. Kristi spoke of how the children who took these photographs understood the photography assignment as well as the concept of community. Josh, she thought, did not. Kristi located Josh's photographs and Jean and Kristi looked at them together. As they flipped through Josh's photographs, Jean noticed two in particular. One pictured three small smiling children of Aboriginal heritage on a sofa. She thought the children were two years old and younger; they were sitting in a row in what was clearly a posed picture. The second photograph Jean noticed was of three guitars carefully positioned leaning against the same sofa. The photograph was carefully composed. Both photographs appeared to Jean to be striking examples of photography. She felt the sense of aesthetic composition and care that had gone into each photograph design. Later, after Vera had talked with each boy, Jean asked her what Josh had said about the two photographs she had noticed. Vera said that he spoke of the three children on the sofa as being his younger sister and her two small cousins. Sometimes his mother's sister came over and the three children played together. He spoke of the three guitars as being a

community because "one belongs to my dad, one to my uncle, and one is mine, and sometimes we play together".

(Interim research text based on field notes, November 2002)

This interim research text served as a marker of a moment where we saw the interaction of a child – a learner, with his teacher – also a learner, with the subject matter of community as part of a Social Studies unit all within the nested milieus of classroom, school, cultural, and social narratives. We saw in Josh's photographs a sense of how his stories to live by of community were ones threaded around plotlines of relationships, extended families, and of seeing himself and all people as related. When asked by Vera to work within a space to hear the children's stories of community, Josh whole-heartedly entered that space, setting aside what he had been taught in the mandated curriculum, filling it instead with stories of his life, stories of his dad, his uncle, his cousins, his younger sister, his aunt, his home, all as expressions of his knowing of community. In this space Josh felt safe to make visible a competing story of community, one that he lives by.

Josh's stories bumped against his teacher's story and the mandated curriculum and created a tension as she viewed his work as an expression of his not understanding the task nor the concept of community. Vera however, as she worked alongside the children, stayed with the visual narrative inquiry as a way to negotiate a curriculum of lives and pushed to have the children compose books in which the photographs were mounted and around which they told their stories. Jean, after looking at the photographs and hearing Kristi's concern that Josh "had misunderstood the meaning of the task" (Interim research text based on field notes, November 2002) spoke with Jeanette. She told Jeanette that she saw Josh's photographs were an expression of his story of community, one that needed to find a place in the classroom story. Jeanette, the school principal, supported Vera in interrupting both curriculum as subject matter only and the story of school in which boys in a learning strategies classroom have difficulty expressing themselves in written forms. Without this kind of support, we wondered if Josh's stories to live by, a competing story to the mandated curriculum, would have been expressed. We also wondered if, without this kind of support, his story might have been turned into a conflicting story and stopped.

Some weeks later, at a school-wide open house for children, parents, and visitors, Kristi displayed the children's visual narrative books of community. It was one of only a few displays of academic work set amidst penny carnival stands, silent auctions, and bake sale items. The work was proudly displayed as the work of the boys in the learning strategies classroom. As Jean wandered through the carnival, chatting with teachers and parents and members of the research group, three other staff members independently approached her and told her to go and look at the amazing visual narrative inquiry books created by the boys in the learning strategies classroom. In that moment, Jean realized that the story of who the boys were in the school context had been interrupted, at least for that time.

Wonderings and thoughts about negotiating a curriculum of lives

One of the things that became particularly evident as we laid the first, second, and third stories in this chapter alongside each other was that the place of speaking of tension is important in the negotiation of a curriculum of lives. In the first story at City Heights, Jean recognized tension at the discontinuities between the children's lives and the mandated curriculum. She did not speak. In the second story at Ravine Elementary School, Lian did speak of the tension she felt writing mandated report cards while at the same time trying to live out her stories as a curriculum maker attentive to children's diverse lives. In the third story, working alongside Kristi, Vera, and Josh, Jean recognized tensions and spoke, encouraging Jeanette to support Vera in keeping this space for negotiating the curriculum of Josh's life open. In the third story, Jeanette supported the negotiation of a curriculum of lives and was comfortable with attending to tension and the ways it interrupted the mandated curriculum and the story of school of boys in a learning strategies classroom.

The curricular moments in this chapter helped us see what it meant and what it might mean to negotiate a curriculum of lives in school. When children with diverse lives come to schools living their stories to live by, it is moments such as these that teach us all how to be attentive to what we are doing in these educative or mis-educative places we call school. We wonder: are schools interrupting children's and teachers' stories to live by? Are their stories to live by interrupted for educative or mis-educative reasons? It is in trying to understand these curricular moments that perhaps we can begin to understand. Attending to these curricular moments as moments of interaction among the four curriculum commonplaces as they intersect might help us begin to understand what it means to negotiate a curriculum of lives for children, teachers, administrators, and families.

> With the narrative perspective, we understand the child's education in terms of the child's and the teacher's dominant narratives embedded within cultural and historical narratives. The child's education, for instance, is seen in terms of his or her personal narrative and of the meaning this conveys of his or her learning experiences in a particular classroom. The child's education is seen temporally in terms of past, present, and future.
>
> (Connelly and Clandinin 1988: 111)

Attending to the lives being composed in these curricular moments helped us both see what Connelly and Clandinin (1988) were writing about and also begin to imagine how we might negotiate a curriculum of lives attentive to all of the lives, teachers, children, families, and administrators as they meet in schools.

Chapter 9

Composing stories to live by
Interrupting the story of school

One day in February, Lian and Shaun were in the classroom talking when Dylan returned, alone, from music class. When Lian asked him what he was doing he told them he went to the office instead of getting into a fight in music with Carson, a classmate with whom he had an altercation during the previous class in gym. Dylan said Mrs Stuart, the principal, told him he had to have something to do while he was sitting in the office. He came to the classroom to get paper to draw on. When Dylan returned to the office Shaun told Lian he would like to talk to Dylan about his stories of school.

(Field notes, February 3, 2003)

Shaun's research in the Year 5/6 classroom focused, in part, on students' knowledge of school and the experiences that shape student knowledge. It was in this space that he met Dylan, an Aboriginal boy who was placed in Year 5 but who was more age-appropriate for Year 7. While Dylan was not one of the initial five students who began to shape the focus of Shaun's research (Murphy 2004) it was in moments such as the one described in the field notes above that Shaun became interested in the ways Dylan expressed his stories to live by in school.

As we met in regular research meetings, Shaun often shared stories about Dylan's interactions in the classroom and larger school. Marni, Anne, and Jean often added stories they heard from Dylan himself, as well as stories they heard of Dylan from others in the school. We realized that Dylan was a central student character in the story of school and school stories at Ravine Elementary School.

In the opening field note, Shaun described what seemed to be a moment of bumping up of Dylan's stories to live by with a school story. In this storied moment, Shaun learned that Dylan had permission to excuse himself from a class and to go to the office if he thought he would get into difficulty with another student. He had permission to interrupt his class attendance when he felt he needed to. We wondered about the ways Dylan's stories of interrupted attendance could help us understand something more about the connections among children's, teachers', principals', and families' lives as they met in schools. We wondered about ways school and class attendance played a part in children's stories to live by in school, and we wondered about ways the dominant stories of school attendance both shape, and might become reshaped, by diverse children's stories to live by.

Listening to Dylan's stories of attending school

Shaun met Dylan at the beginning of the school year when Dylan began to attend Ravine Elementary School. At that time, Dylan was placed in the Year 5 section of Lian's Year 5/6 classroom, although he was already 12 years old. Shaun later discovered the decision was made by Jeanette because Dylan had not attended school the previous year. We were unsure but continued to wonder if Dylan's mother or Dylan himself had any say in this placement decision. We also did not know if Lian's or Jeanette's voices shaped Dylan's placement in Year 5 or if, instead, school board policies in relation to truancy and attendance shaped this decision around Dylan's life.

Later on the February day when Shaun wrote the opening field notes, he and Dylan talked in the office. Until Dylan permanently left Ravine Elementary School in May, Shaun had opportunities for more conversations with him. Often those talks touched on Dylan's attendance at school. Dylan spoke of being in a number of schools. He began school in a First Nations Band school on a reserve near the city where Ravine Elementary School is located. From the Band school, Dylan moved with his mother, older brother, and younger sister to Vancouver Island where he attended a public school in a small town. The family's next move was to a large west coast city where Dylan attended a school near the city centre. Dylan and his family then returned to the reserve and he attended the Band school briefly before deciding to quit. However, this interruption in his schooling was temporary because the family moved again. It was this move that brought Dylan to Ravine Elementary School. When Dylan told of how he quit school before coming to Ravine Elementary School, his grade level was not clear. Shaun thought Dylan quit school in his fifth year. However, in another conversation, Dylan spoke of being in Year 6 but was now back in Year 5.

Dylan's stories of the grades he was in while at various schools were not consistent. It seemed that there were interruptions in his attendance at school when Dylan moved schools, but there were also interruptions while he attended a specific school. As researchers, we began to wonder what was happening in Dylan's stories to live by as he experienced these multiple interruptions, these times of attending, not attending, moving from school to school, quitting, re-enrolling.

In one conversation, Dylan told of advancing to Year 6 because a "kind" (Transcript from individual conversation, February 3, 2003) principal gave him the mark he wanted. However, Shaun later realized the "kind" principal was the principal of the school Dylan attended when he was in Year 4. Possibly Dylan's confusion resulted because he had been promoted at one time to Year 6 and then placed in Year 5 when he began to attend Ravine Elementary School. At another time and in another research conversation Dylan told Shaun he failed twice for being bad. Dylan did not experience school as a smooth progression from grade to grade but, rather, as an uncertain series of schools, classrooms, and grades. We sensed that while Dylan understood attendance was linked to success in schools, Dylan knew success could also be linked with the actions of a principal and the stories s/he lived by. We wondered if Dylan might also have held a similar story of teachers; that his teacher and the stories s/he lived by could also shape his success in school. Grades and success in school could be awarded by people who were "kind" and who honoured his requests. For Dylan, the authority for his school story was in the hands of others. However, we realized Dylan himself saw that he was in authority about his attendance at school.

Oyler (1996) helped us consider multiple ways in which authority might be experienced. She provoked an understanding of authority as something within us, as well as outside of us. Dylan experienced authority in these two ways. Typically in schools, authority for much of what goes on is funnelled down the conduit by others to shape students' and teachers' lives in prescribed, authoritative ways (Clandinin and Connelly 1995). Dylan knew this authority in his life as he experienced success or failure from one grade to another in school. Dylan believed success or failure was bestowed on him through the actions of particular principals and teachers. But Oyler called us to respect children's own authority in authoring their lives at school. By allowing Dylan to interrupt his attendance in music class when he knew his behaviour would not fit a school story of participation in music classes, Jeanette enabled Dylan to be responsive to the multiple stories he lived within. Dylan became responsible to his own story of being in authority over attendance and he became responsible to the school story of participating in music classes without fighting.

When Dylan spoke of quitting school the year prior to coming to Ravine Elementary School, he spoke of other children who beat him up and took his clothes. He also told of a similar incident with clothing when he was much younger. Dylan told Shaun on different occasions that he had moved, that he was bad, that he hit teachers, that he was beaten up, and that he failed. During one conversation Dylan said he could not miss more than five days of school for the rest of the year at Ravine Elementary School or he would not be able to go to junior high school the following year. When Shaun wondered about this with Lian, he discovered that no such deal had been made, at least according to Lian, although there was a plan for Dylan to go to junior high school the following year. However, Dylan told a story of being happy to be in Year 5 or 6 because he was not ready to give up his "kid life" (Transcript of individual conversation, February 3, 2003) for junior high school. As we learned over many conversations with Dylan, he told his school life as one of interruption due to moving, quitting school, school suspension, and missed days at school. We wondered how these interruptions shaped Dylan's stories of his experiences in school.

Attending to Dylan's negotiation of tensions in in-school experiences

When Dylan and Shaun first began to talk about Dylan's stories of attendance, it was in February. They spoke while Dylan was not attending music class. Shaun was intrigued when Dylan chose to excuse himself from music by going to the office rather than getting into a fight with another student. In typical plotlines of discipline in school, teachers send children to the office for inappropriate behaviour. However, Dylan shifted that story by removing himself before he started fighting with one of his classmates, something Dylan felt would be imminent had he chosen to stay.

As Shaun listened to Dylan's stories and as we heard stories of Dylan, we learned there was a story of Dylan often going to the office and drawing. In fact there were several pictures drawn by Dylan on Jeanette's office walls. Jeanette told us how Dylan typically placed the pictures on the office walls himself. For us, this suggested Dylan felt a sense of comfort in relation with Jeanette. When Shaun joined Dylan in the office on the February day described in the opening field notes, Dylan seemed calm. As Shaun and he talked, Shaun asked why Dylan liked to draw. Dylan spoke of how

> it helps me control my mind and clear it ... I like to draw well, it just clears my mind. I just think about drawing way better ... My brother, well it runs in my family. My mom, she was an artist ... And ah, well she taught my brother how to draw, my brother he's like real good at drawing ... He's 13 years old, he just turned 13 yesterday ... And I'm 12 and we, well Jay, he started to draw and I was like, "What are you doing?" And he's just like, "Leave me alone. Get out of my room. I'm trying to think here." And I was like, "Well can you teach me?" And he, he's like, "Yeah, one day I will." And then the next day he taught me how to and he said, "Oh you've got to clear your mind when you draw. You've got to, everything go off your mind. Just draw. It should feel like ...
> (Transcript of individual conversation, February 3, 2003)

As Shaun listened to Dylan's stories of living out a story of drawing, he learned about a family story of being good at drawing, of his mother who was an artist, and of a brother who could draw well. Furthermore, he learned that Dylan learned to draw from his brother who advised him that drawing required focus, a mind that was "clear." Dylan learned that drawing and thinking were connected. Dylan seemed to have learned to tell a story of himself as someone able to draw but he also seemed to be able to use drawing and a clear mind as a way to help him negotiate the tensions he experienced in school. Clearing his mind for drawing seemed to give Dylan a sense of control over the stories he was choosing to both live out and to tell of himself. We saw this in the way Dylan removed himself from the music classroom. Instead of staying in the space and potentially getting into a fight with a classmate, Dylan chose to clear his mind, to focus, and to draw pictures.

Learning that Dylan was comfortable enough to interrupt his time in the music room, comfortable enough to draw, and comfortable enough to put his drawings on Jeanette's office walls, began to shape the stories we were telling about Dylan as a boy in control and in authority of who he was at Ravine Elementary School. We were struck by Dylan's understandings of what seemed to be quite conscious decisions to interrupt the moment-by-moment, particular in-school experiences he was living through when he felt a loss of control or authority over what was happening to him. We wondered about Dylan's self-chosen interruptions in relation with time and place and how these interruptions in his temporal experiences of schools and classrooms shaped and reshaped his identity, his stories to live by, both in- and out-of-school.

As we tried to understand more deeply these interruptions in Dylan's in-class and in-school attendance, we turned to our understandings of narrative unities in people's life compositions. Perhaps we could find a way to think about Dylan's negotiations of his stories to live by in school in that way. Connelly and Clandinin (1988: 74) described narrative unity as "a continuum within a person's experiences ... [that] renders life experiences meaningful through the unity they achieve for the person." They wrote:

> What we mean by [narrative] unity is the union in each of us in a particular place and time of all we have been and undergone in the past and in the tradition (the history and culture) that helped to shape us. It is a meaning-giving account, an interpretation, of our history and, as such, provides a way of understanding our experiential knowledge. Within each of us there are a number of narrative unities. Ongoing life experience creates the narrative unity out of which images are crystallized and formed when called on by practical situations.... . for narrative unities emerge from our past, bring about certain practices in the present, and guide us toward certain practices in our future.
>
> (1988: 74–5)

Although Connelly and Clandinin (1988) were trying to understand teachers' embodied knowledge when they described narrative unities in this way, we found we could think about children, indeed all people, as experiencing, within themselves, narrative unities as their lives unfolded in particular situations. We wondered about the narrative unities in Dylan's life as we thought about who he was becoming as his schooling was interrupted by moves and as he chose to interrupt his time in classes at Ravine Elementary School by removing himself.

Certainly Dylan seemed to be living contradictory plotlines; sometimes in authority and sometimes not. Considering the tension of living this way we were reminded of how narrative unities could interweave both conflicting and competing plotlines within each of us. Different situations called forth different responses. In relation to Dylan, perhaps conflicting and competing stories became visible or faded depending on the landscape he was positioned on. Dylan experienced conflicting stories when his stories were shaped by school landscapes in authority over who he was and was becoming. Yet, when he was able to negotiate and author stories of who he was and was becoming on the school landscape at Ravine Elementary School, a conflicting story seemed to fade and a competing story became more apparent.

By bringing an understanding of narrative unity alongside the unfolding stories we were learning of Dylan's life in the Year 5/6 classroom and in the out-of-classroom places at Ravine Elementary School, we realized that while the temporal interruptions in Dylan's schooling made it difficult for him to tell a coherent story of attendance, that is, a story of attendance in which coherence is understood as being physically present, every day, every year, for twelve years, there is another, much deeper sense of coherence at work in the unfolding stories of attendance both lived and told by Dylan. Many children live a story in school where one grade follows another until they complete Grade 12 in school. Indeed, this was a storyline being lived by many of Dylan's classmates at Ravine Elementary School. Many only ever attended Ravine Elementary School. Others moved maybe once or twice during the seven years (Kindergarten–Year 6) of elementary school. However, for Dylan, this story of school was not possible. Not only had Dylan attended a number of schools, but he had also, at times, lived his life away from schools.

Furthermore, for many children, a coherent story of in-school attendance meant being in class and not in the office. Narrative unities emerged from each child's past, were enacted in the present, and were guides toward certain practices (or ways of living) in the future. A narrative unity threaded around regular attendance in elementary school was apparent for many children, a kind of rhythmic knowing of themselves that provided narrative coherence, in part, to stories lived and told. We sensed something different for Dylan.

As we attended to Dylan's stories around the place of drawing in his negotiation of his stories to live by in school, we saw that drawing seemed to shape a sense of unity for Dylan across his family, home, and school experiences. By removing himself from the music classroom and going, instead, to the office to draw, we sensed that on this February day, and on those days before and after it, Dylan, in those times and places, felt connected with his past experiences, traditions, history, and culture. In this way Dylan was able to reshape a place of tension where he felt out of control and authority to one that enabled him to continue authoring his stories to live by.

While the coherence of Dylan's stories to live by in school was broken by the temporal breaks in his attendance, Dylan seemed to continue to hold onto a story of the importance of school. He often talked about his 13-year-old brother who quit school and how he saw quitting school as a bad choice in his brother's life. Dylan often spoke of how quitting school was a choice he was unwilling to make. His brother was important to him. He had protected Dylan in the past and taught him how to draw. His brother's name came up in most of Shaun and Dylan's conversations. In one of these conversations Dylan told Shaun that his brother intended to return to school at some point. During the research relationship with Dylan his brother never returned to school.

What became apparent to us over the school year was that Dylan was consciously choosing to try to sustain stories to live by that fit within the plotlines of the story of school. He chose when to interrupt in-class experiences in order not to fight with another child. He knew fighting might lead to suspension, an interruption over which he had no control. He knew drawing and establishing relationships with Lian and Jeanette were ways of living within acceptable plotlines of Ravine Elementary School's story.

Trying to understand Dylan's stories to live by in school in relation with dominant stories of school attendance led us to wonder more deeply about the multiple narrative unities, the multiple themes or threads, weaving within, between, and across Dylan's stories. As researchers, we understood that living a story of student in school was just one thread in the stories Dylan lived by. We wondered how significant this thread might have been for him. What other threads shaped his stories to live by outside of school? While Dylan was a student at Ravine Elementary School, the story that began to unfold for Shaun, the story told by Dylan and by the school, was shaped in part by an understanding of attendance. As we thought about Dylan's life, we began to wonder more about narrative unities as a way to understand the identity negotiations experienced by children, teachers, principals, and families as their lives meet in schools.

Inquiring into the meeting of children's, teachers', and principals' narrative unities

We began to deepen our understanding of ways in which Dylan seemed to negotiate tensions in his experiences in school through attending more closely to Lian's and Jeanette's experiences in relation with Dylan. We found it important that Jeanette and Lian supported Dylan's stories to live by in school by making what seemed to us to be shifts in the dominant stories of school. We saw these shifts in the way Dylan was able to leave classrooms at given times, such as his leaving of the music classroom. Returning to the concept of narrative unity, we considered how Jeanette acted based on the narrative unity she developed around respect and care for each student as an individual in her school. As revealed in word images around Robbie's stories in Chapter 6, Jeanette became more attentive to "children's perceptions" after her son Robbie was born. She noticed that often "what was really important to us as teachers was of non-importance to him" (Transcript from individual conversation, January 31, 2003). Jeanette did not find it necessary to treat each student the same, but rather attempted to work with each student in ways that would be most helpful to that child as s/he grew and learned. This thread carried across her relationships with students every day in the school. In encouraging Dylan to come to her office and draw when he needed to, Jeanette was pulling on a narrative unity that ran through her stories to live by.

Another occasion prompted us to think again about narrative unity in relation to Jeanette. On this occasion too, Jeanette seemed to create space for Dylan to reshape the stories he was living to ones where he could continue to live stories of who he was. One winter day at another time during Dylan's year at Ravine Elementary School, he arrived in Jeanette's office without first stopping to inquire if this was okay with the office secretaries, something that was typically part of the office protocol. On this occasion, Dylan had been asked by another teacher to remove a toque he was wearing. We knew that also on this day, Lian was away and a supply teacher was in the class. When Dylan asked the supply teacher if he could keep his toque on, she told him he would need to seek permission from Jeanette. By asking permission, Dylan showed his awareness of the story of school that banned headwear. However, for Dylan, being sent to talk to Jeanette the school principal was also not an event that challenged the story of who he was. As Jeanette recounted the event, she realized it was a student teacher who asked him to take the toque off. Lian's student teacher and the supply teacher said they didn't know what to do and that Dylan had better go talk to Jeanette, the principal. As Jeanette spoke, she described how it was her relationship with Dylan that allowed him the space to sustain stories of who he was.

Not only Jeanette, but Lian, his teacher, created spaces for Dylan to live out his stories. Dylan preferred to dress in baggy clothes, typically wearing large shirts and baggy jeans. He always wore a bandanna folded into a narrow band on his head. At the beginning of the year Lian and Shaun wondered why Dylan wore the bandanna and they assumed it was part of the identity he was cultivating with the wearing of baggy clothing. Dylan's bandanna was not an issue for Lian. Lian never asked him why he chose to wear one. However, when Shaun noticed that no other child in class was allowed to wear a head covering such as a toque or ball cap, he asked Lian why she never questioned or challenged Dylan's wearing of the bandanna. She had no clear reason and said, "I had no idea. I was like, 'Who is this kid with the headband,' and thank goodness I never challenged him on that one the first day." As she and Shaun talked further, she said that even though there was a school rule about wearing hats inside, "there was a part of me that was just like, 'Just leave this kid ... He needs to just be here for a while'" (Transcript of individual conversation, March 12, 2003).

Lian began her teaching career at Ravine Elementary School. Jeanette was the only principal Lian had ever worked with. As principal, Jeanette had spent many hours in conversations with Lian. Together they came to know something of one another's stories to live by. For Jeanette, spending time with new teachers was a way to continue her work as an educator. Her word image in Chapter 6 reminded us that "It's working with teachers ... thinking about teachers and teaching ... where I can make a difference with children." Lian, like Jeanette, seemed to have a narrative unity which grew around a continuing desire to support each student in her class as they composed their own stories to live by, with their own unique strengths and stories. In Chapter 8 we recalled how Lian shaped a space for Kerry's stories of who he was through her improvisatory way of reporting progress through Kerry's found poetry. Not surprisingly, Lian allowed Dylan to keep his headband on in class, for reasons she could not clearly articulate, but which seemed in keeping with this narrative unity in her stories to live by as a teacher who worked to include and encourage the diverse students in her class.

On another day, Dylan, without prompting, asked Lian if she would like to know why he wore the bandanna headband. Lian responded that if Dylan wanted to tell her, she would like to know. Although Dylan planned to share the story after school, he forgot, and so Lian had to wait until the next day. The following day after school Dylan and Lian sat on the classroom couch in the gathering area. Dylan shared that he had a scar on his head, above his ear. He described how, when he was younger, he was teased at school because of the scar. Now he wore the bandanna as a way to cover it. As Lian shared this story with Shaun, she expressed how she was glad she had not pushed the issue of Dylan's head covering and, instead, had let him wear it. In this moment in the classroom, Dylan continued to author his stories by choosing what and when to tell them. We saw him once again negotiating a way to live within the plotlines of the story of school. We did not know what would have happened if Lian had enforced the school rule. We did know she was attentive enough to Dylan's lived stories that she let the moment unfold according to Dylan. She did not interrupt Dylan's stories. This made it possible for Dylan to shape Lian's knowing through their relationship, in turn shaping his stories to live by in school at Ravine Elementary School.

The stories of the bandanna and toque set a further context in which to think about Dylan's relationships with Lian and Jeanette. Without the context of their narrative unities around care and respect for him, some of the interruptions he initiated, resulting in a sense of authority over his unfolding stories, may not have been possible. Through his relationships with his teacher and principal, spaces were created whereby Dylan could negotiate a way to sustain and express his stories to live by within dominant stories of attendance and dress code in school.

Thinking about Lian's and Jeanette's narrative unities as they lived and worked alongside Dylan, we wondered how these might have helped to shape a narrative unity for Dylan, a thread running through his stories to live by, a thread of seeing himself as having a place in school and some authority over how he lived his life in school. This thread, nurtured by Jeanette when Dylan came to draw and spend quiet time in her office, and Lian's willingness to allow him to wear his bandanna in the class, perhaps encouraged Dylan as he lived a competing story which ran counter to dominant stories, particularly around attendance and codes of dress.

Usually there are no competing stories of school attendance. Any stories other than one of being in school daily, yearly, is a conflicting story to the dominant story of school of attendance. Dylan was living a very different story, one filled with interruptions in his attendance, and yet he was able to find a way to be a part of Ravine Elementary School for most of this school year. Perhaps Dylan was weaving a thread of seeing himself as belonging in school, a narrative unity as a school attender, supported and encouraged by the ways that Lian and Jeanette responded to him, ways that were, in turn, influenced by their own narrative unities. By stretching the boundaries of what was acceptable attendance within the story of school, they allowed Dylan to interrupt the story of school.

Lian and Jeanette did not allow others to interrupt the story but, drawing on their own narrative unities about what mattered in school, the value of every individual child's story, they helped Dylan to keep his competing story from turning into a conflicting story. They seemed to recognize that they could easily allow Dylan to disappear from the school landscape if there was no space for who he was. Lian and Jeanette, rather than succumbing to a "one size fits all" story of school where Dylan's identity might be reduced to a single thread, that of "student in school," understood Dylan's stories to live by as a complex unfolding with multiple strands. Attending to a fuller picture of Dylan's life as they could see it, they were able to stretch out a wider school story at Ravine Elementary School for Dylan to live within. Even so, Dylan did not become a model student, according to the dominant story of school, but he was able to keep coming to school most days that year, and to find a place for himself on the school landscape.

Difficult moments – complexity continues

Dylan's stories to live by with Lian and Jeanette were not without tension. Nor was he always in the office by his own choice. Some of the places of tension occurred as Dylan's stories to live by bumped against the stories of other children. When Lian attempted to intervene, sometimes there were interruptions in her relationship with Dylan. For example, Shaun recalled one incident where Lian had spoken to Carson's mother about Carson's friendship with Dylan. During the conversation with Carson's mother Lian did not name Dylan, but it was understood that Lian was referring to Dylan. In the conversation, Lian suggested Dylan was not the best friend for Carson because of the trouble the boys got into when they were together. When Carson's mother spoke to Carson she named Dylan. Carson, in turn, told Dylan that Lian thought Dylan was a bad influence on him and they shouldn't play together. When Dylan found this out he stopped talking to Lian for several days. As Lian spoke about this, she said she tried to "explain to Dylan the whole thing and it takes forever and now Dylan's back, you know I'm back in his good books and everything's okay again" (Transcript of individual conversation, March 12, 2003).

While there were interruptions in his relationships and in his attendance at Ravine Elementary School, Lian and Jeanette continued to attend to who he was trying to be. They were not influenced by stories of Dylan from earlier schools, yet these multiple plotlines appear to have shaped Dylan's story of his school experiences as he was trying to compose stories to live by that were acceptable within Ravine Elementary School's story of school. Dylan missed some days occasionally, except for a period of time in March when he missed over two weeks, and then left the school permanently in May. When the school tried to find where Dylan and his sister were, a roommate of the family said they had returned to the reservation.

Shortly before Dylan left the school in late April, there was another interruption in Dylan's attendance. On this occasion, too, Dylan chose to interrupt his attendance. The Year 5/6 class was attending a week-long field trip at a local sport and fitness centre. The children and Lian were bussed to the centre each morning and returned to school for dismissal. Dylan declined to attend saying, "I don't go out in public with teachers" (Transcript of individual conversation, April 17, 2003). Dylan's refusal to go at first surprised us but as we thought about how hard he worked to sustain his story with places and spaces for safe interruptions in school, we saw how dangerous such out of school places might be. The possibility of an interruption he could not control was too great.

Dylan seemed to know to keep a safe distance from situations where he could lose authority of his stories. He removed himself from music classes when he was in danger of losing control and he resisted going to public places with teachers. It seemed that Dylan knew conflicting stories within him could become visible in these places and he chose not to have these interruptions happen to him. Dylan's resistance to participating in field trips outside school has resonant threads with Julie's stories in Chapter 3 where she kept a safe distance in her interactions in the classroom, not wanting to write the ABCs and wandering off to visit Anne during a group story with the teacher on the rug. Julie, who seemed to come to school with a strong story of who she was, learned in a very short time that her mother's knowledge that Julie was "to go home every time I have a tummy ache" (Field note, September 4, 2002) no longer seemed to count in this new place. Might Julie, like Dylan, have been trying to avoid conflicting with school stories?

In relation with Jeanette and Lian, Dylan was able to sustain who he was for most of the year, partly because of the interweavings of strong threads that ran through both Lian's and Jeanette's stories to live by – threads of respect for diverse children with diverse lives and willingness to support students by creating spaces for them to live out their own stories to live by. The interwoven nature of a teacher's, a principal's, and a student's stories to live by reshaped a mis-educative space for Dylan to an educative space, enabling Dylan to live a competing story of attendance and dress code at the school. In so doing, the interconnected narrative unities seemed to have helped to shape a narrative unity for Dylan, one that helped him compose a story of being a student at Ravine Elementary School.

Last thoughts

As we reflected on Dylan and the way he was able to compose stories to live by at Ravine Elementary School, even as he interrupted the story of Ravine Elementary School attendance and a school story around dress code, we realized how necessary it was for teachers and administrators, like Lian and Jeanette, to continually enable children to compose their stories to live by. Even, however, with their carefully negotiated spaces, Dylan did not end his school year. We later learned from Jeanette that he and his sister spent some months living between the reservation and the streets in another large western Canadian city. We also knew that for the nine months he was at Ravine Elementary School, he was in educative learning spaces at school.

Dylan helped us see how necessary spaces for enabling narrative unity are for children. We saw how important it was to help children compose narrative unities through connecting significant experiences in their past to particular experiences in their present and imagined future. As more and more students around the ages of 15, 16, and 17 choose to interrupt their schooling by dropping out (Smyth et al. 2004), we realized the many things Dylan, Lian, and Jeanette helped us attend to as their stories to live by intersected with Ravine Elementary School's story. As Canadian school landscapes become increasingly diverse, might we consider attending to stories to live by as a way to narratively inquire and understand the complex reality of many school landscapes? Might careful noticing of the bumping places where stories to live by are interrupted help to deepen our understanding so we might reimagine wider school stories that make a space for children who have been left out of dominant stories of school structured around "mainstream" plotlines?

Knowing one another's stories may lead to the kind of relationships seen in this chapter as a child's, a teacher's, and a principal's stories to live by intertwined to interrupt and open up school stories around attendance and dress code to enable a more respectful knowing and living on school landscapes with a boy named Dylan. It is when we can attend from storied lives that we can begin to understand and not dismiss the knowledge embedded in competing stories interrupting and emerging on school landscapes.

Chapter 10

Imagining a counterstory attentive to lives[1]

Maxine Greene in *Releasing the Imagination* (1995) captured our imagination about how we might give an account of our work together when she wrote of seeing small and seeing big. She wrote,

> To see things or people small, one chooses to see from a detached point of view, to watch behaviors from the perspective of a system, to be concerned with trends and tendencies rather than the intentionality and concreteness of everyday life. To see things or people big, one must resist viewing other human beings as mere objects or chess pieces and view them in their integrity and particularity instead. One must see from the point of view of the participant in the midst of what is happening if one is to be privy to the plans people make, the initiatives they take, the uncertainties they face.
>
> When applied to schooling, the vision that sees things big brings us in close contact with details and with particularities that cannot be reduced to statistics or even to the measurable.
>
> (1995: 10)

When we see small, we see a phenomenon such as schooling with patterns or trends, as Greene suggested, through the "lenses of a system - a vantage point of power or existing ideologies" (1995: 11). This system view is primarily a technical view. For example, when researchers see small, from the system point of view, we see some things about the context of schooling. For example, we can see the trends in the school leaving rate, the high school completion rate, patterns of achievement test scores in various subject matter areas calculated nationally, internationally, and in cross-national groups, and the factors that are statistically significant in achievement test scores such as school transience and truancy. While seeing small allows us to see behaviours from the perspective of a system, it does not allow us to see people in their integrity and particularity.

For the most part, this book is about seeing things and people big. But we did not want to reject seeing small, for Greene challenged us to "learn how to move back and forth, to comprehend the domains of policy and long-term planning while also attending to particular children, situation-specific undertakings, the unmeasurable, and the unique" (1995: 11). We try, in this last chapter, to move back and forth from seeing from the perspective of a system (seeing small) to seeing the particular lives of the children, families, administrators, and teachers at Ravine Elementary School (seeing big).

In part, seeing small sets a context and a way for us to understand the research puzzle we are engaged with in this work. Our puzzles did not first emerge from seeing our work within the research generated by seeing small. We did not begin with the patterns and trends on achievement, truancy, or dropout rates. Rather we began with the puzzles that emerged from our own lives, from trying to make sense of our experiences as teachers and researchers alongside children and other teachers. Our passion for engaging in this research came from wonderings about the lives of children, teachers, administrators, and families as we experienced living in close relationships with particular children, particular teachers, and particular families. Over many years lived out in schools, we watched children drop out of schools, watched families and children be treated in what seemed to be culturally disrespectful (and sometimes just disrespectful) ways, and felt ourselves and our colleagues unable to act in ways that would change the situations. In Greene's (1995) words, our puzzles came out of seeing big or, in our terms, out of our life experiences as we lived alongside children, families, and other teachers. As teachers and teacher educators, we live our lives with a desire to see the particularities, the uniqueness of each child, of each family, of each teacher, of each student, and we try to understand the lived and told stories of each child, each family, each teacher, and each student. It was in trying to take up Greene's challenge to move back and forth between seeing big and seeing small, using both points of view, that we hoped to see more about how our research informs our understandings of curriculum making in schools.

Seeing schooling small

We realize we could have situated our research in many lines of inquiry that undertake to do research that sees schooling small. We selected one main line of inquiry, that is, inquiry around school dropout rates, transience, and truancy. Our interest was drawn to this research because often school policy-makers link school transience and truancy to poor achievement scores (Ehrenberg *et al.* 1991). School transience and truancy are often described as creating a kind of crisis in urban schooling and often policy initiatives are undertaken to change these patterns of transience and truancy. We know little about how children and families, labeled transient and truant, view this labeled crisis in their own lives.

Around the time we were working at Ravine Elementary School, new provincial statistics pointed out that one of the local school districts had the lowest high school completion rate in our province. At first we were surprised by this finding but, as we talked more about the finding, it helped us shift between the seeing big of our research and the seeing small of this statistically significant finding. We were intrigued as we wondered about the futures of the children we were coming to know through our inquiry at Ravine Elementary School.

We were inspired by Smyth *et al.*'s (2004) research on the Australian patterns and trends around students' completion of schooling. They undertook a study to explore the decline in numbers of students completing high school, first by looking at the patterns and trends and then by asking 209 youth (147 leavers and 62 stayers) to share their stories. As the title of their book indicates, they heard youths' stories of dropping out, of drifting off, and of being excluded.

As Greene (1995) noted, seeing small comes out of a particular ideology suggested by the system. Smyth *et al.* (2004) drew our attention to that ideology by noting that, rather than referring to dropouts, the term early school leavers is used. This term reflects a "commitment to the view that all young people should be encouraged to stay at school to successfully complete the post-compulsory years" (2004: 15).

We see that Smyth *et al.* (2004) also shifted their lenses between seeing small and seeing big as they described the need to "interrupt stereotypes of early school leavers" (p. 15). They described the stereotypes as problematic in that they "homogenize" (p. 16) those who leave school early, that they "naturalize" (p. 16) early school leaving as "just the way things are" (p. 16), and that they "rationalize" (p. 16) school leavers, relying on "moral boundaries of deservedness that threads research and policies" (Fine as cited in Smyth *et al.* 2004: 16).

Interested in their research on seeing small in an Australian context, we searched for information on the trends and patterns for Canadian early school leavers. Overall we learned that the early school leaver rate[2] dropped from 18 percent in 1991 to 12 percent in 1999. In 1999, 85 percent of those 20-year-olds surveyed met the requirements to graduate, 3 percent were still working to complete their high school diplomas, and 12 percent were considered early school leavers. There was a differential early school leaver rate between males (15%) and females (9%).

In the 2000–2002 *Youth in Transition Survey* (Statistics Canada 2004), a survey designed to examine key transitions in the lives of young people as they moved from high school to postsecondary education and from schooling to the labor market, two cohorts of youth were surveyed: one cohort at ages 15 and 17 and a second cohort at ages 20 to 22. When the 15-year-old youth were resurveyed at 17 years, 3 percent had left without a diploma, 14 percent had graduated, and 83 percent were taking classes. At first glance, a 3 percent dropout rate by the age of 17 might seem low. However, two things are of note. Three percent represented over 9,000 youths across Canada. Secondly, we do not know how many children were, by 15, already absent from school, essentially already school leavers because of truancy and transience. These youth would not even have been included in the survey of 15 year olds. These youth would be ones who, in Fine's research, are described as "disappeared eighth graders who never reach high school" (2004: 250).

When the 3 percent who left by the age of 17 were asked for their reasons, they indicated mainly school-related reasons, such as being bored with school, having problems with school work or teachers, or being kicked out. For girls, while school-related reasons were still cited most frequently, more personal or family reasons such as health, pregnancy, caring for their own child, or problems at home were also cited. For boys, work-related reasons – they either wanted or had to work – were also cited. There was little detail given about these reasons in the context of their lives. We can only wonder about the stories that lived behind these stated reasons. As Fine and Rosenberg noted in their work, "many of these adolescent men and women have been pushed out of school; some have opted out: all are regarded as failures" (1983: 257). This would apply to the 3 percent of students who left by the age of 17. It would also apply to the 12 percent of Canadian 20-year-olds who are considered early school leavers.

Because a number of children we engaged with at Ravine Elementary School were of Aboriginal heritage, we searched out particular data on Aboriginal children in Alberta, information we gleaned from Alberta Learning (2003). The Aboriginal population in Alberta is growing three times faster than Alberta's non-Aboriginal population. Children of Aboriginal heritage account for 8 percent of the school-aged population (5–19 years of age). Seventy-six percent of Alberta's youth of Aboriginal heritage live off-reserve. The success of people of Aboriginal heritage in our schools is significantly less than that of non-Aboriginal people (1.5 times less likely to have a high school education). Furthermore, the average earnings for people of Aboriginal heritage were more than 30 percent lower than the average earnings for people of non-Aboriginal heritage.

These findings are remarkably consistent with Smyth et al.'s (2004) findings. Youth in Canada are also dropping out, drifting off, and being excluded at a rate that suggests, as Fine argued, that "categorizing and stigmatizing young people, their lifestyles and their families as 'the problem' deflects from the real contributing factors and makes them invisible" (as cited in Smyth et al. 2004: 9).

When we adopt an even more focused lens and look at high school completion rates in Alberta schools, the province within which Ravine Elementary School is located, we see that 67.4 percent of youth who began high school in 2000/1 will have graduated in 2002/3 (graduating in three years), 8.9 percent will graduate in 2004/5 (graduating in five years) for a total of 76.3 percent graduating. This leaves 23.7 percent ungraduated. Of course, some of these students will return to complete their high school after five years and we do not yet have those statistics. We do know that the numbers of schools focused on adult learners are increasing in some places in Canada. However, overall, these trends and patterns concerned us. School completion leads to more employment possibilities, more earning potential, and even, some argue, better health outcomes over a lifetime. For example, McCain and Mustard (1999: 69) draw our attention to "what has been called the 'social patterning' of health. Social patterning means, in very simple terms, that the higher people are on the socioeconomic ladder, the healthier they are."

Seeing schooling big

Of course we did not work with high-school-aged youth. We worked with a small number of children who ranged in age from 6 to 13, with a few teachers, administrators, and parents in one urban elementary school. Yet, as we shifted our lenses between seeing small and seeing big, we began to see how plotlines in the children's stories to live by became more sharply illuminated.

We wonder if Dylan has already drifted off, finding it difficult to compose a life that makes sense within the stories of school. Even with Jeanette and Lian's attention to creating spaces for him to take narrative authority (Olson 1993) for his own attendance, he could not sustain himself at Ravine Elementary School for the whole year.

And what of Julie and Aaron? They were already positioned as uncertain characters in the story of school, perhaps sensing they did not fit the possible plotlines for those characters named good students. Aaron already had begun to drift off, only kept alive in the story of school by his teacher's and other children's stories of him as a central character in their classroom story of school. His mother continued to tell a story that schooling was important and that she wanted Aaron schooled. How long would this complex interweaving of stories sustain Aaron before he too drifted off in transience and truancy?

Battiste, a scholar of Aboriginal heritage, raised questions for us about the need for "new relations, new frames of thinking and educational processes, not as mere products or 'wishful fictions,' but as processes that engage each of us to rethink our present work and research" (2004: 1). She calls us to attend more thoughtfully to the lives of Dylan, Julie, and Aaron.

Julie and Sadie were positioned differently in this story of school. Julie, finding herself living a story in competition with the character in the story of school her teacher was authoring for her, tried to sustain herself as living out a competing plotline in the story of school. As we lived alongside Sadie, however, we attended to how the storied contexts in which she lived created dilemmas in who she was and who she was becoming. We attended to her as a story in the making and saw how the story of school was a powerful force in who she wanted to become. With her blond hair and blue eyes, she was drawn to Marni as well as to Gale, her teacher, who both offered her a space and a plotline to live out in the story of school. As we attended to Sadie, to Gale, and to ourselves as our lives unfolded over the year, we slowly came to realize that Sadie was caught between living out the character of good student in the story of school and living out the character of a child in her family story. In some ways we, all of us implicated in composing and living out the story of school, asked Sadie to dress like us and to share similar experiences with us and her teacher. But as Sadie began to live out the story of good student, she came into conflict with the story of who she was in her home, a child who did not have the resources, material or physical, to dress, eat, and engage in activities similar to those needed to live the story of good student. As we watched over the year as Sadie negotiated between these competing, sometimes conflicting, plotlines, we saw her live cover stories such as leaving the school-donated snow pants at school so her mother would not learn of them, and secret stories as she whispered to Marni. Sometimes she moved into the good student character, forming an alliance with Sarah, an acknowledged good student. Sometimes she lived out her story of daycare child as she shifted comfortably into her known relationship with Seeta, another child who lived outside the plotline of good student. We continued to wonder about how long she could sustain herself. At year's end, her mother, feeling that both she and Sadie were seen as not quite good enough characters in the story of school, moved Sadie and her brothers to another school. Was this the start of a pattern of transience that will lead to Sadie eventually leaving school? What, we wonder, could we do? Who were we in this story of school? As Sewall played with the metaphor of shore life as the place educators know and shifting ice floes as the place where children find themselves, he noted, "I live in the frustration of knowing that I teach shore life to so many who live amongst the shifting floes" (1996: 7). We wondered about what we knew and how we positioned ourselves.

We saw similar tensions with other children at Ravine Elementary School. We saw Catrina also caught between competing plotlines in the stories of school and her own stories to live by. Even as she frequently resisted living out a character of good student in the story of school, preferring instead to continue her story to live by, we attended to her yearning to belong as part of the story of school, as one of the children who is storied as someone who fits within the story of school. We wondered as we watched her try to compose other stories to live by that might allow her to fit into the story of school. We wondered whether she too will drift off, finding it too difficult to negotiate a place for who she is and is becoming in the story of school.

At one point, as we read the portraits of the students in Smyth *et al.*'s (2004) book, we began to search for resonance across the stories of those youth and the much younger children we came to know at Ravine Elementary School. We saw a possible kind of resonance between the experiences of

Mark, a school leaver sometime in Year 11 in the Smyth *et al.* study, and the experiences of Dylan when we read Mark's words.

> I did music. In Year 8 and 9, I played the organ; and that wasn't part of the curriculum, so I had to take up the clarinet. And I didn't like that at all so I quit. Blowing into a piece of wood didn't really give me that much satisfaction. The organ was what my grandfather did.
>
> (Smyth *et al.* 2004: 53)

If drawing had been taken away from Dylan, if Jeanette and Lian had not allowed him spaces and places to draw in school, would he have left Ravine Elementary School even earlier? We wondered if Shelby, caught between living a story as a responsible student in school and a responsible child at home, might someday feel like Kelly, a school leaver in the Smyth *et al.* study, who said,

> So if a kid's really stuffing up and doing some terrible things you need to get them and sit them down and say, you know, what's going on? What's your reason for doing it? What do you want to do? Like where do you want to go in life? Because no one wants to be in trouble all the time.
>
> (2004: 63)

We realized, of course, there was no way of predicting how the life experiences of the children we knew at Ravine Elementary School would move forward into the future. As Huber wrote of her own identity making, she noted "the multiplicity of relational positioning, shaped by temporal horizons, continues to unfold" (2000: 124). We cannot predict how multiple contexts, in and out of school, and multiple positionings within these multiple contexts, will continue to shape and be shaped by each of the children we came to know as stories to live by in the midst at Ravine Elementary School. Reading the words of youth in Smyth *et al.*'s (2004) book filled our minds with the uncertainty and necessary acknowledgment of not knowing who these children were becoming. While we realized that "describing dropouts as helpless, trouble making, incipient welfare recipients, or delinquents shifts attention away from the educational institutions from which these youth flee" (Fine and Rosenberg 1983: 257), we also realized that we needed to attend to many perspectives simultaneously.

In the study, we wanted to see big because we wanted to attend to individual lives, lives in motion, lives such as Sadie's, Aaron's, Jeanette's, Lian's, and Karen's. We also wanted to attend to the intersections of those lives, the spaces where lives bumped against each other creating tensions. We knew we needed to attend closely to the bumping places but, thinking narratively about experience, we also needed to attend to each life that was part of creating a particular bump. We wanted to take a multiperspectival approach in our seeing big.

As Anne came to live alongside Julie, we attended to the bumping places as Julie's desire to belong in the story of school as a child who stayed for lunch bumped against her teacher's part to play in the school story of parental responsibility for paying for lunch. We wanted to attend to the stories of both Julie and Laura and the institutional story, the school story that shaped them both. This complex interplay of stories - children's stories, stories of children, teachers' stories, stories of teachers, school stories, stories of school, families' stories, stories of families - are always moving, changing, shifting as one story calls forth an expression of someone's knowing that subsequently calls forth another's and so on. As we watched Julie's, her family's, and Laura's stories to live by interact with the school story of staying for lunch, we gained a sense of this fluid interplay.

One of the dangers is that we and readers of these stories might begin to lay blame. As we attended to the lives in motion, both in the living and as we studied field texts to compose these research texts, we realized that attending in this multiperspectival way to the experiences of all of us caught in, and living out, lives in school does not allow us to lay blame. Assigning blame seems to signal a kind of stopping point in trying to explore the complexity of lives being lived in school. Blaming, we see, is another way of deflecting attention from the complexity of people's lives and, in so doing, making them invisible.

Moving between seeing small and seeing big

Greene (1995: 16) wrote about shifting between seeing small and seeing big as granting

> a usefulness to the disinterest of seeing things small at the same time that it opens to and validates the passion for seeing things close up and large. For this passion is the doorway for imagination; here is the possibility of looking at things as if they could be otherwise . . . Looking at things large is what moves us on to reform.

As we try to shift between seeing things and people small and seeing things and people close up and big, we are hopeful we can enter the dialogue about reform, to begin, first of all, to think about what reforms we might begin to imagine. We are, it seems, in a time of a great deal of reform.

In the United States, school reform is at fever pitch. Policies such as *No Child Left Behind* and policies and practices around high stakes testing were implemented, in part, because of poor achievement scores, high dropout rates, and achievement disparities across racial and socio-economic groups. These policies and practices are designed to set in place strict outcomes, powerful surveillance and monitoring mechanisms, and punitive measures if outcomes are not met. The need for such policies and practices was established by seeing small, with concern for "trends and tendencies" (Greene 1995: 10). The policies and practices were shaped by seeing through the lenses of a system with a vantage point of power. Smyth *et al.* (2004: 16) suggest that policies designed to put education "within the reach of all," a policy we argue like *No Child Left Behind*, opens a "space that makes it difficult to examine the arrangements that are in place," arrangements, they say, that let "the system off the hook and puts the blame on the students." In the case of the *No Child Left Behind* policy, blame is being placed on teachers and administrators as well as children.

While in Canada we are not yet at a place where such surveillance and monitoring are in place to try to correct what are seen as problems identified by seeing small through the system lenses used in the United States, we do see some policies and practices that suggest a similar "categorizing and stigmatizing [of] young people, their lifestyles and their families as 'the problem'" (Fine as cited in Smyth *et al.* 2004: 9). Attendance is more closely monitored using technological means. Individual student truancy that reaches certain levels is often dealt with first by the school principal and, if deemed serious enough, by attendance boards. Schools with lower than expected or falling achievement test scores are more closely watched with requisite monitoring strategies put in place. Superintendents and consultants are brought in to monitor school performance when achievement scores fall or stay the same, that is, do not rise. Increasingly teachers' professional growth plans are checked with reference to government approved lists of knowledge, skills, and attitudes. We wondered if we, too, would soon notice what Ancess has noticed in American schools, that is, that

> The current score-driven high stakes standardized test movement where only scores matter, further undermines intellectual development. Instead of more powerful teaching for in-depth understanding which high standards should imply, all test preparation curriculum prevails.
>
> (2003: 2)

In American schools, "teachers in high-stakes testing states were more likely than those in other states to report that the curriculum is distorted by tests . . . [teachers said] they teach in ways that contradict their idea of 'sound instructional practice'" (Darling-Hammond and Rustique-Forrester 2005: 299). We wonder if the teachers at Ravine Elementary School will also soon begin to express similar concerns about how their practices are interrupted.

Researchers are just now beginning to assess the impact of such reforms in the US. Darling-Hammond (2005) noted, for example, a significant correlation between increasing averages on high stakes testing and the increased number of students dropping out of school. She noted that the average test scores are going up because the students who might have lowered the average test scores are dropping out and are not taking the tests. Fine also noted that "under severe pressure to keep test scores high, these underfunded, high-surveillance high schools [in New York] appear to be discharging students in order to boost standardized scores and graduation rates" (2004: 250). Furthermore, Darling-Hammond and Rustique-Forrester (2005) draw attention to the higher rates of dropout in states with tougher graduation requirements and a widening gap in graduation rates between White and minority students.

We do not think this increased focus on testing, monitoring, and control will have the desired impact to allow us, as Greene (1995: 16) suggested, a "doorway for imagination ... the possibility of looking at things as if they could be otherwise." We want to try to do this, shifting between seeing small and seeing big, with the experiences of the children, teachers, families, and administrators at Ravine Elementary School firmly in our sight. We want to move beyond what Darling-Hammond describes as "a system that seeks to manage schooling simply and efficiently by setting up impersonal relationships, superficial curricula, and routinized teaching. Together these practices overwhelm the best intentions of all concerned" (1997: 15).

Imagining a counterstory

Greene (1995) calls us to use our passion for change as a doorway for imagining how things might be otherwise. As we consider Greene's metaphor of a doorway for imagining, we draw on Sarbin's notion of imaginings as "storied constructions" or "emplotted narratives that carry implications of causality and duration" (2004: 11). For Sarbin, imagining is a series of "narratively constructed events" (p. 11) that serve to "liberate human beings from the constraints of the immediate environment" (p. 11). How might we both attend to the seeing big of our work with the children, teachers, families, and administrators at Ravine Elementary School as well as to the seeing small that has led to school reform focused on managing, controlling, and monitoring schools, curriculum, and achievement? How can we use both seeing big and seeing small to imagine a counterstory of school reform? We must, in order to do this, as Bateson reminded us, pay attention in multiple ways, with "a skillful use of peripheral vision" (1994: 106).

Lindemann Nelson (1995) writes of counterstories constructed against the grain of the taken-for-granted institutional narrative. Counterstories are narratives designed to subvert, to shift, and to change. Lindemann Nelson defined a counterstory as "a story that contributes to the moral self-definition of its teller by undermining a dominant story, undoing it and retelling it in such a way as to invite new interpretations and conclusions" (p. 23). Counterstories are, in some ways, imagined reform narratives. They are narratives composed to shift the taken-for-granted institutional narrative. And so, for us, we begin a storied construction drawing together what we know to compose a counterstory, a story of school composed around the plotline of negotiating a curriculum of lives, a curriculum that is attentive to the lives of the teachers, children, families, and administrators who live on the school landscape at particular times.

Imagine, as we do, that each of the teachers, the administrators, the children, and the families "come to the landscape living and telling a complex set of interwoven stories of themselves … Their individual stories are shaped by living in a narrative landscape with its own network of stories." As they "live together in a landscape, each with their own stories in a landscape of stories," stories of school and school stories begin to emerge that draw from the web of stories. "These stories are rooted temporally as individual stories shift and change in response to changing events and circumstances. Changes in the story of school and school stories ripple through the school and influence the whole web of stories" (Clandinin and Connelly 1998: 160–1).[3]

> The landscape is a living place, a place with a history, with dynamic internal goings-on, with continuing interactions and exchanges with community – all of it aimed into the future in sometimes cloudy and sometimes clear ways. It is a place of relationships among people and their stories positioned differently in the landscape, among the past, present, and future.
>
> (Clandinin and Connelly 1998: 161)

Further, imagine, as we do, that curriculum can be understood as the interaction of four curriculum commonplaces – learner, teacher, subject matter, and milieu (Connelly and Clandinin 1988). In order to understand the negotiation of a curriculum, we need to attend to each commonplace in relation with the others, in shifting relational ways. To understand teachers, we need to understand each teacher's personal practical knowledge, his/her embodied, narrative, moral, emotional, and relational knowledge as it is expressed in practice. We need to attend to the different kinds of stories – secret, sacred, and cover stories – as we attend to stories of teachers and teachers' stories. To understand children, we need to understand children's knowledge as nested knowledge, nested in the relational knowing between teachers and children (Lyons 1990; Murphy 2004). Like their teachers, children also express their knowledge in secret and cover stories and we need to learn to attend to the secret and cover stories that children live in school. Children's stories and stories of children also shape the negotiation of a curriculum of lives.

We also need to attend to the nested milieus, in-classroom places, out-of-classroom places, out-of-school places, storied places filled with stories of teachers, teacher stories, stories of school, school stories, stories of families, and families' stories. In other places (Clandinin and Connelly 1995) we described the out-of-classroom places as shaped by what is funneled onto the landscape via a metaphoric conduit. We also need to attend to this funneled-in prescriptive knowledge. And, of course, diverse subject matters are also part of the interaction within a negotiation of a curriculum of lives. Almost 15 years ago, Clandinin and Connelly wrote that "curriculum might be viewed as an account of teachers' and students' lives together in schools and classrooms" (1992: 392). At that time they attended mostly to teachers' places in curriculum making. Now we are attempting to attend, in multiperspectival ways, to teachers, children, families, and administrators and the lives they compose and live out in the dynamic interaction of teachers, learners, subject matter, and milieu that is curriculum making.

Within this complex fluid mix, lives are what become central. Lives, people's experiences, who each of us are, and who we are becoming are central. Questions of person-making and world-making become central concerns in this counterstory we are composing. By imagining our counterstory and the place of a curriculum of lives within it, we are drawing attention to the importance of staying wakeful to the experiences children and families are living both in- and out-of-schools, to the dreams children hold for their lives, to the dreams families hold for their children's lives, to the gaps, silences, and exclusions shaped in the bumping places children and families experience in schools. The negotiation of a curriculum of lives that stays wakeful in these ways is, then, itself, a kind of living, evolving, shifting counterstory of reform; a counterstory of reform that seeks to continue to engage youth like Mark and his capacity for playing the organ and to create spaces for his knowing shaped in relation with his grandfather; a counterstory of reform that seeks to hear Julie's desires and to create spaces to include her in lunchtimes at school; a counterstory of reform that, through sustained relationships with Aaron and his mom, through listening and love, seeks to continue reaching out so that their lives, their capacities, and their dreams do not drop out of sight.

The negotiation of a curriculum of lives that continuously seeks to reform, to remake the silences, to hear and to learn from children's and families' secret and cover stories about the tensions they experience as they compose their lives in schools, will, we imagine, be complex, tension-filled, and challenging. It becomes even more complex, tension-filled, and challenging when we also continue to attend to the stories of teachers and administrators.

Lindemann Nelson (1995: 38) points out that counterstories are told:

> to resist the authoritarian notion of the 'sure interpreter.' A counterstory that merely inverts existing orders of dominance and submission, seeking to overthrow a reigning interpreter only to put another in his place, is not as good as a counterstory that forbears. And as a most pernicious consequence of authoritarianism is to flatten out or exaggerate differences among people and so to marginalize them, a counterstory that understands, celebrates, and sometimes argues with those differences is

a morally better – as well as a more accurate – story than one that does not.

This imagined counterstory will call each of us positioned as policy-makers, teachers, superintendents, administrators, researchers, and teacher educators to reposition ourselves in relation to one another and, in particular, in relation to children and families. In Smyth *et al.*'s (2004) study, Kelly spoke of her dream of school as a place where teachers might sit down with her and engage in the kind of conversation in which teachers asked her where she wanted to go in life, a conversation we sensed Kelly imagined as a way to sustain herself in school, helping her to not drop out, drift off, or feel excluded.

This narrative, experiential, relational, evolving story of reform fills us with possibilities for conversations where, as Bateson (2004: 407) wrote, even without initial agreement on perspectives, we agree "to go on talking." Further, Bateson wrote:

> Yet we also need to know more about what it takes to get a new idea integrated into an existing system of ideas or values and how this process differs from the prior step of bringing it into conversation; it is this quality of integration that really gives an idea staying power.
>
> (2004: 408)

We continue to wonder about how this counterstory can be integrated into the existing stories of school. What will give it staying power, allow it to be a counterstory that is not silenced?

Within the counterstory, children's and families' life experiences become the central moving force. The plotline of this imagined counterstory must find ways of engaging those lives in ways that compose stories of school that are respectful, meaningful, and educative for all participants. As Darling-Hammond pointed out, these connections between children, families, teachers, and administrators are a means "of deepening the relationships that support child development and of acquiring the knowledge about students needed to teach responsively" (1997: 144). We realize that what we are imagining requires radical shifts in the story of school but we also realize that too many schools now are not educative places for children, youth, and families nor for their teachers and administrators. We see this in the trends and patterns of school leaving, of truancy, of families seeking home schooling, and of families searching for alternative forms of education. We see it in the high attrition rates as teachers leave teaching. We see it in the tensions emerging for children, families, teachers, and administrators at Ravine Elementary School. We need to imagine negotiating curricula, negotiating reform, so lives can be composed with plotlines that allow students, families, teachers, and administrators to live lives of hope and dignity. As Lindemann

Nelson (1995: 38) noted, "counterstories that facilitate our entry into those communities, not as marginalized objects of contempt but as full citizens who may freely enjoy the goods to be had there, ought not only to be preferred to others, but are badly in need of telling." Living alongside the children, families, teachers, and administrators at Ravine Elementary School, seeing big, shifting to seeing small, and all the time trying to imagine how things might be otherwise, might allow all of us to stay at the work, alongside children and families, of bringing into being that which is not yet.

Afterword

Re-narrating and indwelling

Stefinee Pinnegar

Currently, social scientists and researchers in professions like medicine, nursing, law, and business are enamored of narrative. Some look to it as a metaphor of human action and interaction that can be used to organize research findings, understand institutions, or as strategy for psychotherapy. Others look to narrative as data that can be mined, numbered, and charted to reveal and account for pathways and processes of human development about which researchers can assert certainty. Still others name it as a kind of qualitative methodology for exploring human lives and interactions. As each of these groups of social scientists attempt to utilize the power of narrative for exploring and making sense of human life and interaction, each group ultimately shortchanges narrative. These research projects ultimately deny the fundamental power and possibility of narrative for scholarship because the researchers invariably focus on either narrative as methodology for research or narrative as phenomenon of research. Unlike other efforts, the research reported here, founded in the methodology of narrative inquiry articulated and exemplified by Clandinin and Connelly (2000), embraces both. Indeed, this work adds dramatically to narrative inquiry, increasing its usefulness, value, and sophistication. It does so because it increases our understanding of narrative inquiry as research methodology and our understanding of narrative as a phenomenon that provides insight into human interaction.

New understandings for methodology

Our understanding of narrative inquiry as research methodology is enhanced in three ways: first, in the addition of new words or vocabulary for articulating the processes and findings of narrative studies; second, in the addition of new tools for engaging in the research process, and third in a more cogent and comprehensive demonstration of this genre of research report.

The vocabulary of narrative inquiry began by providing ideas like plotlines, narrator, character, actor, genre, image, metaphor, etc. Earlier studies in narrative inquiry gave us additional concepts like stories to live by, cover stories, sacred and secret stories, personal practical knowledge, the professional knowledge landscape, and ideas around storying and restorying lives. Each of these terms enriched the ways in which researchers in teacher thinking and teacher education and curriculum theorists conceptualized both past and future work in these fields. One pair of such concepts is competing and conflicting stories. When competing stories appear on the knowledge landscape they exist together in tension with one another. As long as stories can remain competing they can both continue to exist. In contrast, when two stories can no longer exist together in a professional knowledge landscape, those stories become conflicting stories and ultimately one story must give way to the other. An example mentioned here involves teachers telling cover stories about their use of "phonics" work books when their conflicting stories of a whole language or language experience approach to reading can no longer exist on a professional knowledge landscape in a school story that insists on a more traditional, phonics based approach to reading instruction. An example from my own experience is the competing stories of entrance into the profession of teaching. In teacher education in the United States two competing stories of teacher education include the story of university teacher education coursework alongside the competing story of students whose intellectual and academic prowess and kind hearts allow them to enter the schools as teachers supported with school based mentors and their natural brilliance as students but without university teacher education. The book articulates other competing stories such as stories of school attendance and children "fitting in."

In addition, this study adds new terms that push our thinking about teaching, teacher education, and curriculum making further and enriches our vocabulary for discussing who we are and how we live our lives as researchers using narrative inquiry. One such term is the concept of stories "bumping" against each other. When stories bump against each other the authors suggest tension arises. The stories can move forward to become competing and perhaps even conflicting stories. The researchers articulate the ways in which their own stories as researchers sometimes "bump" against the stories of their participants, the plotlines in their research setting or even their own understanding of who they thought they were as researchers. These places of "bumping" always produce tension. The term itself, since we are not talking about "crashing," certainly suggests tension but also implies the possibility of smoothing which might mean that the researchers begin to tell or enact cover stories about themselves as researchers or decide to doze in their work and not feel the bumping or tension.

We are introduced, here, to additional concepts like staying "wakeful and thoughtful" in listening and decision-making as researchers. Furthermore, the authors talk of the idea of stories of participants, institutions, and researchers being "interrupted." They report "world traveling" to the world of their participants, questioning whether they are using an "arrogant gaze" but trying to understand their participants' world through the eyes and knowing of the participant. They articulate the idea of "living and seeing things from the center and margins." They talk of "narrative unities" in understanding the lives of students, teachers, administrators and schools. They investigate the intriguing idea of "fictionalizing." Finally, they introduce the distinction between "stories of a participant and a participant's stories." We see this initially in Chapter 3 when we are introduced to the idea of the contrast or perhaps conflict between the child's story to live by and the teacher's story of the child. We see it in James whose story of himself as a capable learner and a kind class member bumps up against James's teacher's story of James as a boy who is not fitting in. We can imagine research on the development of pre-service, new, and experienced teachers, which attends more carefully to this distinction, particularly in terms of curriculum making in teacher education, teacher development, and classrooms.

Methodologically, this work provides clearer instantiation of a tool narrative inquirers have seen before: the three-dimensional narrative inquiry space. As narrative inquirers we have met this term and seen it exemplified in Narrative Inquiry (Clandinin and Connelly 2000). However, in this work the tool is applied fluently, fluidly, and aesthetically in ways that move the concept from exotic vocabulary to the everyday language of narrative research. It now flows smoothly into dialogue and conversations of narrative inquiry. In this way, the space and the elements of interaction, continuity, and situation enable the deepening of analysis of field texts and the improvement of research design.

Another tool utilized, explained, and exemplified is the use of word images to capture in an essential but not totalizing way the characters of Jim, Sally, and Suzanne. The word images capture layers of text and chapters and cases in a way that retain the complexity and nuance but make these characters easily and immediately accessible for analysis and understanding.

A third tool for narrative research expanded and strengthened here is the use of wondering as an antidote to and expansion of the more traditional idea of research findings. In this work, we are often presented with a brief narrative with explicit and implicit characters, such as the story of Catrina. Once a story is introduced, narrative inquirers then invite us to become wide awake as readers of this research by engaging us in wondering about the story, the perspectives, the context, and demonstrate the impact of shifting among these for expanding our understanding of the lives of children, teachers, administrators, families, and schools. For example, in Catrina's story we wonder about her desire to belong and live a comfortable and smooth story of fitting in, the potential story her fellow students might tell of Catrina making up stories, the story Catrina's mother might tell of Catrina's school experience, potential misunderstanding or arrogance as the researcher imagines or interprets Catrina's world. Wondering engages the reader in uncovering and discovering research findings leading the reader to imagine alternatives about what was and think more complexly about what is and what might be. Wonderings invite and enable readers to reimagine the story being lived, connect the story to their own lived experience in schools or as researchers, and rethink research, schools, and lives.

A final tool introduced in the last chapter is the introduction of attempting to see situations, trends, and research "small" through the lens of institutions accompanied by evaluation, or positivistic and distanced research studies while we simultaneously see research "big" through an attention to the lives of the individuals we are engaging with. This simultaneous seeing "small" and "big" gives new vigor and expanded relevance to both ways of seeing. Seeing "big" in response to "small" enables policy-makers and quantitative researchers to put individual experience back into the research. It allows them to consider the personal, private, and individual against the institutional. Seeing "small" in response to "big" allows those who focus on the particular to place the particular in a larger context and make connections between the personal and private and the institutional which increase the power of the individual to inform policy and for all to reimagine what schools, families, children's lives, or institutions might be.

Finally, in terms of narrative inquiry as methodology, for me this work introduces a new genre of social science research. Through the use of the research tools explored above, the researcher holds the reader in a narrative space of inconclusivity. Though stories are told in the research study, the researchers artfully hold open both the beginning and endings of the narratives presented. The plotlines of the research extend backwards and forward in time and they often overlap so that going backwards to an earlier experience or connections leads to a jumping forward beyond the moment of the story told. In this way, time is never stable, characters and milieus are dynamic rather than static and the reader often stops reading to consider how a particular future would lead to a reinterpretation of this past or how this present moment supports many futures.

In this genre of research, the authors sieve their lived experience, extracting narratives that are live coals. The stories they presented to us (James, Catrina, Sadie, Julie, Aaron, Dylan, Amit, Jeanette, Sally, Lian, Shaun, Anne) are not so much representative stories or example stories, but glowing embers with a potential to light fires of imagination and understanding. Articulated in ways that avoid arrogance or totalizing and embedded in wonderings, the stories anchor ways of imagining and reimagining both the lives of those being researched but also ways of researching. Because the stories do not have definitive beginnings and their endings never arrive at closure, the reader holds her breath wondering with the researchers whether fragile but potentially positive plotlines might emerge. The aesthetics of this research genre allow us to embrace the findings and allow them to glow in our hearts and illuminate our minds as we consider how to educate teachers, understand and make curriculum, or build a society.

New understandings of narrative as phenomenon

Indeed it is the aesthetics of this new genre of research report that enables us to reach new understandings of narrative as the phenomenon under scrutiny. We understand better the phenomenon of interaction, continuity, and situation in human lives in schools. We are more personally disturbed by the tentative and fragile nature of the potential of children, teachers, administrators, and schools to construct plotlines that will allow them to thrive. We are more hopeful that we can imagine better ways to support current and future children, teachers, administrators, and schools in developing stories to live by that support and sustain us as a society and them as individuals.

Again and again in the unfolding of the chapters of this book our understanding bumps up against the ways in which personal hopes and feelings collide with the conditions that surround us, the ways in which the past is always present in the now and extends into the future, how in the present the hinge between the past and the future is interrupted, renegotiated, sustained, and how the future emerges from the now and reopens the past and the ways in which a particular setting or situation impact what we experience and what we come to understand. The story of the field trip to the fort deepens our understanding of each of these aspects of the narrative space. The experience and voice of the children whose understanding of tepees and bannock and potential knowledge and understanding of their own heritage pry open a mandated curriculum that George the docent considers closed. The stories of the three teachers in Chapter 7 reveal the ways in which current experience can draw forth from past experience threads that allow these teachers to envision themselves as different in the future from who they imagined they were in the past and attempt to wonder about how they can support children's stories to live by.

Dylan's story of wearing a scarf to hide his scar, his rejection of his brother's dropping out, his embracing of his art and his transient life with his sister touches our tender hearts. Amit's being returned to India disturbs us as it disturbed Jeanette. James's potential to become storied as a child not fitting in saddens us. We collectively hold our breaths and hope that the narratives lived in Ravine school will lead these children to compose lives that pull together the positive threads of experience, enabling the children to use the more difficult threads not as a disruption to their lives but as a source of strength for that composition. But it also leads us to begin to imagine different, strengthened, or renewed plotlines for ourselves whereby we find ways to support such children in our own places, in our own ways, in our own lives.

The authors of this book have become our teachers not in a traditional way of giving us new facts but in a way of tacit knowing articulated by Polyani (1967): one of in-dwelling where we have been able to see the ways in which understanding about the narrative understanding of lives in schools "in-dwells" in these authors, our teachers, and thus this understanding comes to "in-dwell" in us. As a result we are changed. We reconsider the plotlines of schooling in our communities. We determine new ways to enter the story of policy-making, bringing our commitment to seeing "big" linked to institutional commitment to seeing "small," allowing us to reimagine the plotlines that the lives of children, teachers, administrators, and schools might animate. Thus we leave this book with renewed visions for narrative inquiry methodology, narrative as phenomenon, and with renewed hope for the children, teachers, administrators, and researchers we know and love.

Notes

1 A narrative understanding of lives in schools

1 Because of the multi-age organization of City Heights School and Ravine Elementary School, our two research school sites, we refer to the children's year in school rather than grade. Year 3/4 refers to the group of diverse 8- and 9-year-old children in the classroom.

2 Ravine Elementary School is an urban school in a western Canadian city. The neighbourhood as reported by Statistics Canada (1996) is ethnically diverse with the largest ethnic population represented by individuals of European descent followed by individuals of South Asian, Chinese, Southeast Asian, Filipino, and Latin American descent in order of percentage of the community population, with other ethnicities represented. A small percentage of people in the community are of Aboriginal heritage. It is a middle to lower middle class neighbourhood comprised of mostly single-family dwellings with an employment rate of 72%. It has many green spaces located adjacent to schools and separate city parks. It is a family community with children 19 years or younger making up 42% of the community population. The immediate area surrounding Ravine Elementary School has a number of multiple-family dwellings including rental apartments and townhouses as well as some housing owned by Aboriginal groups.

3 Children's stories to live by: teachers' stories of children

1 Walking cards were part of the school-wide discipline policy around playground behaviour. Walking cards were given when a certain number of behaviours were judged as outside the acceptable range. A walking card meant that you had to walk beside a teacher on playground supervision.

6 Living alongside children shapes an administrator's stories to live by

1 The Celebration of Learning at Ravine Elementary School was held in place of parent–teacher interviews where parents, teachers, and children met to discuss a child's progress. During the Celebration of Learning children shared their work and demonstrated their learning to parents.

10 Imagining a counterstory attentive to lives

1 We acknowledge the help of Simmee Chung, a graduate student in the Center for Research on Teacher Education and Development, in providing background research for this chapter.

2 The high school leaver rate is defined as the proportion of 20-year-olds who have not completed high school and are not working towards its completion (Statistics Canada's internet site, http://www.statcan.ca/english/freepub/81-004-XIE/2004006/yits.htm, retrieved June 25, 2005). Statistics Canada information is used with the permission of Statistics Canada. Users are forbidden to copy the data and disseminate them, in an original or modified form, for commercial purposes, without the expressed permission of Statistics Canada. Information on the availability of the wide range of data from Statistics Canada can be obtained from Statistics Canada's Regional Offices, its internet site at http://www.statcan.ca, and its toll-free access number 1-800-263-1136.

3 These ideas on narrative understandings of school reform draw on the work of Clandinin and Connelly (1998).

References

Alberta Learning (2003) A profile of Alberta's Aboriginal population: census data 2001 (PowerPoint presentation), Edmonton, AB, Canada: Author.

Ancess, J. (2003) *Beating the Odds: High Schools as Communities of Commitment*, Toronto, ON, Canada: University of Toronto Press.

Arnold, T. (2000) *Parts*, London: Puffin Books.

Bach, H. (1993) Listening to girls' voices: Narratives of experience, unpublished master's thesis, University of Alberta, Edmonton, AB, Canada.

—— (1998) *A Visual Narrative Inquiry Concerning Curriculum, Girls, Photography etc.*, Edmonton, AB, Canada: Qual Institute Press.

Bateson, M.C. (1994) *Peripheral Visions: Learning Along the Way*, New York: Harper Collins.

—— (2000) *Full Circles Overlapping Lives: Culture and Generation in Transition*, New York: Random House.

—— (2004) *Willing to Learn: Passages of Personal Discovery*, Hanover, NH: Steerforth Press.

Battiste, M. (2004) Animating sites of postcolonial education: indigenous knowledge and the humanities, paper presented as plenary address for the annual meeting of the Canadian Society for the Study of Education, Winnipeg, MB, Canada, May.

Baylor, B. (1985) *Everybody Needs a Rock*, Markham, ON, Canada: Simon & Schuster.

Behar, R. (1996) *The Vulnerable Observer: Anthropology that Breaks your Heart*, Boston, MA: Beacon Press.

Belenky, M.F., Clinchy, B.M., Goldberger, N.R. and Tarule, J.M. (1986) *Women's Ways of Knowing: The Development of Self, Voice, and Mind*, New York: Basic Books.

Bennett, W.J. (1993) *The Book of Virtues: A Treasury of Great Moral Stories*, New York: Simon & Schuster.

Borland, K. (1991) "That's not what I said": interpretive conflict in oral narrative research, in S. Berger and D. Patai (eds), *Women's Words: The Feminist Practice of Oral History* (pp. 63–75), New York: Routledge.

Bruner, J. (1986) *Actual Minds, Possible Worlds*, Cambridge, MA: Harvard University Press.

Buber, M. (1937) *I and Thou*, tr. R.G. Smith, New York: Scribner.

—— (1947) *Between Man and Man*, tr. R.G. Smith, London: Collins.

Butler-Kisber, L. (1998) Representing qualitative data in poetic form, a paper presented at the Annual Meeting of the American Educational Research Association, San Diego, CA, 15 April.

—— (2002) Artful portrayals in qualitative inquiry: the road to found poetry and beyond, *Alberta Journal of Educational Research*, 48(3): 229–39.

Caine, V.F.J. (2002) Storied moments: A visual narrative inquiry of Aboriginal women living with HIV, unpublished master's thesis, University of Alberta, Edmonton, AB, Canada.

Carr, D. (1986) *Time, Narrative, and History*, Bloomington, IN: Indiana University Press.

Carter, K. (1993) The place of story in the study of teaching and teacher education, *Educational Researcher*, 22(1): 5–12, 18.

Cisneros, Sandra (2002) *Caramelo*, New York: Vintage Contemporaries.

Clandinin, D.J. (1985) Personal practical knowledge: a study of teachers' classroom images, *Curriculum Inquiry*, 15(4): 361–85.

—— (1986) *Classroom Practice: Teacher Images in Action*, Philadelphia, PA: Falmer Press.

—— and Connelly, F.M. (1988) Studying teachers' knowledge of classrooms: Collaborative research, ethics, and the negotiation of narrative, *Journal of Educational Thought*, 22(2A): 269–82.

—— and —— (1992) Teacher as curriculum maker, in P. Jackson (ed.), *Handbook of Research on Curriculum* (pp. 363–401), Toronto, ON, Canada: Macmillan.

—— and —— (1994) Personal experience methods, in N. Denzin and Y. Lincoln (eds), *Handbook of Qualitative Research* (pp. 413–27), Thousand Oaks, CA: Sage.

—— and —— (1995) *Teachers' Professional Knowledge Landscapes*, New York: Teachers College Press.

—— and —— (1996) Teachers' professional knowledge landscapes: teacher stories – stories of teachers – school stories – stories of school, *Educational Researcher*, 25(3): 24–30.

—— and —— (1998) Stories to live by: Narrative understandings of school reform, *Curriculum Inquiry*, 28: 149–64.

—— and —— (2000) *Narrative Inquiry: Experience and Story in Qualitative Research*, San Francisco: Jossey-Bass.

—— Davies, A., Hogan, P. and Kennard, B. (1993) *Learning to Teach, Teaching to Learn: Stories of Collaboration in Teacher Education*, New York: Teachers College Press.

Connelly, F.M. and Clandinin, D.J. (1985) Personal practical knowledge and the modes of knowing: Relevance for teaching and learning, in E. Eisner (ed.), *Learning and Teaching the Ways of Knowing* (84th yearbook of the National Society for the Study of Education, pp. 174–98), Chicago: University of Chicago Press.

—— and —— (1988) *Teachers as Curriculum Planners: Narratives of Experience*, New York: Teachers College Press.

—— and —— (1990) Stories of experience and narrative inquiry, *Educational Researcher*, 19(5): 2–14.

—— and —— (1999) *Shaping a Professional Identity: Stories of Educational Practice*, New York: Teachers College Press.

—— and —— (in press) Narrative inquiry, in J. Green, G. Camilli, and P.B. Elmore (eds), *Handbook of Complementary Methods in Educational Research*, Mahwah, NJ: Lawrence Erlbaum Associates.

Coville, B. (1997) *The Skull of Truth: A Magic Shop Book*, New York: Simon & Schuster.

Craig, C.J. (1992) Coming to know in the professional knowledge context: beginning teachers' experiences, unpublished doctoral dissertation, University of Alberta, Edmonton, AB, Canada.

Crites, S. (1971) The narrative quality of experience, *Journal of the American Academy of Religion*, 39(3): 391–411.

—— (1979) The aesthetics of self-deception, *Sounding*, 62: 107–29.

Darling-Hammond, L. (1997) *The Right to Learn: A Blueprint for Creating Schools that Work*, San Francisco: Jossey-Bass.

—— (2005) Testing or investing? The influence of test-based accountability on educational opportunity, in J.A. Banks (chair), Educating for democracy and diversity in an era of accountability, Symposium conducted at the American Educational Research Association Annual Meeting, Montreal, QC, Canada, April.

—— and Rustique-Forrester, E. (2005) The consequences of student testing for teaching and teacher quality, in J. Herman and E. Haertel (eds), *2005 NSSE Handbook*, 104: *Uses and Misuses of Data for Educational Accountability and Improvement* (issue 2, ch. 12, pp. 289–319), Malden, MA: Blackwell.

Davies, A. (1996) Team teaching relationships: Teachers' stories and stories of school on the professional knowledge landscape, unpublished doctoral dissertation, University of Alberta, Edmonton, AB, Canada.

Dewey, J. (1938) *Experience and Education*, New York: Collier Books.

Dillard, A. (1995) *Mornings Like This: Found Poems*, Toronto, ON, Canada: HarperCollins.

Ehrenberg, R.G., Ehrenberg, R.A., Rees, D.I. and Ehrenberg, E.L. (1991) School district leave policies, teacher absenteeism, and student achievement, *Journal of Human Resources*, 26(1): 72–105.

Eisner, E. (1988) The primacy of experience and the politics of method, *Educational Researcher*, 20: 15–20.

—— (1991) *The Enlightened Eye: Qualitative Inquiry and the Enhancement of Educational Practice*, Toronto, ON, Canada: Collier Macmillan.

Elbaz, F. (1983) *Teacher Thinking: A Study of Practical Knowledge*, London: Croom Helm.

Ely, M., Anzul, M., Downing, M. and Vinz, R. (1997) *On Writing Qualitative Research: Living by Words*, New York: Taylor & Francis.

Ewald, W. (2001) *I Wanna Take me a Picture: Teaching Photography and Writing to Children*, Boston, MA: Beacon Press.

Fine, M. (1987) Silencing in public schools, *Language Arts*, 64(2): 157–74.

—— (2004) Witnessing whiteness/gathering intelligence, in A. Burns, M. Fine, L. Powell Pruitt, and L. Weiss (eds), *Off White: Readings on Power, Privilege, and Resistance* (2nd edn, pp. 245–56), New York: Routledge.

—— and Rosenberg, P. (1983) Dropping out of high school: the ideology of school and work, *Journal of Education*, 165(3): 257–72.

Fox, M. (1997) *Whoever You Are*, San Diego, CA: Harcourt Brace.

Geertz, C. (1995) *After the Fact: Two Countries, Four Decades, One Anthropologist*, Cambridge, MA: Harvard University Press.

Greene, M. (1995) *Releasing the Imagination: Essays on Education, the Arts, and Social Change*, San Francisco: Jossey-Bass.

Harding, S. (1988) *Feminism and Methodology: Social Science Issues*, Bloomington, IN: Indiana University Press.

Heilbrun, C. (1988) *Writing a Woman's Life*, New York: Ballentine Books.

—— (1999) *Women's Lives: A View from the Threshold*, Toronto, ON, Canada: University of Toronto Press.

Hoffman, E. (1989) *Lost in Translation: A Life in a New Language*, New York: Penguin Books.

Hollingsworth, S. (1994) *Teacher Research and Urban Literacy Education: Lessons and Conversations in a Feminist Key*, New York: Teachers College Press.

hooks, b. (1984) *Feminist Theory: From Margin to Centre*, Boston, MA: South End Press.

Huber, J. (1992) Narratives of experience: voice as evaluation, unpublished master's thesis, University of Alberta, Edmonton, AB, Canada.

—— and Whelan, K. (2000) Stories within and between selves: Identities in relation on the professional knowledge landscape, paper-formatted doctoral dissertation, University of Alberta, Edmonton, AB, Canada.

—— and Clandinin, D.J. (2002) Ethical dilemmas in relational narrative inquiry with children, *Qualitative Inquiry*, 8(6): 785–803.

—— and —— (2004) Scaffolding children's identity making with literature, in A. Rodgers and E. Rodgers (eds), *Scaffolding Literacy Instruction* (pp. 143–61), Portsmouth, NH: Heinemann.

—— Keats Whelan, K. and Clandinin, D.J. (2003) Children's narrative identity-making: Becoming intentional about negotiating classroom spaces, *Journal of Curriculum Studies*, 35(3): 303–19.

Huber, M. (2000) Negotiating stories of courage and hopefulness through relational inquiry: An unfolding story, unpublished master's thesis, University of Alberta, Edmonton, AB, Canada.

—— Huber, J. and Clandinin, D.J. (2004) Narratives of resistance: exploring the continuity of stories to live by, *Reflective Practice*, 5(2): 181–98.

Jackson, P. (1992) Conceptions of curriculum and curriculum specialists, in P. Jackson (ed.), *Handbook of Research on Curriculum* (pp. 3–40), New York: Macmillan.

Johnson, M. (1987) *The Body in the Mind: The Bodily Basics of Meaning, Imagination, and Reason*, Chicago: University of Chicago Press.

—— (1989) Embodied knowledge, *Curriculum Inquiry*, 19(4): 361–77.

Kennedy, M. (1992) Narrative journeys: a mother/teacher story, unpublished master's thesis, University of Alberta, Edmonton, AB, Canada.

Kerby, A.P. (1991) *Narrative and the Self*, Bloomington, IN: Indiana University Press.

Lincoln, Y.S. and Guba, E.G. (1989) Ethics: the failure of positivist science, *Review of Higher Education*, 12(3): 221–41.

Lindemann Nelson, H. (1995) Resistance and insubordination, *Hypatia*, 10(2): 23–43.

Lugones, M. (1987) Playfulness, "world"-travelling, and loving perception, *Hypatia*, 2(2): 3–37.

Lyons, N. (1990) Dilemmas of knowing: Ethical and epistemological dimensions of teacher's work and development, *Harvard Educational Review*, 60(2): 159–80.

—— and LaBoskey, V. (2003) *Narrative Inquiry in Practice. Advancing the Knowledge of Teaching*, New York: Teachers College Press.

McCain, M.N. and Mustard, F. (1999) *Reversing the Real Brain Drain: Early Years Study Final Report*, Toronto, ON, Canada: Publications Ontario.

Merriam, E. (1991) *The Wise Woman and Her Secret*, New York: Simon & Schuster.

Mickelson, J.R. (2000) *Our Sons are Labelled Behaviour Disordered: Here are the Stories of our Lives*, Troy, NY: Educators International Press.

Miller, J.L. (1990) *Creating Spaces and Finding Voices: Teachers Collaborating for Empowerment*, Albany, NY: State University of New York Press.

Mitchell, W.J.T. (1981) *On Narrative*, Chicago: University of Chicago Press.

Murphy, S. (2000) Stories of teachers and technology, unpublished master's thesis, University of Alberta, Edmonton, AB, Canada.

—— (2004) Understanding children's knowledge: a narrative inquiry into school experiences, unpublished doctoral dissertation, University of Alberta, Edmonton, AB, Canada.

Murray Orr, A. (2001) Facilitating caring relationships through book talks in a year two classroom, unpublished master's thesis, St Francis Xavier University, Antigonish, NS, Canada.

—— (2005) Stories to live by: book conversations as spaces for attending to children's lives in school, unpublished doctoral dissertation, University of Alberta, Edmonton, AB, Canada.

Neumann, A. (1997) Ways without words: learning from silence and story in post-holocaust lives, in A. Neumann and P. Peterson (eds), *Learning from our Lives: Women, Research, and Autobiography in Education* (pp. 91–120), New York: Teachers College, Columbia University.

Noddings, N. (1984) *Caring: A Feminine Approach to Ethics and Moral Education*, Los Angeles, CA: University of California Press.

—— (1986) Fidelity in teaching, teacher education, and research for teaching, *Harvard Educational Review*, 56(4): 496–510.

—— (1992) *The Challenge to Care in Schools*, New York: Teachers College Press.

Olson, M. (1993) Narrative authority in (teacher) education, unpublished doctoral dissertation, University of Alberta, Edmonton, AB, Canada.

Osborne, M.P. (1998) *Magic Tree House*, Toronto, ON, Canada: Scholastic.

Oyler, C. (1996) Sharing authority: student initiations during teacher-led read-alouds of information books, *Teaching and Teacher Education*, 12(2): 149–59.

Pearce, M. (1995) A year in conversation: negotiating relationships, unpublished master's thesis, University of Alberta, Edmonton, AB, Canada.

Personal Narratives Group (1989) *Interpreting Women's Lives: Feminist Theory and Personal Narratives*, Indianapolis, IN: Indiana University Press.

Phillips, D.C. (1987) Validity in qualitative research, or, why the worry about warrant will not wane, *Education and Urban Society*, 20(1): 9–24.

Pillay, G. (2003) Successful teachers: A cubist narrative of lives, practices, and the evaded, unpublished doctoral dissertation, University of Durban-Westville, South Africa.

Polacco, P. (2002) *A Christmas Tapestry* (1st edn), New York: Philomel Books.

Polanyi, M. (1958) *Personal Knowledge: Towards a Post-Critical Philosophy*, Chicago, IL: University of Chicago Press.

—— (1967) *The Tacit Dimension*, New York: Doubleday.

Polkinghorne, D.E. (1988) *Narrative Knowing and the Human Sciences*, New York: State University of New York Press.

Raymond, H. (2002) A narrative inquiry into mother's experiences of securing inclusive education, unpublished doctoral dissertation, University of Alberta, Edmonton, AB, Canada.

Rose, C. P. (1997) Stories of teacher practice: exploring the professional knowledge landscape, unpublished doctoral dissertation, University of Alberta, Edmonton, AB, Canada.

Rylant, C. (1992) *An Angel for Solomon Singer*, New York: Orchard Books.

Sarbin, T.R. (2004) The role of imagination in narrative construction, in C. Daiute and C. Lightfoot (eds), *Narrative Analysis: Studying the Development of Individuals in Society*, Thousand Oaks, CA: Sage.

Schön, D. (1983) *The Reflective Practitioner*, New York: Basic Books.

Schwab, J.J. (1969) The practical: a language for curriculum, *School Review*, 78(1): 1–23.

—— (1970). *The Practical: A Language for Curriculum*, Washington, DC: National Education Association, Center for the Study of Instruction.

—— (1971) The practical: arts of the eclectic, *School Review*, 81: 461–89.

—— (1973) The practical 3: translation into curriculum, *School Review*, 81: 501–22.

—— (1983) The practical 4: Something for curriculum professors to do, *Curriculum Inquiry*, 13(3): 239–65.

Sendak, M. (1986) *Chicken Soup with Rice*, Toronto, ON, Canada: Scholastic.

Sewall, I. (1994) The folkloral voice, unpublished doctoral dissertation, University of Alberta, Edmonton, AB, Canada.

—— (1996) Blessed be the spirit that carries us from day to day, paper presented at the Center for Teacher Education and Development, University of Alberta, Edmonton, AB, Canada, Sept.

Smyth, J., Hattam, R., Cannon, J., Edwards, J., Wilson, N. and Wurst, S. (2004) *Dropping out, Drifting off, Being Excluded: Becoming Somebody Without School*, New York: P. Lang.

Statistics Canada's Internet Site (2004) *Youth in Transition Survey (YITS)*, Ottawa, ON, Canada: Statistics Canada, Human Resources and Skills Development Canada. Retrieved from http://www.statcan.ca/english/freepub/81-004-XIE/2004006/yits.htm, on 26 June 2005.

Steeves, P. (1993) An exploration of voice in the research process in a primary classroom, unpublished master's thesis, University of Alberta, Edmonton, AB, Canada.

—— (2000) Crazy quilt: continuity, identity and a storied school landscape in transition. A teacher's and a principal's works in progress, unpublished doctoral dissertation, University of Alberta, Edmonton, AB, Canada.

—— (2004) A place of possibility: the Center for Research for Teacher Education and Development, *The Alberta Teachers' Association Magazine* (Summer): 16–17.

Stine, R.L. (2000) *Goosebumps*, New York: Scholastic.

Thorndike, E.L. (1927) *The Measurement of Intelligence*, New York: Bureau of Publications, Teachers College, Columbia University.

Trinh, T.M. (1989) *Woman, Native, Other: Writing Postcoloniality and Feminism*, Bloomington, IN: Indiana University Press.

US Congress (2001) No child left behind act of 2001, *Public Law 107–110. 107th Congress*, Washington, DC: Government Printing Office.

Veugelers, W. and Veddar, P. (2003) Values in teaching, *Teachers and Teaching: Theory and Practice*, 9(4): 377–89.

Vinz, R. (1997) Capturing a moving form: Becoming as teachers, *English Education*, 29(2): 137–46.

Witherell, C. and Noddings, N. (1991) *Stories Lives Tell: Narrative and Dialogue in Education*, New York: Teachers College Press.

Wood, D. (2002) *A Quiet Place*, New York: Simon & Schuster.

Young, M. (2003) Pimatisiwin: walking in a good way, unpublished doctoral dissertation, University of Alberta, Edmonton, AB, Canada.

Index

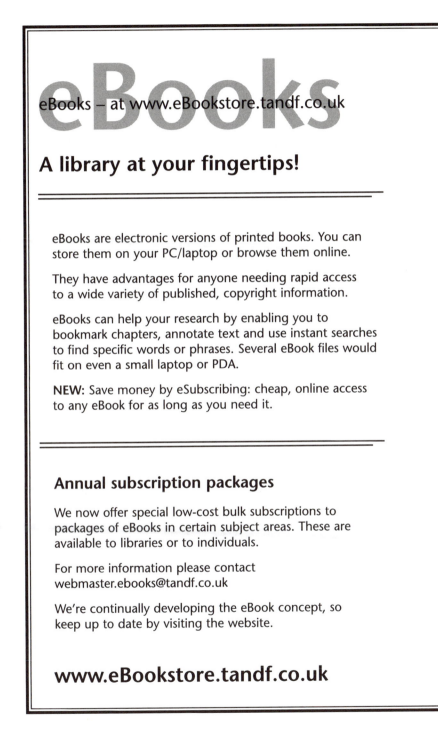